A

JOURNAL OF A TOUR

TO THE

UNITED STATES.

A *LOG HOUSE* drawn from *INGLE'S REFUGE* State of Indiana U.S by W. Faux.

Published by W. Simpkin & R. Marshall, June 1823.

MEMORABLE DAYS IN AMERICA:

BEING

A JOURNAL OF A TOUR

TO

The United States,

PRINCIPALLY UNDERTAKEN TO ASCERTAIN, BY POSITIVE EVIDENCE,

THE

CONDITION AND PROBABLE PROSPECTS

OF

BRITISH EMIGRANTS;

INCLUDING

ACCOUNTS OF MR. BIRKBECK'S SETTLEMENT IN THE ILLINOIS:

And intended to shew Men and Things as they are in America.

By W. FAUX,

AN ENGLISH FARMER.

AMS PRESS
NEW YORK

105193

Reprinted from the edition of 1823, London
First AMS EDITION published 1969
Manufactured in the United States of America

Library of Congress Catalogue Card Number: 71-95144

AMS PRESS, INC.
NEW YORK, N. Y. 10003

TO

HIS GRACE, THE DUKE OF BEDFORD,

AND TO

THOMAS WILLIAM COKE, ESQ., M. P.,

THE

DISTINGUISHED PATRONS OF THE AGRICULTURE

OF THEIR NATIVE COUNTRY,

THE FOLLOWING FAITHFUL PAGES,

INTENDED TO ENABLE

THE CAPITALISTS, YEOMEN, AND LABOURERS

OF ENGLAND,

TO FORM A JUST AND WELL-FOUNDED ESTIMATE

OF THE COMPARATIVE ADVANTAGES

OF BRITISH FARMING

AND

AMERICAN EMIGRATION,

ARE,

WITHOUT PERMISSION,

BUT WITH THE GREATEST RESPECT,

INSCRIBED,

BY THEIR ADMIRER, FRIEND, AND COUNTRYMAN,

THE AUTHOR.

PREFACE.

In any other point of view than with reference to the facts and observations which are here submitted to the public, who I am, and what I am, is certainly a matter of small moment; nor shall I detain the reader with any observations on that subject, on which sufficient information, through the medium of the following pages, will probably be found.

The motives which induced me to visit America, and afterwards to give to the public the results of my experience, originated in many favourable prepossessions for that country, and in a strong desire to ascertain the naked truth, in all particulars relating to emigration to that land of boasted liberty. When I saw thousands of my countrymen hurrying thither, as though they fled for life, and from the city of destruction, I became very anxious to know the real nature of their prospects. To them, I felt assured, that a statement, containing, to the best of the writer's belief, the truth and nothing but the truth, plainly and fearlessly spoken, and calculated to give a correct impression, would be of the most essential service; and, upon those subjects to which my inquiries were particularly directed, I may, perhaps, be allowed to say, that I was, in some measure, qualified to judge, by experience, and by the habits of my life. With these views, I have endeavoured to retrace my many steps, and to take the reader with me, that he may see, taste, and know, *things as they are;* the rough with the smooth; the bitter with the sweet; the good with the evil. That he may go where I go; hear all, see all, and, by evidence, judging all, form his own resolutions and conclusions.

I may truly say, that throughout the whole of this enterprize, I have been, in a great degree, influenced by a sense of patriotic duty. The same sentiment impels me to the completion of my task, in the hope that the truth, so long perverted and concealed, may contribute to destroy the illusions of transatlantic speculation, and to diffuse solid, home-bred satisfaction amongst my industrious countrymen. Deeply sensible, as I am, of all the kindness which I met with in the United States, and fond, as its natives are proverbially known to be, of unmixed praise, I shall yet speak of them and their country, as I, from first impressions, corrected by subsequent reflection, thought, found, and felt, alternately and impartially blaming and praising, where I believe censure and encomium to be honestly due.

To my many subscribers in both the old world and the new, some apology for the delay which has taken place in the publication of this volume, may be thought necessary. It is simply this; and found in one circumstance, over which I had no control — a long and painful paralysis, contracted in America, which seemed, for some time, to threaten my life.

Throughout the work, I have studiously avoided every thing which might savour of systematical or methodical arrangement; it being my wish to give, as nearly as practicable, my Journal, as it was begun, progressively continued, and ended; and thus to make plain delineations and convey correct impressions—Pictures from life—Things as they are!

Somersham,
June, 1823.

LIST OF SUBSCRIBERS.

A.

ATKINSON, Rev. John, *Somersham.*
Asplan, Mr. William, *Bluntisham.*
Asplan, Mr. ditto, for three friends, *ditto,* 3 copies.

B.

BEDFORD, HIS GRACE THE DUKE OF, *Woburn Abbey.*
Butler, Rev. Mr. *London.*
Bonfield, Rev. J. *Chatteris.*
Bonfield, Mr. *Wimblington.*
Bird, Mr. Thomas, *London.*
Blake, Mr. John, *Yarmouth.*
Biggs, Mr. *Linton.*
Brown, Mr. John, *Earith.*
Brown, Mr. Samuel, *Somersham.*
Barley, Mr. Edward, *March.*
Betts, Mr. *Potton.*

C.

COKE, T. W. Esq. M. P. *Holkham.*
Curwen, J. C. Esq. M. P.
Chowns, John, Esq. *Welches, near Welwyn, Herts.*
Chatfield, Rev. Dr. *Chatteris.*

Cooper, Rev. Mr. *Potton.*

Chaplin, —, Esq. *Fulborn.*

Culledge, —, Esq. *March.*

Cockle, George, Esq. M. D. *St. Ives.*

Cockle, George, jun. Esq. *Willingham.*

Cole, Mr. G. *Norwich.*

Cole, Mrs. *St. Ives.*

Cooche, Mr. *ditto.*

Coote, Mr. William, *ditto.*

Coote, Mr. John, *Wisbeach.*

D.

Dudley, Sir H. B. Bart. *Ely.*

Day, G. G. Esq. *St. Ives,* 4 copies.

Dawes, Frederick, Esq., M. D., *Washington, America,* 100 copies.

Dumbleton, Mr. E. *Coppingford Lodge.*

E.

Emery, Mr. T. W. *Potton.*

Ellis, Mrs. *ditto.*

F.

Fiske, Rev. Mr. *Fulborn.*

Farre, J. R., Esq. M. D. *Charter-House Square.*

Fryer, John, Esq. *Chatteris.*

Fryer, Thomas, Esq. *ditto.*

Fryer, Mr. Daniel, *ditto,* 6 copies.

Faulkner, William, Esq. *Potton.*

Freshwater, Mrs. *ditto.*

Fisher, T. E. Esq. *St. Ives.*

Fountain, Mr. J. *Norwich.*

Faux, William, sen. *Sutton.*

G.

Gurney, John, Esq. *Serjeant's Inn, London.*
Gifford, Mr. J. *Cambridge.*
Gray, Mr. Nathan, *March.*
Grey, Mr. G. *Wimblington.*
Groocock, Mr. W. A. *St. Ives.*
Gell, Miss, *ditto.*
Gray, Mr. *Buckworth,* (for the Kimbolton Book Society).

H.

Hunt, Henry, Esq. *King's College, Cambridge.*
Hardy, Johnson, Esq. *March.*
Hammond, John, Esq. *Fenstanton.*
Hatchard, Rev. John, *Chatteris.*
Holmes, Rev. Mr. *Wisbeach.*
Hill, James, Esq. *ditto.*
Hallack, Mr. *Cambridge.*
Huckberry, Mr. *Spalding.*
Harris, Henry, Esq. *Peterborough.*
Howson, Mr. sen. *Huntingdon.*
Hutchinson, Mr. Stoakley, *Colne.*
Hagger, Mr. *Potton.*
Hall, Mr. *Biggleswade.*

I.

Isaacs, Rev. Mr. *Chatteris.*
Johnson, Hardy, Esq. *March.*
Johnson, Mr. Catlin, *Potton.*
Jecks, Mr. *Wisbeach.*
Ilett, Edward, Esq. *Chatteris.*
Ilett, Mr. Jonathan, *Earith.*
Ingle, John, *Somersham.*
Ingle, Mr. *Willingham.*

K.

King, Rev. —, Prebendary of *Ely*.

L.

Lloyd, John, Esq. *Potton*.
Leeds, Mr. John, *Somersham*.
Leigh, Mr. Thomas, *Earith*.
Livet, Mr. Richard, *Cumberland Street, New Road, London*.

M.

Moseley, L. Esq. *Somersham*.
Mason, William, Esq. *ditto*.
Martin, —, Esq. *Potton*.
Martin, Downes, Esq. *Godmanchester*.
Margetts, Thomas, Esq. *Hemingford Grey*.
Margetts, Mr. P. *ditto*.
Morton, Mr. *Potton*.
Manning, Mrs. *ditto*.
Masters, Mr. *ditto*.
Massey, Mr. *ditto*.
Martin, Mr. sen. *Somersham*.
Mayfield, Mr. John, *St. Ives*.

N.

Nicholls, Mr. *Buckworth*.

O.

Osborne, J. Esq. *St. Ives*.
Orris, Rev. —, *Somersham*.
Owen, Mrs. *Mepal*.

P.

Pinchard, Dr. *Haddenham*.
Prince, —, Esq. *Balsham*.

Pittiss, Edward, Esq. *Newport,* 2 copies.
Pryme, George, Esq. *King's College, Cambridge.*
Pratt, William, Esq. *March.*
Pratt, Mr. *Norwich.*
Pierson, Mr. *Kimbolton.*
Potto, Mr. Carter, *Earith.*
Peake, Mr. *St. Ives.*
Patrick, Miss, *Potton.*

R.

Rugeley, W. P. Esq. *Potton.*
Rugeley, Mrs. *ditto.*
Rugeley, Mr. H. *St. Ives.*
Robinson, Mr. Noble, *ditto.*
Rogers, Mr. John, *Potton.*
Robinson, Captain, of the Electra Packet.

S.

Smith, Major, *Somersham.*
Smith, Mrs. *Coppingford Lodge.*
Sewell, Thomas, Esq. *Chatteris.*
Sparrow, Mr. *Norwich.*
Starling, Mr. *Yarmouth.*
Sutton, Mr. G. *St. Alban's.*
Setchfield, Mr. D. *St. Ives.*
Shaw, J. jun. Esq. *King Street, Cheapside,* 2 copies.
Smith, Mr. J. *Chatteris.*
Steed, J. *London.*

T.

Tillard, Rev. Richard, A. B. *Bluntisham.*
Thomson, George, Esq. *Somersham.*
Tebbutt, M. Esq. *Bluntisham.*

U.

Underwood, Mrs. *Potton.*

Underwood, James, Esq. *Ordnance Office, Tower.*
Underwood, Mr. *Somersham.*
Upsher, Mr. Thomas, *Sutton.*
Upsher, Joseph, Esq. *St. Ives.*

V.

Vipan, Benjamin, Esq. *Mepal.*
Vipan, Joseph, Esq. *Sutton.*

W.

Wilson, Thomas, Esq. *Houghton, St. Ives.*
Wilson, John, Esq. *Somersham.*
Wilson, Mr. J. Oakes, *ditto.*
White, Mr. Thomas, *Bluntisham.*
White and Medcalf, Messrs., *Oxford Street, London,* **2** copies.
Wallis, Mr. R. *Hemingford Grey.*
Wells, Mr. Samuel, *Huntingdon.*
Wittingham, Rev. R. *Potton.*
Warner, Charles, Esq. *Somersham.*
Wright, Mr., Chemist, *Wisbeach.*

Y.

Youd, George, Esq. *Wisbeach.*

JOURNAL.

———

HAVING, through the medium of the public prints, advertized my intended departure, and made the necessary preparations, I bade farewell to my good and venerable father, whom I never expected to see more, and tore myself from the embraces of my wife, and of one dear and only child. On the following day, being the

27th November, 1818, I reached London, on the Defiance coach, after riding all day in the rain. On the next day, I boarded, in the King's Dock, the good ship Washington, which carried out Mr. Fearon and Mr. Lancaster. The former gentleman was, I found, disliked by the captain, and, indeed by all Americans, on account of the fidelity of his Sketches. I called on him and thought him an interesting and intelligent man. I requested of the tourist, letters to his friends; " No," said he, " my book has destroyed them: you will confirm my reports."

December 16th.—I, this day, boarded the good ship Ruthy, and paid 15l. in part of passage, to

B

Captain Wise of Boston, to Charleston bound:
" We are," said he, " short of money in America;
but sure of living."

21*st*.—Insured 120*l*. on my luggage with Butler
and Wade, and tried in vain at several offices to
effect a life-insurance, the climate to which I was
destined being doubly hazardous. Received from
my physician a prescription, costing and really
worth three guineas, and fit for both land and sea.
Take two-thirds of Cheltenham salts, and one-
third of Epsom salts, mixed; a quarter of an ounce,
dissolved in a pint of hot spring water, and drunk
an hour before rising, is a dose which may be
often repeated, if necessary, by patients disposed
to indigestion.

January 1*st*, 1819.—On Monday last, five days
since, I came on board the Ruthy, then lying in,
and now creeping down the Thames; nothing remarkable having yet transpired. On Wednesday,
I showed myself at the custom-house at Graves-
end. Now, twenty-five miles from the Downs.
Our crew and passengers consist of three Englishmen, one Welshman, one Spaniard, and nine
sprightly Americans, including our youthful captain, twenty-five only, of very energetic habits, manners, and aspect; possessing an air, an eye, and a
voice which say, *arm*; which create or annihilate;
which say *be* or *not be*. What a pity that so much
natural manly talent and efficiency should be mixed
up with so much frightful profaneness! The ship

has yet no motion, nor is there any sickness,
except amongst the poultry, and first mate, who
seems sick and ready to die. I began an epistle
to my father, and assured him that my heart is a
compass, which will ever truly point towards England, and that a ship is a prison, a house without
land, where life is most uncertain, and death always at hand.

Sunday, 3rd.—Under weigh at half past eight,
but soon stranded; struck and stuck fast on the
shallow sands above Margate roads. Somewhat
alarmed, but providentially off again at three o'clock
tide, losing only an anchor and cable worth 100*l*.
Terrible language even on this day; but Sabbath
none here!

4th.—Safely anchored in the Downs, off Deal;
where at six, p. m. the pilot left us. Boarded by
smugglers, offering best Hollands at 14*s*. and 12*s*.
6*d*. per gallon, which they keep sunk in the sea.
The captain traded, and thereby saved 100*l*. per
cent. Wind full south, right a-head; rough sea;
felt squeamish, not sick.

5th.—In company with the captain, visited
Deal Castle, the seat of Lord Carrington, an ancient fortress, and fortified, during the reign of Eli-
zabeth, against the Spanish Armada. Called on
Edward Iggledon, Esquire, the American vice-
consul. The captain here evinced a laudable, and
obliging, yet barbarian curiosity.

6th.—Under weigh at noon. Passed Dover

Castle. Distinctly saw the coast of France. Parted with our old friends, the Deal smugglers; sea-
robbers, whose constant prayer is, " Give us a
good *south-wester:*" a wreckful gale in the fatal
Downs. Boarded by Lloyd's agent, who reports
the time of coming in and leaving the Downs. Saw
two bright light-houses, shining from the South
Foreland. At eight, p. m. came on, right a-head,
a strong wind on a leeward shore, and a very
heavy, swelling, rough, angry sea, such as I had
never before seen, alternately lifting me on my
head and heels, while in bed. No sleep, all night.

7th.—Both wind and sea more violent than
ever; the latter running deep, right over the ship,
and falling like claps of thunder on the roof of my
cabin. Continued thirty-six hours in bed with but
little sleep, drinking neat Hollands, and eating biscuit only, so avoiding sea-sickness, though morally
sick at heart.

8th.—Rose at eight. Fine morning, wind N. W.
The Isle of Wight a-head. Visited the steerage, a
hole unfit for either man or beast. My simple
Cambrian friend found himself robbed of his dollars, by the sailors artfully borrowing his keys.
Passed the Isle of Wight. At six, p. m., off the
Isle of Portland, another tremendous gale came
on, worse than the last, on a leeward shore; no
port; a dismal atmosphere, with all the horrors of
Thursday night doubled. From the captain's
dark physiognomy I saw our danger, though not

willingly admitted by him. We could see no land from the mast-head, only a dismasted vessel; and knowing not where we went, suffered the ship, without sail, to drift back. Felt my nervous system greatly shocked and impaired; passed a most dreadful night, admitting of no sleep, but a fearful looking out for death and swift destruction on the rocks. At nine, p. m., the gale abated, and hope dawned; and we hailed an Isle of Wight pilot-boat, which led us to *Mother Bank*, Portsmouth-harbour. Great and general was the joy of all on board, some being sick, and all worn down with fatigue and excessive watching. Thunder this morning. Off Ryde, at anchor, by eleven o'clock, a. m. Felt great gratitude, but not commensurate with the deliverance. The feeling during the gale was that of overwhelming fear, and as one under sentence of death, in dreadful suspense, waiting the moment which was to sink us all in old ocean's deep unfathomed caves. It was the most miserable 24 hours of my life, but worse were to follow. I was near resolving, that if I reached shore, I would abandon my mission! My hopes, objects, prospects, and all the bright visions of the future, seemed only as things passed away. When safely anchored, I felt as one risen from the dead; and, though my fears tried to seduce me towards home, shame, and my little remaining courage, impelled me to proceed.

11*th*.—The gale continues: how happily auchored! Infinite mercy calls for infinite gratitude! In the gale, we damaged our cargo, and lost nearly all our water; the bung-holes of the casks being left carelessly unclosed. If this had happened in the midst of the western sea, we must have returned, or have perished with thirst.

12th.—In the stage for Newport, Isle of Wight, to the hospitable board of Messrs. J. and Edward Pittiss, where we were regaled like princes. This town is London in miniature; it contains 6,000 people, and is as beautiful as any in Britain. Viewed Carisbrook Castle, with its wonderful well, 250 feet deep. Visited Mr. Barnet of Cowes, who has wild cattle on his estate. Left our good and hospitable friends, and promised to ourselves to return such kindness with interest, when opportunity occurred.

19th.—Reached Roxhall-farm, near God's Hill, to dine with John Arnold, Esq. whose house and estate are delightful. Mr. Arnold has resolved on emigration, with handsome property, good agricultural knowledge, and first-rate general intelligence. He farms 400 acres of good land at 20s. per acre, but has lost on it 300l. per annum for some time past, which he thinks is an argument in favour of emigration.*

25th.—For the first time in my life it has been

---

* This gentleman and family, with 10 of the Pittiss family, sons and daughters, brave and fair as Britain boast, have emigrated to the Western wilds.

my lot, while on board the Ruthy, and that too
in Portsmouth Harbour, to partake of chicken
which had died diseased, and pig killed because
it could no longer live, though well nursed during
its sickness. I, in consequence, dread starving
if I remain here; the recollection of having thus
fed, quite destroying appetite. Mr. Pittiss this day
came on board with the present of a hare, which
was barbarously boiled, and slush (or melted fat)
poured over it for dinner. This was my last inter-
view with this respectable man, to whom I gave
introductory letters to friends in America.

27th.—To dinner this day at the Cornish Arms,
Portsmouth, the landlord of which always pre
sides, and at table toasts Bonaparte, by saying
aloud, " God bless Bonaparte, the man of the
people, the Frenchman's hope, and the glory of
the world!" Splendid portraits, too, hang in almost all parts of the house; and one in particular,
in the drawing-room, must only be approached
bareheaded and bowing. Mr. Cole is quite an
original. At noon, a S. E. wind hurried us on
board, to prepare for sea. Received a pilot.

28th.—Weighed anchor at five, and dropped
into Cowes harbour at ten, a. m., having in view
the beautiful hills of the Isle, adorned with castles
and mansions. Spoke the ship Plato, from Baltimore to Bremen bound, and recently exposed to
the worst gales and weather, and much damaged

on the banks of Newfoundland, where the crew were frost-bitten and lost their toes and fingers' ends.

29th.—Sailed at six this morning. Wind at S. E. Passed Yarmouth, Lymington, and Christ Church, in full view, and, at one, p. m., those sublime romantic rocks rising high out of the water, and therefore called the Needles. Here the pilot left us.

30th.—Now off Plymouth, but no land in view. Made, since yesterday, 130 miles. Felt possessed of more courage than when last at sea, or rather a sort of desperate, not pious, resignation. On leaving St. Aldhams head, yesterday, saw no more of poor old England. Peace to my dear native land!

31st.—In lat. 48°. Saw two Yankee brigs, for England bound. Rose at midnight, and beheld the pale moon illuminating the dark sea, which looked like an infinite lake of quicksilver.

To my sorrow is it known, that the captain finds his beef and porter (bought for good) good for nothing, the former having been a voyage to the East Indies! Navigators up the Mississipi river, frequently steal from 10 to 20 sheep at once from the farmers, and think it no crime; it being more convenient to steal than to buy. Captain Wise, when there, acknowledges he saw his crew dressing several sheep so stolen, but forbid them not; only telling them they should not let him know of such thefts. Alas! poor honesty, how art thou discarded!

February 2nd.—Fine day. Wind none. Eleven sail in view: a dead calm. Lat. 48°.

3rd.—Almost a gale, and right a-head all day. I perceive my fears lessen as I proceed. Huge mountainous waves of a mile in length, but as they do not break, as in the Channel, the ship gallantly rides over them. Saw a fine mast afloat, recently fallen from some ill-fated ship. Lat. 47°, and on the skirts of the Bay of Biscay. A large shoal of sea-hogs, alias porpoises, played round our ship; we harpooned one, which instantly became a prey to its fellows. Its blood invites them to destroy and devour it.

4th.—Bad weather, wind west, right a-head; lat. 47° 30′ at noon. At a recent anniversary in Boston of Free Blacks, met to celebrate the abolition, or as they term it the *Boblition* of the slave-trade; the chairman rose after dinner, and said, " Gemmen, I be Massa Peter Guss, and give you this toast, That President Madison be no more like General Washington than puté finger in the fire, and haul it out again!" great applause. And another toast was, " Mr. Wilberforce be the blackyman's friend, and may he never want polish to his boots." I give this anecdote, as I heard it from an American; but contempt of the poor blacks, or niggers, as they are there called, seems the national sin of America.

5th.—Squally, and almost a gale all day. Felt no fear, but hope and confidence in the good hand which can deliver. Our first mate turned into the steerage for disobedience this morning, and a fight near at hand between himself and the captain. Our black steward is known as a champion of champions, having conquered a hero of his own colour by butting on all fours, like two rams, a mode of fighting common amongst blacks.

7th.—In the bay, off Spain, and 170 miles from the port of Corunna.

8th.—Lat. 44°. Bad day, wind a-head, blowing hard. Black superstition. Our steward has this moment lost a drop of red blood, which involuntarily fell from his black pug nose. " There," said he, " I have lost my mother—a good friend." This blood-losing he considers as a sure omen of death taking place, having more than once proved it.

9th.—All's in the wrong. Head wind. No fire in the cabin. So cold, that I am compelled to wear two pair of hose, and my large box-coat. Coals are few and our captain stingy, being one of those Yankees (says our first mate) who, in the Southern States, are said to skin a flea for the sake of its hide and tallow. My liver, however, seems on fire, through want of exercise and wholesome food. I am pained in all positions, and every breath is costly. This is an evil day. A small jug of water fell of itself to the floor from the table, at

which the captain in high rage rang for the poor
absent broken-backed steward, and accused him
of doing it. Then, doubling his fist, he knocked
the steward down twice, by violent blows on the
head, and, when down, set his foot on his neck,
and stamped three times on it violently. The
poor fellow gave no provocation, but only begged
for mercy, and said, " Captain, you must do as
you will with me now." He is a faithful creature,
and the captain's conduct brutal, but somewhat
national.

15th.—Turned in this evening, much indisposed,
and in want of every good. Hapless is the prospect; a long passage yet before us, with but little
water, no fire, weather cold, provisions bad and
few. The sailors already on short allowance
both of bread and water, and wind yet a-head.
At two this morning greatly scared by several
frightful squalls, one of which bellowed like loud
thunder, and nearly laid the ship on her lee side;
insomuch that I expected a visit from the grim
king of terrors, clad in his most dismal attire. At
eight, a. m. rose from my bed of horrors after a
racking of 38 hours; sad, as ever fell to the lot of
man! In a gale, and laid to, for the two following
days.

19th.—Wind still a-head. Find that the steerage, through want of cleanliness, swarms with
creeping things. Now, 3,000 miles in a direct
course from our destined port, Charleston city,

We are off those beautiful Western isles, the Azores,
abounding with herds, grapes, wine, oil, and earth-
quakes. Summer, this morning, suddenly burst
in upon us; the air being, in the shade, warmer
than May in England.

20th—Fine day, dead calm, lat. 38°; therm. in
shade 65°, in the water 61°, at night 70°. Have now
taken leave of old winter. It is June; no chilling
breezes. How delightful, to an Englishman, is
weather like this in February. Now, within 70
miles of the Azores, to which ship-loads of maho-
gany are annually drifted along the gulf stream,
from the bay of Honduras.

23rd.—Day-light from six to six in this delightful climate. I saw, during the day, what
sailors call sun-dogs, a species of rainbow, without either pillar or arch, having only a base, and
being thought symptomatic of windy, squally weather. The horizon at sun-set glowing with crimson,
pink, and blue, the perfection of beauty. This
being the 60th day of our passage, we have yet 3,000
miles to sail, and stores for 10 days only. Distress and famine are predicted. The men grumble
about long days' work, and short allowance of
food and sleep; more of the latter is given, and as
to the former, they intend redressing themselves.
At this distance from land, we saw a land-
bird.

25th.—Met a fine Grampus. Rose at five, a. m.
and laid aside my winter dress. Saw a few dol-

phins.　I find my eyes glisten with returning
health, after a week's fine weather and a favourable wind, which has done more for us than the
three preceding weeks.

28*th*.—Lat. 28°, and a fine trade-wind, N. E.
Every thing outward wears a propitious aspect,
but not so within.　Only one ounce of ham for my
breakfast, and no meat for dinner; but soup made
of lean, dry, and dirty salt beef, stewed to rags,
and pudding made of flour and water only.　Feel
however my spirits healed, and find mercy mixed
in this bitter cup, to be long remembered with
blessings and praise.

March 1*st*.—Stripped to my shirt all day.　Sailing eight knots an hour, in lat. 32°.　Saw this night
the young moon in a position new to me, lying
horizontally, flat on her back, as the sailors say,
with her horns upwards; a sign of fine dry weather.　A regular trade-wind, and at sunrise and
set, the sky full of beautiful blushing amber clouds,
of indescribable richness, but common in this latitude.　The sea, by reflection, becomes a flood of
gore, especially while these clouds fly round the
expansive horizon.　The effect was greatly heightened by a huge rainbow at noon, which gave to
the waves all the changeful hues of the camelion.

2*nd*.—Therm. 72°, lat. 26°.　Find it necessary to
seek shade under the awning all day, and at the
second and third watch of the night to take an air-
bath, quite undressed; when I saw Venus, the

bright morning-star, lighting the sky and sea like
a moon, casting a long broad shadow over the
bosom of the wave, and yielding a light nearly
equal to the moon in her first quarter. Being
now nearly in the tropic of Capricorn, all the lumi-
naries of Heaven blazed with a light and brilliancy
quite novel to me. Horrible dissatisfaction openly
reigns amongst the crew, because hard worked
and half starved. The captain, in reply, kindly
called them damned gluttons, and bid them go and
fare better if they could. He complained of my
talking to them, a condescension on my part
which, he said, teaches them insubordination, and
a liberty taken by me not allowable in a cabin
passenger. Saw many flying-fish, winged as a
bird, and also several beautiful tropical birds, a
species of sea-gull, having sharp long tails, formed
of only one quill, and called by sailors *Neptune's
children.*

Our brutish captain this day beat and bruised
the poor steward with a thick rope about his
broken back, head, and face, until a torrent of
red blood gushed from his thick black nose. For
what? Because the poor fellow had been smoking,
and could not by washing make his black face
white!

5th.—Therm. 78°, lat. 22°, long. 40°, and now
midway between London and Charleston. Saw
a fine whale, reflecting in its course from the sun
all the hues of the rainbow; and a large flock of

flying-fish, bright and silvery, and at a distance easily mistaken for the feathered tribe.

Sunday, 7th.—Wind dead a-head; a rather singular circumstance in the trades. The men busy making coffee of roasted barley. Eat the pig, the last killed yesterday. The captain full of dark, savage thoughts. It is now a fortnight since a sail was seen, and as all seems wrong, we droop and hang our heads like bulrushes.

9th.—Lat. 21°, therm. 78°. Met a huge shark, two dolphins, and a grampus. All hands now go nearly naked, and quite stockingless and shoeless, and frequently jump into the brine. A passenger, being once seized with the cramp, soon found himself drowning; on which a line was thrown out, and he seized it with his teeth until it was tied round his arm, and he could be so hauled up.

11th.—S. W. wind blowing a gale all day, a rather remarkable thing in this latitude, being within the tropic line, where a regular trade-wind is expected from either the N. E. or S. E. All hands now brought to short allowance; one biscuit only, in 24 hours, for the crew; and one and a half for each man in the cabin. When I, as now, omit the latitude, it is because we cannot get an observation, and are driven backwards, and tossed to and fro. Our hopes are very low. This evening, immediately after the sun sunk, the full moon rose from a huge pillowy cloud, and shone with an angry redness and largeness, casting an awful splendour on the dark sky and mountainous sea. Still a gale, in direct opposition to the generally received theory of the trades, which should blow as above mentioned, says Captain Wise; but at the command of God, how his works laugh at the theories of man!

12th.—Lat. 22° 15′. A beautiful fat flying-fish flew on board this morning, and furnished us with a delicious breakfast.

Sunday, *14th.*—In lat. 22°, long. 45°. Wind due west, dead a-head; a hope-blasting wind. I continued nearly all last night on deck during a strong gale, it being better to see the worst than to imagine it. This is the sad seventy-eighth day, from the port of London. At three o'clock, p. m. saw, distant from us 10 miles, a large Indiaman; hailed her with a signal of distress. At four, the captain boarded her, the good ship Hamilton of Boston, from Canton 92 days, returning from a trading voyage round the world, manned and commanded by Captain Martyn and a fine, efficient crew of 30 men, and armed with 20 guns, musquetry, swords, and pistols, and a large magazine. Our captain now returned from the Hamilton, with his boat laden with bread, pork, and hams, tea, coffee, sugar, and rum. What a providential supply! What joy shone in the faces of all on board, who till now were greatly suffering, and constantly meditating on what should be their conduct in case of extremities. Captain

Martyn being told that a passenger, meaning myself, was very anxious to quit the Ruthy for his
noble ship, instantly ran on deck, and through
the mouth of a loud sounding brazen trumpet,
said, " Sir, come on board, you are welcome; I
shall charge you nothing, although yet 3,000
miles, in a direct course, to sail." Seeing I
hesitated a little, he sent off his boat and first
officers for me, and through them pressingly renewed his invitation. I now took my leave of the
Ruthy, and returning with them, found my new
captain a generous, gentlemanly man, having a
noble vessel stored with pigs, poultry, turtles,
and goats (for milk), all alive and fat, from Canton city. There was besides on board, a profusion
of China sweetmeats, Jamaica rum, old oily brandy
and wine, and new bread, on table daily; and, at
night, a Chinese bed of down to receive me, all
from Asia, the Sandwich isles, and the north-west
coast of the American continent, where during
the last four years, this adventurous ship has been
trading to its awful hazard but great advantage.
It has netted to its owner in four years 20,000l.;
to the captain seven and a half per cent., and to
the first mate one per cent. The present cargo
being composed of China silks, crapes, and teas,
is rich, and valued at 20,000l. It was received in
exchange for furs and skins, purchased by barter
from the Indians and South Sea islanders, who
gladly take in exchange train-oil, powder, shot,

knives, simple toys, and gaudy printed cottons. This is a fine trade for men of capital.

16th. — Fine day; wind fair, N. E. lat. 22°. Owing to want of science, and inability to take lunar observations, on board the Ruthy, I discover, by Captain Martyn, our longitude to be 48 instead of 45°. We have on board a beautiful white Chinese mouse working a wheel, like a squirrel; and a cage full of Java sparrows, with crimson beaks. Caught this morning three beautiful dolphins, which we fry and eat as a luxury. We now sail nine knots an hour with little motion, and I amuse myself with reading *General Washington's invaluable Legacies.* Beautiful silk umbrellas and huge parasols from Canton, on board; prime cost, two dollars; and portraits, large as life, in elegant frames, at eight dollars each. Living in style at Calcutta, costs for a mess (several in number) one dollar per day.

18th. — Fine breeze, lat. 24°, long. 52° 15'. Caught a fine fat porpoise weighing 200 lbs., which supplies us with beef-steaks, fried in oily fat. Saw beautiful Canton crape, three dollars a piece, sufficient for two dresses; shawls of it equally low and very rich, such as in England are almost unattainable except by the rich. Pictures, too, four of them coloured, four feet in length, and one fan, all for one dollar. These Chinese pictures want expression or impress of mind, yet display great ingenuity.

20th.—Lat. 25°, long. 56°. As to-morrow is Sunday, we this morning kill a fat Canton pig with little head and short legs, a delicious thing at sea. It weighs 100 lbs. (or 40 lbs. Chinese), and is fatted on rice-bran only, food on which an English pig I suppose would starve. Saw a whale almost the length and breadth of the ship.

The owner of the Ruthy, which I quitted, though now a very rich man, the Honourable Wm. Gray, of Boston, who has a ship at almost every port, was once very poor, a little shoemaker. His first mercantile speculation was a shipment of warming-pans to the West Indies, which some wag advised him to send thither; it was, of course, a very successful shipment in so cold a country, but not for the uses intended; the pans were used as ladles for molasses or treacle.

Sunday, 21*st.*—Saw two sail to England bound, and two whales sporting by our ship. What a glorious transfer I have made, and how timely and unexpected, just at the moment when, on board the Ruthy, all our hopes had perished! How merciful is the God on whom I called! For instead of drowning, starving, or eating each other, I am living on the new and interesting luxuries of the east, and surrounded with many rare curiosities of unseen lands; a bleating goat of Owhyhee supplies me with milk; and in the morning, the shrill clarion of Canton cocks, the cack-

ling of geese, and the grunting of swine early
rouse me from my warm and downy bed; and, all
together, make me fancy I am in my farm-yard,
although 4,000 miles distant.

22nd.—Lat. 27°, long. 61°. Now about 11 days
sail from Boston. The captain this morning turning out first, cast a cup of cold water into the
bosom of his clerk, who was yet in bed, and promised him a pailful if necessary. The clerk is
a pleasant young man of about 25, and only said,
" Captain, if you expect perfection of me you will
be disappointed; I am not perfect." Republicans
seem uncommonly tyrannical, and sometimes aristocratical. We sail swiftly, and sometimes 228
miles in a day.

I now sleep in high style every night, having
under my pillow a bottle of madeira and a basket
of China sweetmeats; at my side nine muskets
and a huge broad-sword; and underneath me a
magazine of gunpowder and balls.

24th.—Warm day, wind S. W. almost a calm,
lat. 30°, long. 65°, now opposite to and distant 40
miles from Bermuda, and 720 from Boston, our
destined haven. In this port (says our captain)
there is an old hump-backed pilot now living, to
whom some British officers once waggishly said,
"What's that on your back ?" He answered,
" What do you think? Bunker's hill, to be sure,!"
a reply which silenced the facetious inquirers.

26th—Lat. 32°, long. 66°, sailing all day 7, and at night 10 knots an hour. The old Southern goat, kid, Canton cocks, geese, hogs, and turtles, begin to quake with northern cold. In the winter of 1817-18, the fish generally experienced a vast mortality; the shores and water, quite out at sea, were literally covered with countless tons and ship-loads of dead and dying fish: much to the discomfiture of shipping, dependent on them for a supply of food. The cause is unknown, but supposed to be volcanic; as very frequently, loud subterraneous, or rather subaqueous sounds, like the discharge of artillery, were heard in these desolate regions.

27th.—Now only 440 miles from Boston, wind a-head. At midnight it blew a gale, and we were in serious danger of losing our masts through not taking in sail in time. I rose at this awful hour, and saw the horizon wearing a singularly angry aspect. It is predicted that this gale will continue three days. It did, in fact, last just three days: some men are truly weather-wise, and—

> " Old experience doth attain
> To something like prophetic strain."

Saw three sail; one, a Frenchman, who seemed disposed to conceal his colours, when we shewed him the star-spangled banner, and then loaded, pointed, and fired a cannon over, not at him, just to teach him good manners. He now hoisted the dirty white flag of Louis 18th, but would not speak us. Spoke a Yankee brig, out five days from Boston, and compared her longitude with ours, by exhibiting both on a board, from the bows of each ship. They agreed ; and so proved the nautical skill of our captain to be of the first order.

It is now so cold that three coats are necessary, although only six days since it was too hot to wear one, or any thing else: we are now anxious to see land. Saw the moon distinctly at noonday. In stores for a long voyage, the Americans take out roasted geese, ducks, fowls, partridges and pigeons, in casks secured from external air by closing the tops over with melted lard or mutton fat, so keeping all good for several months: when any are wanted, they are heated over the fire or in an oven. As a luxury, pickled oysters are taken for stewing, which eat as good as if then opened alive from the shell.

30th.—At eight last night came on a strong breeze from S. W. carrying us from 8 to 10 miles an hour, and increasing through this day, to a gale of unprecedented fury. Lat. 36°, long. 68°, by a correct lunar observation. At five this evening, the affectionate mother of one dear and only child was, by the violent rolling of the ship, impelled overboard, and sunk to rise no more, being buried instantly in a huge billow. She was a native of Owhyhee, and is deeply lamented by all on board, who had shared in her kindness, for she was milk and honey to all during a long passage from Asia. But what pen can depict the mad, shrieking sorrows of her now motherless child, who witnessed this sad catastrophe, and who became a poor orphan, dependent on the humanity of the captain or owner of the Hamilton! By force only was the frantic child prevented from plunging into its mother's grave. Its agonies made the following night memorable. The gale, too, continued with unabated fury, ready to blast all hope. At midnight, we found ourselves in the midst of the gulf stream, a current 60 miles broad, and running eastward, in a calm, three miles an hour. Here, until and after the dawn of day, we experienced severe thunder and lightning, forming altogether a horrible tempest; a perfectly novel scene, such as I had never witnessed. Up all night.

31*st*.—The morning dawns, with a most dismal frowning aspect; the air being full of blue fire and crashing thunder, and the sea rising and falling over, on, and around us, like swelling mountains of liquid fire. The captain apparently bewildered, not knowing how to act, and seemingly overwhelmed with doubt and indecision.

At nine, a. m. we tried for soundings, but found none, the gulf being unfathomable. At ten, fell a smothering rain, succeeded by a short calm, when the wind veered to N. W. and the air became suddenly cold and clear, though in the gulf it was singularly, warm and foggy; the salt water was there as warm as milk from the cow, and very steamy, and sparkling like burning sulphur or volcanic lava, having luminous particles large as a hazel nut; but these, when touched by the finger, disappeared. Lat. 39°, long. 70° 50'. Saw several pieces of wreck. This is the last day of March, and was expected to be the last of our lives.

April 1*st.*—Wind N. W. dead a-head, brisk, and colder than I ever felt it on a winter's day in England. I resume my winter dress, but cannot be warm. Tried for soundings, but our line of 140 fathoms found no bottom. At present we know not where we are. The captain, during yesterday's gale sulked, and would eat nothing, nor suffer any thing eatable to be cooked; I was therefore pining 24 hours on tea, coffee, wine, China sweetmeats, and dry, hard biscuit. These brave circumnavigators state, that during the last four years' voyage, they met not a worse gale than the equinoctial tempest of yesterday; and the captain says, that at six, a. m. he saw the most dangerous sea he had ever witnessed. It was mounting 15 feet above the ship, and ready to burst over her stern; a mighty mass of water, more than sufficient to have swept the deck of every man and beast and mast upon it, if not to sink the ship itself. My fears were not great;

but I felt rather loth to die without telling my own tale, or enabling others to tell it for me. " The chamber where the good man meets his fate," seemed indeed a matter of envy, and " privileged beyond the common lot." I desired and prayed it might be mine, instead of sinking in these dark, desolate, unfathomed waters.

At noon, we saw several indications of land; a land-sparrow on our rigging, and several fat Yankee ducks and geese near us. At four, p. m. got soundings in 100 fathoms water, on a sandy bottom, by which we knew we were only 70 miles from land; Gay-head lighthouse. Loaded a cannon, ready for calling a pilot, when we make the said lighthouse; which we hope to do by four to-morrow morning. At six, p. m. saw one sail to the north. At eight, ten, and twelve, p. m. sounded again in 40, 35, and 30 fathoms. Still extremely cold.

2nd.—Fine clear morning; in 10 fathoms white water, just on the edge of a dangerous wrecking shoal, but soon plunged into 20 fathoms.

At ten, a. m. blessed with the heart-cheering sound of *Land, O!* and saw the island of Nantucket from our topmast, distant 15 miles, and marked by three windmills and a few high white houses. My heart now rebounded with gratitude, at being made so signal a monument of providential mercy.

At eleven, a. m. saw distinctly a beautiful island,

16 miles round, of red and yellow ochre, called Martha's Vineyard, now occupied principally by civilized Indians, pilots, and fishermen. We hoisted the patriot colours of South America, the best signal for a pilot, who soon boarded us, and conducted us to an anchorage in the bay, formed by the above island and by a cluster of other smaller isles, smothered with small hardy sheep, which graze all winter upon them. Passed a huge group of wreckful rocks, (some in and some out of the water) called *The Old Sow and Pigs.* At six, p. m. a fishing-boat came along side, and brought us a fine fry in exchange for putrid South-Sea pork. The head fisherman seemed a mighty fine independent fellow, both in manner and conduct. Found our fine huge China turtle (a present for the ship-owner) quite frozen to death; indeed I was myself half frozen, being colder than ever I felt in England in my life. Absence, distance, and difficulty, seem to enhance the value of the unprized comforts which I leave behind me; my heart is thereby enlarged for those too little loved objects whom I have quitted, perhaps, to see no more.

3rd.—At six this morning weighed anchor in *Holm's Hole* harbour, a beautiful little port of Martha's Vineyard. On leaving this pleasant vineyard, we fired a salute of five guns, which nearly shook me out of bed. Saw a beautiful fleet, of 10 sail, around us. The island of Nantucket

alone sent out last year 60 sail of whalers round
Cape Horn.   At noon, we made Cape Cod, a
long neck of land running 100 miles into the sea,
and having four light-houses on it, offering to the
eye a singular scene; an immense bank or ridge
of dirty white sand, quite naked, and bare, without grass, shrubs, or trees; it is the most perilous
part of the coast.   By midnight we made Boston
light, and fired two cannon for a pilot, who soon
came to us, and took the helm.

Sunday, 4th.—At daybreak passed *Fort Independence*, *Fort Strong*, and *Fort William*, which
are all founded by nature, and built upon two
little islands, a fine cluster of which surround and
ornament the mouth of this noble harbour of Boston, now lying, with all its towers, spires, and
masts, in full view before me; the hills around are
all capped with snow.   At eight, a. m. we saluted
this town, the grand emporium of Yankee land,
with 16 guns.   At nine, a. m. our ship was
boarded by its fortunate owner, —— Lyman, jun.
Esq. one of the richest men (says the captain) in
America.   'I was introduced to him by a polite
and friendly shaking of hands, in the presence of
the captain, who said I was an English gentleman
taken out of a ship in distress, belonging to his
neighbour, the Honourable W. Gray.   He then
invited me to his town mansion, and saying that
he would see me again next morning, in the kindest
and most gentlemanly manner took his leave.   I

now shaved and arrayed myself in the costume of
London ; and at ten o'clock, in company with the
captain, went on shore.   With great gratitude, I
felt my foot press the earth once more,—the free
earth of America!   On landing, curiosity brought
many gay, cheerful, free, easy, good-looking faces
to behold, and gaze, and guess, what I, the foreigner, was, whence coming, whither going, and
why?   Of the women whom I saw at first, I
thought but meanly, all being old or ugly; but
the men fair, and in their Sunday dress; the town,
too, though full of melting snow, was highly interesting, especially when associated with the recollection of its having so bravely fought for liberty,
and preferred it to English tea, sweetened with
taxation, and the milk of maternal monarchy.   I
feel much nearer home than I am, and find good
fare, good wine, and good company at my boarding-house, the cost of which is one dollar per day.
My fellow boarders are moderately social.   I accompanied one gentleman to church, an edifice
inwardly and outwardly splendid, and the congregation fashionable; but I thought the service and
sermon very dull and insipid, and the worship
altogether inanimate.   As Sunday here vanishes
with the daylight, I went in the evening to the
Town-hall, to Caucus, a grand political meeting
of thousands of the *Mobocracy*, met to deliberate
upon the choice of a state governor, &c.   The
orators, on the present occasion, being principally

well educated federalists, seemed, some of them, eloquent and ingenious abusers of the democrats, who angrily retorted on their opponents. Thus I found two strong parties, which I am at present unable to define, except as mutual haters of each other, like Whigs and Tories in England.

5th.—The people here seem thankful for nothing, or rather, they do not shew it. Mr. Smith, my landlord, a pleasant Scotsman, advises his and my countrymen to keep at home, if they cannot bring from 500l. to 1,000l. The poor, he says, are not wanted here, nor any where in the state of Massachusetts, where many are unemployed, and nobody is satisfied. According to promise, I met Mr. Lyman again, at his large commercial office, who renewed his kind offer of any needful services while in Boston. He then accompanied me to the exchange, and there introduced me to the richest merchant, save one, in America, the Honourable Wm. Gray, a gentleman of kind manners, but of an eccentric look; with long withered features, pale complexion, white hair, and dressed in an old cloak, and a hat, seemingly 20 years old. Notwithstanding all this, he appeared on change to be an influential object of attraction. He kindly offered me a letter of introduction to his friends and bankers, at Charleston, S. Carolina.

6th.—Seemed pleased with every thing and every body, and every body with me. Visited the State house, where assembles the legislature, and governor at its head. From the top of the dome of this stately structure I surveyed the university of Cambridge and Bunker's Hill, about two miles distant. Boston, from this elevation, appears to be encircled by the sea, and by broad rivers, over which are bridges nearly a mile in length. The beauteous hills and contiguous valleys shine with villas, villages, and towns, which, together, make the perspective rich and inviting to an English stranger. Of churches there are here plenty; but churches create not religion. The new part of the town glitters with elegant mansions, which strike the eye of the stranger with surprise. In these live rich or retired merchants.

7th.—My trunks and person, this day, exposed at the custom-house to a gentle scrutiny only, not a British searching. This establishment is superior and well conducted. At noon very politely introduced by Mr. Jonson to the *Reading Rooms*, where I found nearly all foreign and domestic newspapers. The morning's first salutation from a gentleman to a young lady is, " Miss Lucy, you look smart," or " you come out bright this morning." Fine man,—smart man, or woman, seems the highest praise amongst the commonalty. Took leave of my friendly guide, Mr. Burnham, who left me for the interior. He presented me, at parting, with a keepsake; an elegant burning-glass, for kindling segars; and, in return, carried with him my esteem and regards.

8th.—By appointment I met on change and returned home with Mr. Lyman to dinner, where all,
within and without his establishment, is attractive.
The lady of my host is an accomplished daughter
of —— Otiss, Esq. the celebrated oratorical senator in congress from this state. In politics Mr.
Lyman is a very strong federalist, and his lady
also. She thinks America and its government far
inferior to ours, regrets the loss of the British
yoke, and ranks our Courier and Post amongst
her favourite papers. " And then," said she,
" how pleasant are even the cottages of your
poor!" Mr. Lyman and his lady seemed on all
subjects unanimous, and especially in giving preference to England, and every thing English. His
brother is now in England, on a visit to Holkham,
the seat of our illustrious commoner, Mr. Coke.
Mr. Birkbeck and emigration now became the
theme: " At that gentleman," said he, " I am astonished. He is intentionally or unintentionally de-
luding your English farmers, who, if they come to
America, must drive their own carts, waggons,
and ploughs, into the field and to market, and
work here as hard as labourers work there, or not
live. And even in this state, you see, as to-day,
our farmers hauling their own produce, such as
hay and corn, to market, where they have to stand
all day, or hawk it about from house to house.
What would your smart English farmers think of
this, and how would they like it? If however, Mr.

Birkbeck and others must emigrate, why should they go into our wilderness, far from society, or at best mixing up with the refuse of our population, with men of stained names, thieves, and insolvents, who go thither to hide themselves; voluntary exiles, of whom society is well rid, because unable to endure them. The Caucus which you attended on Sunday night, embodies the respectable part of the citizens, federalists, and democrats, who differ but little in real principle: the former are always most favourable to England, and think a war with her always unnecessary, and an evil to be avoided, the latter prefer France and the French." My host seems to regret that his freehold and other large estates give to him no more power than that of the humblest citizen, and says that my countryman, Joseph Lancaster, will be forbidden to instruct the black people of the South, it being indispensably necessary that they should remain in ignorance.

9th.—Agreeably to promise, I this morning visited the Honourable Wm. Gray, a moderate democrat, a hoary honest patriotic chronicler of America long before the revolution. He is, in other respects, a kind-hearted, intelligent, grandee of this republic, highly influential both in commerce and politics, filling and having filled the most responsible stations in the state of Massachusetts. He seems the exact reverse of Mr. Lyman, in state matters and opinions: he feels sure that British farmers and labourers, of steady habits, must, and do benefit by emigration, to so good and flourishing a country as America, and says, that Englishmen are esteemed far above all other Europeans. I said I thought that feeling was mutual between the people of both countries, but that little good-will existed in our government towards revolted America : he thought so too. "I wish you to call on the British consul, an amiable man, to whom I will introduce you ; he lives near my country seat ; and, sir, any advice or money of mine, is much at your service. I regret I cannot pay you better attentions, for I am greatly pleased to see English gentlemen come amongst us, to witness, as to-day, the fairness, freeness, and openness of our elections, which you see are conducted in an orderly, respectable manner. Here is no con-fusion ; a voter has only to choose his ticket, and give it as and to whom he pleases, and that secretly, and unknown, if he thinks proper." While I was thus snugly closetted with my honourable friend, a gentleman abruptly entered and joined our conversation. He was at the head of a manu-factory of broad cloths, equal, he thought, to any imported. An establishment of this kind, till lately, was almost a novelty ; he wished me to view it. I now said, for the present, farewell ; and was introduced by a professional gentleman, to the floor of the supreme court, then in judgment as-sembled, in a large and goodly building. I heard

D

but little eloquence, and saw nothing interesting about their proceedings; all seemed plain, simple, and undignified, like a vestry meeting in England. The lawyers or counsellors were easy and colloquial, and the judges by no means awful, nor in anywise distinguished, but by a higher bench and a silk gown. The former gentlemen are both wigless and gownless. A wig is thought superfluous, when nature has given hair to the head, whether of a judge or a barrister.

10th.—By Mr. Gray I was this day introduced to the most respectable bookseller in Boston, in order that he, Mr. Armstrong, and others, might view my friend Heath's sample of English quarto Bibles, of unequalled elegance. I sent them; but a note, politely written, soon accompanied their return; stating that on account of the extreme scarcity of money, the gentlemen declined purchasing, but wished to do me service.

Intending to quit Boston on Monday, Mr. Lyman called on me, and took a formal leave, but wished me to revisit him, now or at a future time; saying that his brother, a large proprietor and farmer in the district of Maine, wished to see and communicate with me on agricultural matters. I also called on, and bid a final farewell to my friend, Mr. Gray, who very kindly put into my hand an introductory letter to his bankers and agents at Charleston, with a liberal purse of dollars, which he thought I should need before I

could arrive at my destination. This purse was
unsolicited, and received without absolute necessity on my part, and without giving him any security for it. I took it principally for the sake
of the singular confidence and liberality shewn
in the circumstance, and for the same reason I
here record it. "Take, sir," said he, "more
money."—"O this is more than enough," replied
I,—"What! enough? Take more, and repay it
at your own time and convenience. I shall be happy to hear of your happiness and safe arrival; my
son and his lady sailed last week in one of my
best ships. I wish you had come in time for it:
you should have sailed with him to the south,
whither he is gone on a tour of health."

Sunday, 11th.—To chapel, once. Thought less
meanly of American worship than on Sunday last,
the sermon being rather eloquent, and containing
something more like religion. Sunday commences
here on the Saturday eve; or, at any rate, ends at
sunset on the following eve. Taught three of my
fellow boarders, (revenue captains,) good manners.
They were all standing spread out before the fire,
to the complete exclusion of all around. I reached
two or three chairs for them. They all took the
hint, and were immediately seated at a fit distance
from the fire, while all the rest of the company
seemed greatly amused by the silent lecture which
John Bull had so smartly given them.

12th.—Left the good Yankee town of Boston,

this morning, full of blessings on it and America, but scarcely hoping to find another Boston, where I wished a longer stay, because people of all ranks and colours are so generally disposed to please and be pleased. Left behind me a letter of thanks to Captain Martyn of Cape Ann, who so generously snatched me out of the vile and starving Ruthy, and kept and conveyed me well and safely so many miles, without charging or wishing to charge a single cent. At nine, a. m. got under weigh on board the packet schooner, Swiftsure, for Charleston, S. C. about 1,000 miles passage. Met seven comical fellow passengers, besides a country-woman of mine, Miss Jane Compere, an ancient maid, who states that all emigrants with whom she is acquainted, are disappointed ; but that they settle in an unfit neighbourhood. She is going to her reverend brother, a missionary, living at Bethel town. I learn from her that the Rev. Mr. Keeling, late of Woburn, Bucks, Old England, and known to J. Ingle, the patriarch of Somersham, is now with his wife and children settled in a church near Boston, and likely to succeed. Many of the followers of Mr. Keeling, who accompanied him thither, felt and feel greatly disappointed.

The captain discovers a few stray vermin in the cabin, and I, two whales in sport, spouting water at each other.

12th.—Awoke this morning and found myself

out of sight of land, and 150 miles from Boston,
lat. 40° 59'. At nine, a. m. caught a fine fat ha-
libut, a most valuable fish, weighing 180 pounds;
the flesh of which partakes of fish, flesh, and fowl,
and is fit for broiling, frying, boiling, or stewing.

14th.—The price of passage, in this vessel, to
Charleston, is 15 dollars; to Havre, in France,
100 dollars. Picton, near Halifax, Nova Scotia,
is a good place for cheapness of passage to England; 12l. and found in cabin. At three, a. m·
spoke a schooner, the Eloisa, 17 days from New
Orleans, to Boston bound, requesting our latitude
and longitude, and what distance from the south
shoal of Nantucket. It is no unusual thing for
some of the people of this country, on going to
Charleston, to take their free negroes with them
and sell them for slaves, by way of turning a
penny, or as they say, of making a good *spec.* of it.
Two white gentlemen, I was told, determined on
a plan to benefit themselves, and cheat the planter,
or slave buyer; one blackened his face and body
and became a negro; the other was his owner and
salesman, and sold his friend to the planter for
800 dollars, but in less than three days he returned, a white free-man again, to divide the spoil,
nor was the imposition ever discovered to prosecution. Our captain had green peas, on the 1st
March, in abundance at Charleston. From two
passengers, (shoemakers), I learn that first-rate
hands will turn out from five to six pairs of

ladies' shoes, per day, and earn from 10 to 12 dollars per week.   One of these gentlemen, a staunch republican, Mr. Atman, of Lynn, near Boston, and an intelligent man, says, in reference to the federalists, that for every Julius Cæsar, there is a Brutus.

16th.—Spoke a brig, the James Monroe, from New Orleans.   Recommended my ship-mate, Mr. Atman, to read Mr. Fearon's *Sketches*, which he promised to do, but learning they were unfavourable to America, he said he thought he should not read them.   My Yankee friends love nothing but unmixed flattery.   My fellow passengers, one a colonel, and the rest of the most respectable order of the middle class, all seem of uncleanly manners and habits; with unwashed hands, and grossly indelicate in language.   To the honour however of this section of the land, there seem few or no idle hands; from the richest down to the poorest, meanest citizen, none are seen eating the bread of idleness; even my rich friends, Mr. Lyman and Mr. Gray, are no exception to this remark.   The former gentleman is found at his office after dinner, till sunset; and the latter, by sunrise throughout the year.

17th.—Lat. 36°, long. 74°, a beautiful morning, after much lightning and thunder, at six, a. m. when all sail was taken in, in expectation of a terrible squall.   Saw an immense number of dog-fish round our stern.

Sunday, 18*th*.—A very warm dense fog to-day, at noon, and therefore unable to get an observation ; but judge ourselves to be off Cape Hatteras, 260 miles from Charleston ; and, on sounding, found 20 fathoms ; saw four sail ; the wind very variable.

19*th*.—Rose at eight this morning, becalmed in the gulf stream, and therefore drifting back with the current, three miles an hour. The air and water warm and steamy, and the sky summerish and gleamy, and ornamented with huge pillar-like thunder-clouds, from which we saw one small and one very large water-spout, about one mile distant, and dipping into the sea. It was formed like a tunnel, bottom or tube upwards. Nine of these phenomena are sometimes seen at once in this tempestuous latitude, 34° 40′, long. 76°, from Greenwich. A fine breeze immediately followed the bursting of these two spouts.

At midnight came on a terrific tempest, filling the horizon above, and the sea beneath, with blue forked lightning, and stunning the ear with loud-sounding, crackling, rattling, crashing thunder, presenting a scene more sublimely horrific than I had ever seen ; the lightning might almost be handled, being what our captain calls " *double-twisted ropy*." The gulf seemed, literally, a lake of boiling fire and brimstone.

20*th*.—Warm, calm, bright day, and 13 sail in sight. Yankee sailors, says our captain, are now

so badly paid (14 dollars per month), that they
leave the sea, for ploughing land, and therefore
half the crews of our vessels are composed of British seamen. I find that watches, costing from
three and a half dollars to 20 dollars each, are
selling at Massachusetts from six to 30 dollars
each; made in Geneva, but marked *London*.

21*st*.—At two this morning we were providentially prevented from running our ship ashore, on
those dangerous shoals off Cape Look-out, by a
singular dream of the captain's, who awoke much
alarmed with the dream, in which he saw both
sides of the ship falling out, a complete wreck.
He rushed on deck, took soundings in 15 fathoms,
and again in only nine fathoms, just on the edge
of these fearful shoals, where, in less than twenty
minutes, we must, perhaps, have gone to pieces,
and sunk like lead in the mighty waters. But in
all this deliverance, there were none who seemed
to see and acknowledge the hand of Omnipotence.

Now, 120 miles from the city; spoke a schooner,
26 days from North Carolina, and in distress for
provisions, yet only bound to Savannah, about
400 miles from her starting.

22*nd*.—After safely passing Cape Fear, again
greeted with the blessed sound of *Land, O;* and
saw the beautiful isles round Charleston where
I arrived at six, on the evening of this day; so
finishing a passage of 112 days, the longest, perhaps, ever known between London and this city.

Presented my kind introductory letter from Mr. W.
Gray to Messrs. Prescot and Bishop, two eastern
gentlemen, who politely introduced me to Mr. Bird,
landlord of the Planters' hotel, where I became
immediately acquainted with the high-minded General Young Blood, then boarding at this house,
and on a visit to the city, to meet his excellency
the governor, and also the president of the United
States, who, on the morrow, was expected to make
his entry here.   The general and I became very
friendly, and held a long and interesting conversation, and that without a formal introduction, which
is generally held to be indispensable amongst almost all ranks in this country.   In our politics,
foreign and domestic, we seemed one.   At nine
this evening, I plunged into a warm bath to wash
off all marine impurities, paying for it half a
dollar.   I was then introduced by Mr. Bishop, to
the grand hall, where his excellency is to dine in
public next week, with all the grandees of this
aristocratical state.   During my walk to and fro,
and on my landing, I felt immediately impressed
with the respectable, happy, and healthy appearance of the slaves, with which the city seems to
swarm, and of whom I have now six or seven
males, and as many females, in constant attendance, and one or two at all meals, surrounding
the long table, waving over it plumes of peacock's
feathers, to fan away hungry flies from eatables
and eaters.   It is commonly asserted, and main-

tained, that slaves are happier here and better off
than free blacks. There seems, indeed, in this
city, no want of happiness amongst them.

23rd.—Accompanied by my courteous and
obliging friend, Mr. Bishop, to my bankers, Mess.
Lovent and Wulf, Germans, of high commercial
repute, and to Mitchell King, Esq., now Judge
King, a Scotch gentleman of high reputation, to
whom, with several others too numerous to name,
I brought letters of introduction. At three o'clock
I returned to my hotel to dinner, where I again met,
in the chair, General Young Blood, —— Watts,
Esq., the Secretary of State, the French consul, and
many other grandees of this state, civil and military.
Besides turtle-soup and turtle-steaks, the number
of our viands was to me countless, and at present
indescribable; and to every plate stood two half-
pint decanters of rum, brandy, or Hollands, to
drink at dinner, instead of ale. After dinner
came claret, champaigne, and cider, all of the best
kind, for those gentlemen who gave an order for
it, and to those who did not, the bottle seemed to
pass with the name of its proprietor, when both
socially drank to each other. In the evening,
after supper or tea, I was taken by —— Prescott,
Esq., to the grand new steam-ship, the *Savannah*,
a beautiful and superb vessel, then about sailing,
for the first time, to Liverpool and St. Petersburgh.

24th.—Bought a piece of fine India bandanas,
seven in number, for 34s. Fixed on William, a

fine young yellow slave, as my body guard, to attend my person within or without, and to dress or undress if necessary. He so offered himself, agreeable to the custom of this establishment, and is considered always at command and faithful to his trust. The population of this warm city seems above half black and yellow. Called on the venerable Nathaniel Russell, Esq., residing in a splendid mansion, surrounded by a wilderness of flowers, and bowers of myrtles, oranges, and lemons, smothered with fruit and flowers. This gentleman is near 90 years old, very courteous and friendly, and willing to give any assistance in promoting the object of my mission, being the original trustee to the estate of my late matrimonial uncles, Rowland and Henry Rugely, Esqrs. These gentlemen were merchants here and in London, previous to the American revolution, in which they bravely fought as colonels under Lord Cornwallis. The former, Rowland, a poet of some celebrity, died a natural death in this city, and the latter (Henry) at Potton Beds. Old England lost in them two generous fellows, of whom I shall hereafter say more.

Sunday, 25th.—Conducted by Mr. Bird to the seat of Patrick Duncan, Esq., a Scotsman, who emigrated 36 years since, and is now the head of a bank in this city. He is a rich, knowing old gentleman, living in a garden of the choicest flowers and fruits, breaking down the trees with their

weight. Although, nine days ago, I was freezing
amidst an icy, snowy winter, yet here is summer
in all her gay luxuriance, and down every street
is the Pride of India (a tree so called) in full
flowery perfection, forming an ornamental colon-
nade on every side. Met and parted with Dr.
Osgood, a physician of Boston. He kindly left
me introductory letters to two of his friends here,
a physician and a counsellor, each in his profession, the most eminent man in the city.

26th.—Met my countryman, G. Beale Brown,
Esq. of the respectable firm of Bainbridge and
Brown, London, and gave him my introductory
letter from England. Thought him a clever, smart,
and efficient young gentleman, willing to further
the interests of my mission. Walked several miles
on a dusty, sandy road, under a scorching sun, in
expectation of seeing and meeting his excellency,
the President of the United States, who, this morning, made his public entry into this city. But he
passed by me in the tumultuous crowd, quite unobserved. So many civil and military characters,
more imposing in figure, quite eclipsed the supreme
magistrate. We therefore returned as we went.
By Mr. Bishop, introduced to two noble young
fellows, Mr. Richmond of Philadelphia, and Mr.
Dodge of Providence, who kindly pressed me to
visit them in the north.

27th.—Promenaded round the city with Mr.
Brown, who introduced me to F. Fleming, Esq.,

and to the respectable firm of Messrs. Broadfoot and M'Neale.

28th.—After rising this morning, from my hot and feverish bed, I found, by the inflammatory eruptions on my hands, legs, and feet, that I had been stung by the mosquitoes, which, in New Orleans, are said to kill more men than the pestilence; as a remedy, I bathed the parts stung and swollen in brandy, and, at noon, took a warm bath. A leno net, fine as a lady's veil, surrounded my bed in future, and protected me from these midnight blood-thirsty assassins, which seldom annoyed me more.

May 1st.—A waggoner, on the day of the president's entry to this city, was commanded, by the military, to move out of the road, and give place to the coming show. " Pray," said he, " by what authority do you stop me?—It is more than the president dare do. Shew me your authority. If you had civilly asked me, I would have driven into the ditch to *obleege* you." During the few days spent here, several robberies, burglaries, and attempts at murder, have disgraced and alarmed this city. In the street where I sleep, for two nights successively, our slumbers have been disturbed by the cries of *murder!* At the theatre. a gentleman has been stabbed by a Spaniard. This morning presented a poor fellow lying all night until nine, a. m. in the street, in a hot, broiling sun, 110° by the thermometer. He was found nearly murdered, having his legs both broken, and otherwise terribly bruised about his head and breast, and robbed of all he had, 15 dollars. To the disgrace of the nightly watch and city centinels, and to the open day humanity of the citizens, here was he suffered to lie, saturated with pestilential dew, and, in the day, left to roast and be devoured by flies, until an old Prussian colonel offered a dollar to have him removed as a nuisance, too disgusting to delicate nerves and sensibilities. Mr. Brown, a landlord in Church Street, then called out to two black men, " Here, June and July, come and assist, and tell August to help you." These three men were so named ; and but for them and the colonel, the poor forsaken sufferer must have taken three months, literally, to effect his removal.

Sunday, 2nd.—Went in grand procession to the elegant Scotch church, where I met, and was seated near his excellency the President, James Monroe, Esq , an amiable, mild-looking gentleman, of about 60, dressed in a common hat, plain blue coat with gilt buttons, yellow kerseymere waistcoat, drab breeches and white silk stockings, and a little powder in his hair, just a sober grey. His eyes beam with an expansive kindness, gentleness, and liberality, not often seen in persons of his elevated station, and his physiognomy, viewed as a whole, announces a noble, well-judging, and generous mind.

3rd.—Paid my hotel bill, 28 dollars and a half for 11 days. The business of the bar-keeper, an influential character, seems to be, to make a bill. One bottle of madeira, in the bill, more than 1 ordered or drank. It is charged 2 dollars or 9*s.* sterling a bottle, and cider half a dollar, the finest in the world, and first cousin to champaigne; it is made in the north. Strong cider is procured thus: set out a large cask, during winter, until the whole body seems frozen; then bore into its centre, from which runs an unfreezeable quantity, highly spirituous. It is then bottled and closely corked, and in summer comes forth, the pure sparkling soul of the barrel. Parted with Mr. Richmond for the north, a sober, sensible, honourable man.

5th.—Wrote to J. Ingle in Illinois, and to my cousin, Major Rugely, of Camden, S. Carolina, apprizing them of my intended visit. General Young Blood, the lieutenant governor of this state, took his leave of us this morning for his country seat. Introduced this day by my friend, Colonel M'Kinnon, to a young gentleman, —— Edwards, Esq. of Savannah, and others, who, with the young colonel, had all there met as gay proud birds of a feather; men, I mean, who, in duels, had killed their man each!!

6th.—Colonel M'Kinnon was this day refused claret at dinner. The landlord was called to account for so refusing, and instructing the bar-keeper. He appeared, and said, " You, colonel,

have referred me to your father for payment of
your bill of 250 dollars, contracted here during
the last three weeks, but he says he cannot and
will not pay any more for you.   And that I know
from your father's friend, Captain Bell of the ship
Homer, now in port." After this, the colonel
looked thoughtful, and requested I would accompany him to the captain.   I did so.   After the
captain had politely spread out his brandy, the
colonel, with pistols in his hand, said, " If you
will not meet me I will shoot you instantly." The
captain, with an angry laugh, replied, " O fear
not! I am ready with either sword or pistol, and
to-morrow morning, at ten, expect me at the hotel."
He fulfilled his promise, but the colonel had cooled
and fled.   After our return from the ship, the colonel wanted to shoot the landlord, and then attempted to shoot himself, but had no prime.   He
then begged round for prime, but could get none.
I endeavoured to reason with him, but with as
much effect as with a woman possessed with seven
devils.   " I have a right, sir," said he, " to do as
Brutus did. ' What Cato did, and Addison ap-
proved, cannot be wrong.'   I am a blasted lily
and a blighted heath." This young gentleman,
naturally witty and highly gifted, has married and
abandoned three wives, and yet is only 22 years
of age.

7th.—Visited the supreme court, over which
preside six judges on the bench, but, from my

not understanding the nature of the cases under consideration, the speeches of the several young advocates seemed jargon, and little short of nonsense. In court I met Patrick Duncan, Esq., who knew a young gentleman, who once bought a negro wench, the only slave he ever purchased; but, at his death, his heirs divided 70 slaves amongst them, all her offspring and posterity, during a period of only 35 years. Increase and multiply is here the grand first order of the day. Two men were this day sentenced to die; one for the murder of a white man, and the other for stealing a negro. A man may, here, murder a negro almost with impunity, or by paying a paltry fine to the state; but, if he steals one, he must be hanged for it, and almost without benefit of clergy.

I find, that James Gregory, Esq., a gentleman to whom I brought an introductory letter, stands at present much in the way of my mission. Visited Judge King, my constant friend and adviser. He came hither from lean-landed Scotland, bringing nothing with him but his capacities. He began as a schoolmaster, but, during his leisure hours, gained a knowledge of law, in which, though not great as an orator, he has become eminent as an advocate and judge, because he is wise, honest, and good. He came hither in his own proper name of Michael Kinggo, which, at the request of his American friends, he changed into Mitchel King,

his right name being obnoxious to national prejudices.

Sunday, 9th. Accompanied Mrs. Atkins, a
countrywoman of mine, once of St. Ives, a lady
of good fortune, and amiable mind and manners,
to the new Episcopal church, to which a female
friend of hers has subscribed 4,000 dollars. Met
a small genteel auditory, in a splendid edifice;
but the parson seemed dull. He prayed not for
George IV., but for the President; nor for lords
temporal and spiritual in parliament assembled,
but for the congress, &c. I walked nearly all
day through a dissolving heat, and thought myself
the better for it. So necessary is exercise to the
continuance of health.

10th. Leaving Planter's hotel for a season, I
took my place in the Columbia mail, 15 dollars
for 70 miles, and slept at the mail-house. Met
several travellers who knew my friends in the interior, and found them talkative and agreeable on
subjects interesting to me. after I had told them
who I was, what I was, whither going, and for
what purpose.

12th.—At four this morning we left the city by
the mail, four in hand, and drove on to a team-boat,
worked by eight horses, by which we were ferried
over the Ashley river, large and broad as the
Thames. We soon entered what seemed to be an
interminable forest, and rode 28 miles to breakfast,
in company with his Excellency J. Geddiss, Esq.,

Governor of South Carolina, an Irish gentleman of much style, but apparently of easy, kind, sociable and polite manners. We met accidentally; and he presided at table, frequently helping and inviting me to beefsteak, chicken, cakes, coffee and tea, for which we paid three quarters of a dollar. We passed a large deep black-looking pond, on the banks of which are sometimes seen as many as ten huge alligators, ten feet along. A puppy carried thither and made to cry, calls them instantly up from the bottom of the pond, when they seize and eat it, as they would the carriers, if they remained. 1 saw no plantation on which I should like to live; but the best are not viewed from the road. Many, however, I observed cleared, cultivated, worn out, and abandoned, with their houses burnt down, or otherwise in ruins. Passed, during the day, General Young Blood and other gentlemen-travellers, who all invariably bowed politely to me and to my fellow-travellers. On inquiring the cause of this bowing to strangers, I was given to understand that this state boasts of a supereminent degree of civilization. We slept and supped at a farm-house, on roast leg of pork hot, price for all, one dollar; but we longed for some of the many squirrels and other game which we passed all day.

13th.—This day's journey of 80 miles lies through a valley of sand, nearly on a level with the sea, and without any hills, stones, or pebbles

105193

on its surface. Roused at two this morning from
my refreshing bed in the bosom of this vast wilderness, which, during the night, seems awfully dark
and still. Intermitting sounds are, however,
heard, something like the noise of a distant water-
fall, and produced (a poet would say) by the
trees becoming vocal and talking all together.

Language is inadequate to describe a journey
through this interesting, romantic, fantastic forest.
At one time the eye beholds large fleets or groves
of naked masts, trees which have been girdled,
and by time stripped of all their bark : at another,
roads apparently conducting to the houses of great
men ; spots, too beautiful for description, into
which the traveller enters by infinite serpentine
windings. To find what? Miserable negro huts,
and negroes, (if by night) with blazing torches in
their hands. The roads and paths are so constantly and suddenly winding, and withal so
beautiful, that common mortals might fear to
proceed further, expecting to meet some mighty
prince or celestial spirit in these sacred haunts ;
or perhaps some gigantic monster, rushing out of
these dark shades to annihilate all. Imagination
is here highly and almost fearfully excited. It
is, therefore, difficult to rid one's self of the idea
that one is certainly moving into some castle or
palace, by favourite concealed paths, ornamented
with magnolias. An archbishop seems conse-
crating the spot ; but, as I approach nearer, I find

the most reverend father is only the black stump
of a burnt tree, variegated with ashes. Immense
snakes, alligators, and hydras, appear in burnt
serpentine arms of trees, waiting to fall on and
destroy the poor traveller. But it is impossible
to convey a just idea of the beauties and deceptions of these singular regions.

A little before sunset, this day, we crossed the
fine river Wateree, a little below its falls and
rocks.   On the banks of this river, stands Columbia, the capital of South Carolina, and the
seat of a flourishing university. Here, too, my
friend, Governor Geddiss, sits enthroned as king
over his parliament or state government annually
assembled. I sup and sleep at the house and
sumptuous table of Mr. Randolph, where for the
present I say good night.

14th.—At breakfast, I found five or six sorts of
bread, hot and cold, with boiled rice and *hominy*,
Indian corn husked and boiled. Visited the
university and its president's house; Dr. Max-
well is the head. There are here 125 students who
are very disorderly, frequently disturbing congregations on the Sunday, because the Doctor is too
idle to preach, and thereby keep them together.
Saw several of these learned young gentlemen
stretched on a table, with their learned legs carelessly hanging out of their chamber windows,
which seemed nearly all broken. Want of discipline is here too palpable, but there is no lack

of whiskey. In company with the ladies of Mr. Randolph's family, I attended a lecture given at the house of the minister, an able man, who very impressively said, " The Christian must swear on the altar of his God never to forgive sin; never to be its friend; as did Hannibal against the Romans."

15th.—I left sweet Columbia this morning, well pleased with the compliment paid to me and my distant country, by Captain Strode, now here on a visit from Fayette-Ville, who entrusted to me, though a perfect stranger to him and all here, an unsealed letter full of cash for his lady, to whom I was requested to forward it by the first safe conveyance. " Before my marriage," said the captain, " I had a splendid carriage and a pair of the finest horses in the world, given me by a friend, but now gifts are few and unwanted." He seems to love his old mother-country, and says, " I think king, lords, and commons to be the best system of government for Old England, if the commons were but good and faithful."

Arrived at fair Camden at six o'clock, p. m. First and again crossed the Wateree river, in the stage, on a flat. Called on I. K. Douglas, Esq., who was not at home. Took a hasty view of this good and growing town, sacred to revolutionary blood and battles, and where my uncle Henry, the loyal British colonel, lived, loved, fought, ran away, and lived to fight another day.

Sunday, 16th.—Called a second time at the

mansion of Mr. Douglas; not at home. I thought myself slighted, but found, on meeting him at the Presbyterian church, that I was mistaken. He had called at my hotel, and waited at the church-door for me, where he kindly engaged to drive, or find guard, horses, and carriage, to conduct me, to his and my late uncle's friend, General Cantey. From two gentlemen present, I learned many anecdotes of my uncle, Colonel Rugeley. He was a favourite royalist, but often hesitated; yet, by the advice and reasoning of his friend, Colonel Chesnut, (lately dead) it was mutually agreed, that Colonel Rugeley, being a man of influence, and then the richest of the British, should remain true to his party, and that Colonel Chesnut should adhere to the side of the rebels, in order that each might be useful to the country, and serve the sufferers on both sides, which they did in an eminent degree, during that long day of trial and unnatural strife. Attended three times this day, at Presbyterian and Methodist churches, where I met small congregations, little talent, and, as I thought, less devotion.

Very politely waited on and invited to ride, this evening, with five young, dashing, generous Carolinians, who all came on horseback, with a horse in their hand for me, in order to shew me fields of revolutionary battles, and the solitary house which Lord Cornwallis made his head-quarters, during the battle of Camden.

I saw, with some surprise, churches and the tombs of citizens, all exposed on the common, uninclosed, and without a grave-yard ; as though man had died accidentally and was buried in like manner. Some graves were distinguished by shrubs, laurels, and flowers, planted on them, and had rails around them, to prevent swine and cattle from offering indignities to the dead, who here seem to slumber in unregretted forgetfulness. But it is patriarchal " to bury my dead out of my sight."

Negro's food.—All that some planters deem necessary is one peck of corn-meal and a little salt for an adult, and six quarts for a child, without either milk or bacon. Such is the allowance for a whole week ! What gluttony! What extravagance in a land of scarcity! Famine surely is at hand.

17th.—With a handsome introductory epistle from Mr. Douglas, I met General Cantey, Captain Cantey, and ladies, at one of his mansions, seven miles off in the wilderness, on a beautiful plantation of several thousand acres of cotton and corn, and full of well-treated negroes. I went thither on horseback, attended by a horseman (a slave of Mr. Douglas) riding behind me, and remaining with me all night until I returned. Graciously and heartily received and entertained by the hospitable general, who was a prisoner to the British during the revolution, and was very rudely treated. He is one of the finest old fellows I have met with

in the South. " I once," said he, " told Colonel
Rugeley that I thought we rebels should succeed."
" What! they succeed?" rejoined the colonel,
" Aye! you may as well expect the sky will fall,
to catch larks." What a miserable prophecy, my
uncle! How soon didst thou find thyself mistaken,
and fly, a refugee, to the West Indies, to return
no more, until all was peace and pure republicanism.

18th.—A splendid breakfast this morning, with
the general, of tea and coffee, flowing from the
most elegant urns of silver, and other vessels of
corresponding beauty and costliness. Returned
to Camden after viewing the plantation, on which
I saw a small village of negro-huts well peopled,
and, in the garden, a long and beautiful dark
bowery walk, formed by grape-vines, laden with
fruit. Visited Messieurs M'Caws' store, where
I saw British broad-cloths, second quality, costing
seven, and selling at ten dollars, or 45s. per yard.
" A mighty fine price!" At a late hour this evening, came an invitation from Mr. Douglas, for-
bidding my departure on the ensuing morning, and
insisting on my company to dinner at his house,
with General Cantey and family, and a large and
splendid circle of friends. I, being nothing loth,
obediently complied.

19th.—Dined, this day, at four, p. m. at the elegant and hospitable table of Mr. Douglas, where I
met General and Captain Cantey, and ladies, and

James S. Day, Esq. a Yankee, one of the most intelligent and superior men I have ever seen in this or
in any country. He married a daughter of the late
Colonel Chesnut, an old friend of my late uncle, and
received a fortune of 25,000*l.* with his lady. His
attentions to me were very marked and kindly dis-
tinguishing. I know not that I have ever met
with in any other man, so happy a stock of ideas,
and so appropriate and pleasant a flow of language,
with which to express and adorn them. Our
table was rich, and groaned with a variety of
viands, wines, and cordials, finely coloured. Many
fine fruits garnish the table and tempt the palate
in Carolina. The whole of our dinner party retired to the neighbouring house of Mr. Martin, to
tea and coffee, where the number of our ladies was
quadrupled. The mode of spending the evening
is here highly interesting. No cards nor any species
of gaming are introduced; but the ladies, as all are
connoisseurs in music, take in turn the grand piano,
and play and sing to it delightfully; while conversation goes round in tête à tête groups, as though
the voice of music were not heard. At a rather
late hour the party breaks up; none of the ladies
walked home, but their family chariots were thick
in waiting round the door, and into them were all
led with great homage and attention, yet without
any formality. Thus they meet and part, pleasing
and well pleased with each other.

20*th*—Just as I was mounting my carriage and

leaving Camden, Mr. Douglas called to say that he had engaged me to ride over the rich and matchless plantations of —— M'Cray, Esq. in company with the proprietor, Mr. Day and Mr. Weatherspoon, who all waited on me at my hotel for that purpose. I found from 1,000 to 2,000 acres planted with cotton and corn, and all in a state of high cultivation on a gardening system. Cotton in good times is worth 100 dollars, or 22*l*. 10*s*. an acre, and costs 25 dollars, or 5*l*. 12*s*. 6*d*. This gentleman (M'Cray) derives a net profit of 10,000*l*. to 12,000*l*. sterling a year, and is the proprietor of 5,000 acres of valuable land. General Cantey possesses 30,000 acres. Their black cattle (alias slaves) do not breed freely, but destroy their young in embryo, because they are slaves, but still they are considered to be the best cattle kept. Their treatment appears to be humane; their day's work or task being done by one o'clock, if they labour well. Their condition seems in some respects better than that of the paupers of my native land. It is said that the blacks are unconscious of any degradation, but of the truth of this assertion I greatly doubt. The planters generally profess to abhor the force and cruelty of the task-master or overseer, but still think both indispensable, and that their estates could not be cultivated without them.

This evening, in consequence of a polite card of invitation from the stewards or managers, Captain Cantey and J. M'Caw, M. D., I attended a gay and glittering hymeneal ball of the gentry of this town and neighbourhood. Soon after the marriage of any couple of distinction, it is customary for the bachelors to give a ball to the recently wedded pair. The ladies, were almost all interesting in person and manners, and superbly dressed; and it was said, sure of large and good fortunes.

21st.—Paid my bill, 16 dollars, and quitted Camden, where many flattering marks of respect constantly attended me. I wrote a few notes, expressive of my gratitude, and of my most sincere desire to return all their kindness.

I now re-entered the wilderness, in which both myself and guides were several times lost; but, at length, found my destination, the lone log-house and plantation of my cousin, Major Rowland Rugeley, eldest son of the late Colonel H. Rugeley. He was not at home, but his wife, a young thoughtful woman, with two babes, received me kindly, and, in a patriarchal style, found food for me and my guides, and provender for our beasts. The house has only three rooms; no chambers nor any windows of glass. To my hostess I was quite a stranger, and kept myself so a considerable time. I merely said, that I supposed her quiet was seldom disturbed by the approach of a strange guest like me. "Strangers," said she, "sometimes call for refreshment, because this house was once open for their accommodation." "Where," said I.

"is Mr. Rugeley?" She artlessly replied, "He is gone to the bank at Columbia, to get money if he can; for he is unable to sell the crop of cotton, and is therefore much harassed for money." "Where lives Mr. Henry Rugeley?" "He, sir, lives near; both families have long been accustomed to drink at the same spring." I felt delighted with this primitive simplicity; it seemed to carry me back to the beginning of time. I now gave her my introductory letter from her aunt, Mrs. S. Rugeley of Potton, in Old England, relict of the late —— Rugeley, Esq. high sheriff of Bedfordshire. She read it; the secret was now out; I was no longer a stranger; she seemed highly pleased, and said, "How happy will Mr. Rugeley be to see you!"

22nd.—Major Rugeley, during the last night, returned; and this morning he received me, a welcome guest. He spread a table full of good things for me in the wilderness, and well garnished it with ingenuous kindness. I was immediately at home and treated as one of the family. After breakfast we rode to the house of his brother, Capt. H. Rugeley, a sprightly young planter with a young wife, two babes, and 14 negroes, all his own. Returned and dined with both, very patriarchally. Met several ladies and gentlemen of the wilderness.

Rugeley anecdotes.—Our uncle, the late Rowland Rugeley, Esq. the facetious poet, and much-loved companion of the ducal family of Montagu, married a beautiful but poor girl, and both soon after died of the yellow fever, within a month of each other.

Before, in, and after the long revolutionary war, the late Colonel Rugeley lived one of the most esteemed of men. Although on the British side, he was thought to be an American at heart; and his extensive influence, as a first settler at Camden, was generously exerted in doing good, and procuring mercy for and from both parties. His good opinion and favourable representation, were life and salvation to hundreds on both sides, often under confiscation and sentence of death, the fruits of a hasty court-martial. Many Americans when taken prisoners by the British, were suffered to be at large on their parole of honour, never to fight more; but having broken their parole and being taken again in arms, they were hanged and shot instantly in great numbers. But if there were any, on either side, who happily knew Colonel Rugeley, that knowledge, and his confirmation of it, was complete redemption. He was a favourite, also, because he never suffered his soldiers to plunder, as others did. Being once in an extremity, he cut and marked some pine blocks, so as to resemble cannon on an intrenchment, and in consequence surrendered his regiment on good terms to the republicans. In the consideration even of a generation unknown to him, his memory is precious. After the peace, and the establishment of independence, he returned home, and was prosecuted 36 times in the American courts by men, whom, it was alleged, his revolutionary troops had injured ; but he was victorious in his defence of all the suits, out of which he came, says a survivor, with honour un-spotted.   He was the most friendly and indulgent of men towards neighbours and negroes, for he loved and served all. He would not have returned to die in England, but for the infidelity of his lady, during his flight to the mother country. Her guilty paramour was the colonel's confidential overseer, who, after the final departure of his master, married the lady. This affair, it is here thought, broke the noble heart of the colonel ; who soon after his return, slept, and was gathered unto his fathers.

Sunday, 23d.—I dined, this day, at my cousin Captain Rugeley's, with Mr. Irvin and family. At sunset, I visited the negro-huts, in which I found small nests or beds, full of black babies. The women were cooking corn-cakes in pans over the fire. Oak-leaves were laid over the cakes, and then hot embers or ashes on them : thus they are speedily baked. All seemed happy, having kind treatment, full bellies, and little thought ; be-ing unconsciously degraded, to the level of the beasts that perish. Saw no church, nor heard any thing of a sabbath. Slept at the Captain's in a good bed, curtainless, alongside the one in which himself and lady and children slept ; all in one room, the only one in the house ; with

a fine negro-wench on the floor, at our feet, as
our body-guard, all night, in readiness, to hush the
children. Thus patriarchally did I and my cou-
sins dress and undress, talk and sleep. What
lovely simplicity! It is all pure, unsophisticat-
ed nature—a shining contrast to all I saw at
Camden.

24th.—All the morning hunting deer, but killed
none. Visited Captain Rugeley's rich plantations.
One negro to 12 acres of land, and one horse to
every 24 acres, are thought to be sufficient. Met
a large and social party, including Mr. J. Rochell
and Mr. M——, two intelligent and gentlemanly
men, brothers-in-law of the Rugeleys. All these,
and many others, are here living in great ease and
independence, but still they seem dissatisfied, and
on the wing for another and better country, the
Alibama territory, where they have made purchases of fresh land and new homes. An awful
tempest darkened and illuminated the mountainous forest this evening, during which I noticed
large luminous sparks of fire in the trees, which I
found to be *fire-flies*, or as they are here called
lightning-bugs. These curious insects have been
seen in clusters, hanging on two trees on each
side of a road, and at a distance resembling two
lamps.

Introduced at Mr. Rochell's to an ancient black
woman of about 80 or 85, a favourite negro of the
late Colonel Rugeley, and once his cook. They

told her I was one of his English children. The
good old creature shed tears, and would have
kissed me for joy.

25th.—Dined with Mr. Irwin, and a kind family
party. Two gentlemen, planters, came this morning to the major to make for them the conveyance
of a negro, whom one had just bought of the other,
and who was warranted to him sound wind and
limb, and to be defended against all other claims.
If a negro dies soon after sale, or at the end of six
months, the physician is called in, not to restore
life, but to open the body, and thereby ascertain
whether the slave died from unsoundness and old
diseases, or from recent sickness. If from the
former cause, the purchase money is returned.
Negroes occasionally ride their masters' horses all
night, to the distance of many miles, on trading
excursions, selling what they have stolen during
the week. About three weeks since, a gentleman
planter of this neighbourhood, had one of his
slaves, a strong fellow, whipped to death for stealing. The party who presided over this horrid
execution, were all, as well as the owner, drunk,
a circumstance which is here offered as an excuse
for murder; or rather for whipping away 1,000
dollars, the prime cost of the victim.

26th.—Much alarmed last night, while in my
bed in the state-room. Something jumped on my
dressing table, drank up the water, broke the glass,
and disappeared. It was a rascally rat. I was

awakened again by a singular rustling, rattling noise underneath my bed, and suspected it must be a huge rattle-snake. What a bed-fellow! It came not however into bed, but continued to annoy me all night with intermitting noises. What, gentle reader, dost thou think it proved to be? A good motherly old hen on her nest, full of hatching eggs, which she found it necessary to turn over frequently. She disturbed me no more, but remained my well-known companion.

27th. — Dined this day with Mr. J. Rochell, a fine hearty Carolinian, who promises me a handsome cane of ironwood as a keepsake. Here, where slavery prevails in perfection, which Carolinians call their curse, it is calculated that the labour on a plantation costs nothing; and that by breeding freely, and by the consequent increase of saleable slaves, the planter is even a gainer, exclusive of the costless labour. The market price of negroes fluctuates with the price of produce.

Buffaloes, which herd together in vast numbers, are thus decoyed and taken; but not alive. A man dresses himself in one of their skins, and walks on all fours to the brink of a stupendous precipice, so concealed as to be unobserved by the hurrying animals. The decoy steps aside, and **down** rush and tumble the herd, and break their necks or legs in falling. The skins and tongues are then taken and the carcases left.

28th. — Took leave of Captain Rugeley, and ac-

companied Major Rowland Rugeley to the seat
and goodly plantation of his wife's venerable father,
—— Mickle, Esq. to dine and spend the day and
night; being now on my return to the city, by
way of Columbia. Here I found a rich patriarchal
table, and at it, Major J. Jo. Mickle and J. Elliston
Pea, two only sons and favorites, young gentlemen
of fine fortunes. After dinner we went a hunting
but caught nothing, except one of the most venomous serpents, called a Mocoson, and the rattle
of a rattle-snake. Examined a vegetable, said to
be efficacious as a remedy for the bite of these
deadly serpents, and received a root of it. It is
cultivated in gardens, but taken originally from
the forest. It resembles a fleur-de-lis, and the flag
which grows in English marshes, and is called
the Rattle-snake's Master-piece. When the leg or
hand of a man is bitten, the limb is buried in the
earth, until a milky decoction and fomentation can
be made from this herb, which, if promptly applied
externally and internally, is an unfailing specific.
The burying the parts affected, prevents, it is said,
the poison from circulating through the system to
the heart. I witnessed, at a late hour this evening, a tempest remarkably awful, during which the
good old man prayed to the God of thunder, while
all the family surrounded its domestic altar. This
gentleman (Mr. Mickle, sen.) appears to me to
be a rare example of pure and undefiled religion;

kind and gentle in manners, and much resembling
good old Ingle, the Patriarch of Somersham.

Seeing such a swarm, or rather herd, of young
negroes, creeping and dancing about the door and
yard of his mansion, all appearing healthy, happy,
and frolicsome, and withal fat and decently clothed,
both young and old, I felt induced to praise the
economy under which they lived. " Aye," said
he, " I have many black people, but I never
bought nor sold any in my life. All that you see
came to me with my estate by virtue of my father's
will. They are all, old and young, true and faithful to my interests; they need no task-master, no
overseer; they will do all, and more than I expect
them to do; and I can trust them with untold
gold. All the adults are well instructed, and all
are members of Christian churches in the neighbourhood; and their conduct is becoming their
professions. I respect them as my children, and
they look on me as their friend and father. Were
they to be taken from me, it would be the most unhappy event of their lives." This conversation
induced me to view more attentively the faces of
the adult slaves; and I was astonished at the free,
easy, sober, intelligent, and thoughtful impression,
which such an economy as Mr. Mickle's had in-
delibly made on their countenances. Blush, ye
black whites of America, when ye behold these
white blacks !

29th.—At nine o'clock, after receiving the blessing of this family and its venerable head, I moved towards Columbia, greatly regretting that I could stay no longer. I shall, perhaps, see him no more; but wheresoever this humble page shall bear his honoured name, liberty, justice, and truth, shall bless him, and make him a blessing.

At noon, we were overtaken in the forest by a tremendous storm of wind, hail, rain, thunder and lightning; huge trees fell around us; houses were unroofed; and we were exposed to all its fury in our chaise under a tree. The air seemed full of thunder-bolts, insomuch that I fancied myself shot through and through. Hail-stones, large as pigeons' eggs, smote us and our horse, but were not permitted to do us harm.

About 20 miles west of Columbia, we saw a party of jurymen and other citizens, digging up the body of a slave, who had been wantonly whipped to death, and buried privately about a week since, and that too by the hands of his own master. As this is the second man thus murdered, the first being left unburied for dogs to eat, I hereby resolve to give publicity to all the particulars of the last case when I reach the city. The gentleman who disclosed to the Coroner the secret of this outrageous murder, came to us, stated the case clearly, and invited us to go with him and behold what was once man, but then a mis-shapen mass of putrescence. At sunset we reached Columbia, and bid farewell to the kind and generous Major Rugeley. I promised to revisit him, but could not; a circumstance which I much regretted, because he and his sire had collected a museum, containing many natural curiosities of the state, in readiness for my return to them and England.

Sunday, 30th.—Off by six o'clock. Saw a large field of wheat ready for the harvest, and white plums, dead ripe, in great abundance. Four young negroes were offered for sale at 1,000 dollars the lump, but found no customers, although they would some time since have sold for double and triple that amount. Saw a large venomous Mocoson. Slept this night 68 miles from Columbia; a dreadful tempest, all night, almost equal to that of yesterday. I found my bed alive with bugs, fleas, and other vermin; rose at two, a. m., to shake myself, and enjoy a sort of respite from these creeping, tormenting bedfellows. On opening my window, I was annoyed by frogs innumerable, of two species; some loudly whistling or chattering, like English sparrows at pairing-time; others, bitterly lamenting, like thousands of chickens deserted by their mother hens; others, bellowing like cows in sorrow for weaning calves. This confusion from within and from without, from above and from below, spoiled my night's rest, and seemed to carry me back a few scores of centuries,

into Egyptian plagues. I was not a little pleased
and surprised to find that none of my restless bedfellows accompanied me.

31st.—I started at three this morning. Noticing
during the preceding day, a large number of young
naked negroes, male and female, all very healthy;
I praised their appearance. A gentleman, standing
by, seemed to enjoy and take that praise to himself. " They are mine, sir," said he, meaning
that he had bred them. " I treat them well. When
hungry, I feed them ; when sick, I send for a
doctor for them. My care over them is money
well spent. As to clothing, you see they want
none." We changed horses and stopped half an
hour at Mrs. Chandler's mail-house. At eight
o'clock, this evening, I once more found myself at
the Planter's hotel, to sleep in a bed without a
mosquito net, and to rise, growling at my old
negro chamberlain and landlady. Saw, during
the day, moss hanging in large ropy lengths from
the forest trees down to the earth ; a certain in-
dication of rich land, but of a sickly and pestilential situation.

June 1st.—Closetted with Judge King. This
good and honest man deems a monarchical syste
of government, having a limited monarchy, the
best for all countries. The poor are kept in better
order by it. He believes also that the republican
system is not yet fairly tried in America ; the
people being scattered over a wide surface, and

therefore unable to concentrate or organise them-selves against the system yet. He thinks also that the national debt of England is a national good! " A good," rejoined I, " from which may the Lord deliver both us and you!"

2nd.—Waited on Doctor Benjamin Huger, with my introductory letter from Dr. Osgood. These gentlemen were once fellow-students at the uni-versity of Cambridge. I thought the doctor a clever and interesting man.

3rd.—Rose, this morning, stung and lamed by mosquitoes. As a remedy I bathed the parts af-fected in brandy, and then lay half an hour in a warm bath, at 95° by the thermometer. Two of my fellow-boarders, one a rich German Jew, a jeweller, and the other a German quack-doctor, came to me and requested that I would " make a duel" between them. They had quarrelled about a horse running in the Jew's curricle. " I want, and wish, and will," said the doctor, " throw a bullet into the Jew's shoulder." I declined com-mencing manufacturer of duels. —— Robertson, Esq., from Scotland, a near relative of the cele-brated Dr. Robertson, the historian, came to invite me to a dinner at Mrs. Monroe's to-morrow. The party to be composed of Scotch and English merchants only, and the dinner given by one of the party in honour of King George.

4th.—The birth-day of George III. Agreeable to engagement, we celebrated this anniversary at

a sumptuous table, surrounded principally by
dashing Scotchmen, at which, in a shower of champaigne, nearly all present were loyally drunk to
the honour of Great George. As this feast was
too highly seasoned with loyalty, no Americans
were admitted.

5th.—My resolution, made on the 29th, was
this morning carried into effect in the following
letter to the editor of the Courier, copies of which
I saw printed in other papers, nearly 2,000 miles
from this city.

From the Charleston Courier of June 5.

" The well taught philosophic mind,
To all compassion gives,
Casts round the world an equal eye,
And feels for all that lives !"

Mrs. Barbauld.

" Sir,—On my way to this city, from a short
tour through the interior of this state, a few days
ago, 20 miles west of Columbia, I was suddenly
attracted to a spot of earth, over which a respectable company of citizens were deeply intent on witnessing the exhumation of the body of an animal,
costing 1,200 dollars; but which its humane
owner, (one Kelly) and three other persons like-
minded, had seized and tied to a tree at midnight,
and each in turn wantonly whipped until sun-rise;
when, from excessive lashing, *its bowels gushed
out,* and it expired, and was instantly buried in a

private corner on Sunday, the 23rd ult. But, on inquiry, the said animal proved to be of the negro, and by some was thought to be of the human species; and stood " guilty of having a skin not coloured like our own." An offence for which these arbiters of life and death, doomed it to die! To their honour, it should be told, that, when fainting, they threw cold water on its face, and poured whiskey down its throat, in order to *prolong the sport*. It, however, for several minutes before it was untied, became speechless and motionless, as the tree to which it was bound. It could feel and writhe and smart under the merciless lash no longer.

" Good God! exclaimed I, where am I? on the earth which thou hast created, and didst once pronounce blessed; or in the Pandemonium of the heathen? Heaven, I knew it could not be, for a cruel task-master, his hands imbrued in human blood, had just crossed my path! Is it then, I continued, free America? an asylum for the distressed and oppressed of all other lands; the land of my adored Washington; the adopted country of my dearest friends; the only country on this huge cursed earth, where liberty finds an ark, or rest for the sole of her pained foot; and the country to which I came with every fond prejudice and predilection! What! free, and yet offer up human sacrifice! Monstrous anomaly! Go; fly these hasty lines through the world! Challenge offended

humanity to produce a spectacle so genuinely
hellish, or so purely demoniacal! Did, sir, ever a
sabbath-sun dawn on a catastrophe so abhorrent
to your feelings, or those of

>   " Sir, your most obedient servant,
>   " W. FAUX.
> " *Planter's Hotel, Charleston,*
>   *June* 2, 1819."

A great noise was heard as soon as the Courier
appeared; some approving, others disapproving,
as interest or humanity prompted. James Gregory, Esq. first called this morning, regretting
that I had thus written. He then introduced me
to a noble Marquis, now the French consul here,
with whom I dined, and who very condescendingly
offered to introduce me to his friend the British
consul. " I love England," said he, " in either
peace or war; in peace she is more friendly than
America; and in war, she is a brave and noble
enemy. There is much honour in beating her,
and consequently but little disgrace in being
beaten by her." Soon after dinner came a gentleman, a candidate for legislatorial honours, Mr.
Condy, aid-de-camp to his Excellency the Governor, bearing a message and compliments to me
from the Governor, begging to know when I could
wait on the Attorney-General with Mr. Condy, to
make an affidavit of facts, touching the case stated
in my letter of to-day. I replied, I was engaged

for the present, but would accompany him to the mansion of the Attorney-General next morning. He then politely took his leave, promising to re-visit me in the morning.

Sunday, 6th.—At ten o'clock this morning I went in due form with the governor's aid-de-camp to Colonel Haines, the young Attorney-General, who, when I entered, after a polite reception, ad-dressed me as follows:—" Now, sir, will you please to open to me your sources of informa-tion, touching this alleged murder? But, sir, give me leave to say, that I think that you have acted imprudently in publishing it so hastily, inasmuch as it interferes with the province of a jury." I replied, " My motives are good, and they must shelter me. I fear not the conse-quences. Too little publicity, I think, is given to such cases: what I have done is calculated to prevent a recurrence of such enormities." "But, sir, you have stained the character of South Caro-lina, and what you have thus written will be gree-dily copied and extensively read to our injury, in the northern and eastern states, and all over Eu-rope. But, sir, let me tell you, further, that such offences rarely occur in this state, which is always prompt to punish the offenders. Will you or can you give personal evidence?" I answered, "I can-not. I can do no more than I have done. My publication and my conversation with you, sir, are sufficient. From what I have said to you now,

the matter is tangible enough." "Well, sir," rejoined he, "if that is all that you will do and
say, we must leave it, and I will write immediately
to the district attorney, and get Kelly indicted."
This conversation or examination occupied about
an hour, and was politely conducted. There is
no evidence, that the learned gentleman redeemed
his promise here given. A well written pamphlet
by my friend, J. Wright, reproaches Mr. Attorney-
General with direct breach of promise in this affair.

Dined and spent the day with Mitchel King,
Esq., at whose table I met the reverend minister
of the Scotch church, and heard him preach in
the evening.

The most eminent advocates in the law here,
rarely make above 2,000*l.* sterling, and the salaries
of the judges are under 1,000*l.* per annum.

I thought the reverend gentleman above named,
neither eloquent nor very interesting. Our conversation turned from lawyers to divines. We all
united in praising and admiring the Rev. Robert
Hall, of Leicester, who through the medium of the
press seems intimately known and highly valued,
here. Specimens of his oratory, from some of his
printed sermons, are given for examples to young
students in the ministry, and may be seen in a
work called, *The American Pulpit Orator.*

7th.—Met my venerable friend Nathaniel Russell, Esq. and his son-in-law, Mr. Middleton, living
in a nest of roses, and both regretting the cause of

my letter respecting the negroes, because it would
make a deep impression to their prejudice in the
northern states. I saw and ate ripe figs, pears, apples, and plums in abundance, the rich productions
of this generous climate, which now fill the markets, as though it were Autumn instead of June.
Terribly stung by mosquitoes, fleas, and bugs.
Feeling inflammatory symptoms, something like
bilious fever, I took two grains of calomel, and a
very warm relaxing bath, and found relief. I drank
also less toddy and punch, which, in this country,
are certainly bilious.

I noticed to-day the galley-slaves all singing
songs in chorus, regulated by the motion of their
oars; the music was barbarously harmonious.
Some were plaintive love-songs. The verse was
their own, and abounding either in praise or satire,
intended for kind or unkind masters.

8th.—This morning, at the command of the Governor, and under the direction of the Attorney-
General, appeared in the Courier some vague
paragraphs on the subject of my examination,
before the latter gentleman on Sunday. It was
a vain endeavour to obliterate the deep impression made, and still making by my negro letter.
Soon after I began my morning walk, I was met
and rather rudely catechised by a Mr. Bee, who
much importuned me to accompany him to the
Times Office, and see the above reply, which appeared in both papers. This tart republican de-

fender of slavery, seemed disposed to quarrel with
me, but I had seen the article and declined his
invitation. " Go," said he, " and do justice to
injured Carolina." To do that would be to make
negroes and planters, for a few years, exchange
places and stations.

I dined, and spent the day and night on Sullivan's healthy island, four miles in the sea, east of
the city. On landing I found the elegant chariot
of Mr. Gregory, with two negroes in waiting on
the beach to take me up, and when I returned, I
was attended in like manner. At this gentleman's
summer seat, washed by the ocean, I met with an
agreeable dinner in the English style. But as I,
in the execution of the objects of my mission, had
called on Mr. G. to give an account of his long
stewardship, in the affairs of the Rugeley property,
and wanted money from him, I was not a very
welcome guest, nor he to me the most agreeable
host. His lady seemed a superior woman.

9th.—On my return to the city, this morning, I
found a silly and ill-natured epistle in the Times
paper on the subject of my negro letter. It is
certainly honourable to this state that so much
excitement is seen, on touching its sore and
vulnerable part. Judge King regrets that I should
have so written, and says I must not answer my
opponents in the way I wish. It will be thought
time-serving, and be read to my prejudice on both

sides of the water. "And moreover," says he,
"the Carolinians are chivalrous, and will pursue
you with the most determined animosity, if you
continue to provoke and wound them on this tender point." Such being the state of public feeling,
in this free country, I was cautioned against being
out late in the evening. "Take care of yourself,"
said my friends, "for dirking is the fashion." I
therefore declined further controversy; merely
saying, that though the paupers of England were
by the planters thought to be worse off than their
negroes, yet in England, bad as things are, not even
a lord may kill a man without being hanged for
it; a specific which I could recommend to all
negro-killers in America.

10th.—I visited the high court of justice, where
but little talent seems necessary, and where the
judge upon the bench and the counsel and crier
below, all seem upon an easy, familiar footing
of equality; consulting together, tête-à-tête, about
the time of opening court next day. His lordship
then left the bench, and stepping into his sulky,
with a negro-boy behind him, drove off. No ceremony, no trumpets told the multitude that he was
a judge, and that it was judgment day.

11th.—Thomas Ferreand, Esq., a Frenchman,
and an eminent merchant of this city, shot himself
on the eve of this day; pecuniary embarrassment
was the cause. He had endorsed bills to a large

amount, for the accommodation of a friend in the
city, who had just failed and deceived him. Ferreand sent a challenge in consequence, but was
advised to wait three days for an answer. Before
the end of April he shot himself in the following
manner. Accompanied by his servant, a male
negro, he went down to the battery hanging over
the sea, at ten o'clock at night, taking a pair of
loaded pistols with him. On his arrival, he took
off his coat, and gave the negro two letters just
written, one for his chief clerk, and the other for
his lady. The negro, now suspecting evil, began
to give an alarm ; when Ferreand, to hush him,
pointed one pistol at him, and discharging the
other into his own mouth, fell instantly dead over
the battery into the sea.

12*th.*—I spent this day in the Court of Common
Pleas, witnessing the eloquence of the American
bar. The cause a negro wench, to whom two citizens laid claim. Twelve witnesses on both sides
swore to her identity. This trial, being the sixth
on the same case, lasted four whole days. Colonel
Haines, the young Attorney-General, displayed
a pleasant species of eloquence, quite conversational. Mr. Barrister Hunt was low and stormy.
The jury, unable to come to an unanimous decision, were locked up till midnight, when they could
dissolve themselves, but they remained until eleven on Sunday morning. Food was furnished to
them by stealth. The state immediately altered

the law to compel juries to sit until they can decide, or be liberated by consent of parties. On the Monday, the jury again met, and were locked up again for four days, and liberated by consent of parties without giving a verdict. The case therefore remains to be tried a seventh time.

Sunday, 13*th.*—Accompanied Nathaniel Russell, Esq. (whose son-in-law was a bishop) to an excellent church, this morning, but saw, as I thought, little piety or devotion.

14*th.*—Again at court, to witness the form of passing sentence on a criminal, the turnkey of the prison, who was convicted of aiding the escape of a murderer. He seemed a genteel or *smart* young fellow, and with little emotion heard himself doomed to be branded with the letter M on the thick of his thumb, and imprisoned one year. The judge, in a black silk gown, a very judicious, kind-hearted man, shewed how just and reasonable was the sentence pronounced.

I left the Planter's hotel, (Charleston,) where funerals begin to be frequent, owing to pestilential air, and took up my abode on Sullivan's cool, salubrious isle, to which I go with an agreeable young Yankee, Mr. Coffin, bound to New Orleans and Natches.

16*th.*—I find myself delightfully situated on this island of White Land, where not a blade of grass is seen; only hedges of *bagonet* plants and myrtles. It is a naked island, of about eight miles in cir-

cumference, variegated with summer mansions,
refuges from pestilence. The sea is tumultuously
roaring about one's ears all night, and kissing one's
feet all day. The houses are of wood, and built on
wooden posts or pillars, so that the sea may flow
(at high-tide in winter) underneath.

17th.—In the city, to which I can go by steam
four times a day, I saw large flocks of vultures,
called turkey buzzards, because they are of the size
and form of a turkey. At a neighbouring city,
Savannah, there is a law to enforce the fine of five
dollars for every bird of this species, wantonly
killed. They fly about like carrion-crows in England, but so tame that you may walk amongst
and kill them easily. This, however, is not permitted, as they devour all filth and putrescence,
and are considered as friends to the community
at large.

The judges, counsellors, senators, and representatives, down to the constables, in this state,
are, it is said, the slaves of popularity. Laws are
therefore enacted and decisions made, unfriendly to
the public good. In the courts, the influence of
the bench over the bar is scarcely seen or felt; or,
if at all used, it is done in the most gentle and
delicate manner, both seemingly mutually obliged
and obliging. The same conduct also exists in the
bar, towards witnesses, who audaciously mount
the judge's bench to give evidence. This love of
popularity is deemed by some an enemy to the

general weal.　My landlady, Mrs. Calder, a Caledonian, grumbles greatly, because her billiard table pays a tax of 100 dollars annually.　How hard !

The Scotch people, of whom there are many in this city and state, are the most successful merchants; yet they abuse America violently, and never become citizens.　In time of war, they are therefore very properly deemed and treated as aliens and prisoners, and ordered out of the seaports into the interior, where they must quietly continue until peace is made.

My landlord, Mr. Calder, during his last visit to Scotland, was imprisoned on a charge of endeavouring to force his negro back to America.　The poor negro's chains fell off, when he reached old Scotland, where he now lives, a free man.

At sunset, a few evenings since, while among plantations, suddenly burst upon my ear an earth-rending shout.　It proceeded from negroes shouting three times three, on finishing their task.

20th.—The ladies of Carolina, it is said, prefer a fair effeminate kind of man to one of a robust habit, and swarthy dark complexion.　This preference of delicate complexions originates in their antipathy to any colour approaching to that of the negro or mulatto, or yellow man, whom it is sometimes difficult to distinguish from a white or brown person.

Squatters are natives who squat or settle on

vacant, unoccupied lands in the interior of the
country, and claim a title thereto by long undis-
turbed possession, in which the government protects them. The heirs of the late R. and H.
Rugeley have lost 80,000 acres, now in the hands
of Squatters. On the verge of barbarism, near the
Indian territory, when a respectable settler comes
with authority to occupy the lands, these squatters are known to dress and disguise themselves
as Indians, and present themselves, with the rifle
and tomahawk, to the servants of the settlers,
whom they threaten with destruction. This is
intended to scare away all new comers, and has,
in some instances, had the desired effect. To
remedy this, it was proclaimed that the first Indian
seen, mock or real, should be shot without ceremony. Hence no more sham Indians were seen.

21st.—I sailed over to the city with his Excellency Governor Geddiss, who seems friendly, and
generally known, shaking hands with nearly all in
the boat. It is a pleasing feature of this people
that all are outwardly social, bordering on something like equality. This feature, though delu-
sive, strikes, and is highly interesting to strangers
from old countries, and is beneficial to America,
to which it particularly attaches them ; and, perhaps, both natives and adopted citizens are thereby
fraternised.

In the Washington City Gazette, I saw the good
speeches of Mr.——, while chairman of the

forum. My prophecies respecting this distinguished friend and excellent man are, I see, fast fulfilling. With fair play, such men as he and Mr.
Pittiss, late of the isle of Wight, must succeed any
where, and therefore furnish no fair criterion of
success in emigration generally.

22nd.—My countryman, Mr. Beaumont of
Huntingdonshire, called, and introducing himself
to breakfast with me this morning, continued two
hours in conversation. He states that he came an
unrecommended stranger to this town, only two
years since. He advertised his wishes, and had
immediate offers of first-rate situations on plantations. He engaged at 500 dollars the first year;
half the profits of the dairy, all the poultry: and
advances every year, either by an increased salary,
or by a per centage on the produce. He saves
money, and doubts not of being able to realize a
competency as an overseer; but he thinks clerkships in stores much more desirable and beneficial.
Any young man who is steady, must, he is sure,
do well there. Mr. Beaumont has introduced the
English system of agriculture, so far as practicable, with success. The value of one acre of rice
is 100 dollars, or 22l. 10s. sterling, and its cost
about 30 dollars.

23rd.—Yesterday, as a mark of special favour,
I received a present of a female slave from my
hostess, Mrs. Calder. Her name is Cassandra.
She was to be dressed as a man and pass for my

body guard to England, and then to be given to my neighbour George Thompson, Esq. of Somersham, who had requested me to procure a pair of negroes for the use of his establishment.   On communicating the news of this transfer to the fair and youthful Cassandra, she wept bitterly, and tore her curly wool; the thought of leaving her old mistress and many young acquaintances, was death to all her hopes.   When I heard this, I proceeded with her owner in due form to take possession of my fair property.   She looked piteously at me.   I told her she was mine and must accompany me to England.   She sighed and cried, and said, " What, Massa! Go to dat far off country?" " Yes."   " O, Massa! let me go and see, and bid good bye to all my dear children, and grandchildren, and great grandchildren.   I do love 'em dearly."   When I declined to accept the gift, her tears vanished, like dew before the sun, and joy lighted up her black wrinkled countenance ; for she was turned of 80, and her woolly head was white as snow.

24th.—— Broadfoot, Esq., a merchant in the city, informed me at dinner, that he was once on a jury, in a cause where a female sued a white man of this state for 60l., the amount of 12 years maintenance of her and his natural child.   She gained the cause, but he not being able to pay debt and costs, or give security, was actually sentenced to be sold for a term of years, until his labour had paid the demand. How equitable! how patriarchal!

I am here paying 3*s*. 6*d*. a bottle for bad London porter, just 700*l*. per cent. above cost, and 18*s*. 8*d*. a gallon; three times dearer than real French brandy, or any other spirits, the best of which is sold at a dollar and a half a gallon.

At Charleston, no black man, though free and rich, and having horses and carriages to let, as for instance, John Jones, the landlord of the best house in the city, is permitted to ride them for pleasure as his own, nor to be seen out of his own house after ten at night, when the thundering drum and the centinels from the guard-house, go round to clear the streets of all men, women, or children, stained with negro blood.

Sunday, 27th.—It was reported this morning that the pestilence, called the yellow fever, had made its entry into this city, and that the board of health had, as is usual, requested all strangers and visitors to depart. This report was, in part, untrue; one man in the hospital had just died of it, but he brought it with him from the Havannah. This disease in its nature seems at present not understood, nor correctly defined by the faculty here. Disputes have arisen only to darken the subject. Some hold it to be contagious, others infectious. The houses, in which it first appears, are generally pulled down; while others are fumigated and washed with strong lime-water, and the families removed from the street to the fields and kept in tents. This disease seems confined to the western world, and to have been known there, from the time of its discovery by Columbus; but it prevails most in the southern states, cities, and swamps. It sometimes extends as far north as lat. 40°. In rainy seasons, and during a long westerly wind, it is more fatal than common. In Charleston, it is said not to be contagious. Its first symptoms are a pain in the back and head ; then a vomiting of black fluid, resembling coffee grounds; a mortification next ensues, and the patient dies quickly and easily in about three days after its commencement.

My friend, Mr. Kelsall, a visitor at my hotel, states that he lately met at the Planter's hotel a party of thirteen gentlemen, eleven of whom had each killed his man in duels. A military officer, living in this city, kept a mistress, who knew and disliked the friend of her gallant, then living at New Orleans, and of whom she said many evil things to her gallant, which he fully credited. The New Orleans friend was then instantly challenged by letter, to which he answered personally, saying the charge against him was false, and, in explaining, he could prove it to be so. They met, and the New Orleans man, with the first shot, killed the accuser ; and that, says my informant, deservedly. The survivor went up to shake hands with the dying man. " No," said he, with a bitter oath, " Have I missed you?" The seconds then asked him what were his last wishes. " I have a pair of pistols, given me by a brave fellow and I should be sorry that they should fall into the hands of a coward; put them, I pray you, into my coffin with me." The point of honour is maintained here in high perfection. A scoundrel, who has cheated his creditors, if reproached with it, calls out his man and kills him if he can.

28th.—I quitted for ever Sullivan's pleasant isle of myrtles, a sure refuge from pestilential heat and poisonous mosquitoes, in the hot, sandy, stinking city of Charleston, where the elements, earth, air, and water, swarm with all that is noxious. At 11, a. m., we got under weigh in the good packet *General Wade Hampton*, Captain Baker, commander. I paid 30 dollars for my passage in the cabin, full of genteel and agreeable passengers, male and female, of the first rank and quality, all bound to the city of Philadelphia. I left letters of thanks behind me for the many civilities received from Messrs. Prescot and Bishop, N. Russel, Esq., (now no more) and several other gentlemen, to whom may this page carry my grateful regards. So great was the difference in exchange between north and south, that I had to pay my banker 4*l.* per cent. for New York paper, and 7*l.* per cent. for specie, silver dollars. Southern paper is somewhat ragged in reputation at New York. Our good captain, who is an honest gentlemanly man, knows, in Carolina, a poor master-builder from England, who landed without money, but who in the course of a few weeks, by jobbing about among the planters, saved money enough to send over for his large family, now all with him, flourishing together to all their hearts' desire. As surely as the sun shines, so will industry prosper in any almost untaxed community.

30th. — In the gulf-stream all last night, and passed, unseen, Cape Hatteras, having sailed 400 miles since Monday. J. W. Ancrum, Esq. with his lady and family, and six black servants, are on board. Mr. Ancrum's lady is a branch of the Washington family, a niece of the late General, and he a senator of Carolina, to whose civilities I acknowledge myself indebted. " At a recent contested election," says he, " I saw a candidate soliciting the vote of a gentleman freeholder in our state, where freeholders only, by the bye, have a vote. The answer was this : " Why, colonel, I always reckoned you was an independent man, quite above begging. I now find I was grossly deceived and mistaken. I came here purposely to give you my vote, which is now in my hand ; but as you have demeaned yourself so much as to ask me for it, I shall not give it to you but to your opponent." What a lesson is this to the old world. But think not that candidates and electors are, here, all incorruptible. A barbecued

hog in the woods, and plenty of whiskey, will buy
birthrights and secure elections, even in America.

July 1*st.*—We were greeted with the sight and
sound of *Land a-head O !* the coast of Pennsylvania and Philadelphia light-house; thus passing
from Charleston light-house to this, in the short
space of 60 hours, a distance of between six and
seven hundred miles, averaging ten miles an hour.
At six this evening, we anchored in the spacious
Bay of Delaware, 20 miles broad, dividing the
two states of Jersey and Delaware. At nine we
passed the quarantine establishment, (a noble
asylum) with but a slight scrutiny by the doctors,
although we expected detention, on account of
the sickness on board and of the pestilence left
behind us.

2*d.*—At six this morning we reached Newcastle,
on the banks of the river Delaware, 40 miles from
Philadelphia. The scenery here, on both banks,
is enchanting. The hay and oat harvest, now
general along these lovely banks, perfumes the
air of the river with odours. Here, too, the contrast is heightened by the recent view of parched,
bare sands in the south; for here all is green, gay,
and flowery; and fine commodious farm-houses
and rich pastures, full of cattle and sheep, variegate the perspective in every direction, quite up
to Philadelphia. In the south are no pastures;.
in the north, plenty, well stocked with beeves or

bullocks of enormous size and weight. We passed
the bare Hessian bank, a sandy bluff on the river,
so called ; where, during the revolutionary war,
a post of poor hireling Hessian soldiers was surprised and destroyed by the rebels. This spot, it
is said, is haunted by spectres, and the grass,
therefore, has never since grown upon it. We
landed in the city, at one o'clock, p. m. having
travelled 800 miles in four days, with a rapidity
seldom equalled. The city, viewed from the river,
is neither imposing nor interesting, nor does it
present any thing striking, until you reach its
centre. Quitting the good ship *Wade Hampton*,
which is formed of a part of William Penn's noble
tree, under which he made peace with the Indians,
I put up and dined at Jud's good hotel, with my
southern Irish friend, Moses Wood, Esq. an agreeable and kind-hearted young gentleman, of a
good temper. In the evening, attended by a free
negro, I called with my several introductory letters to Messrs. Price, whom I saw ; —— Krugg,
Esq. gone to Kentucky ; Jerry Wardour, out ;
Edward Wilson, at Baltimore ; Joseph Lancaster,
at Boston ; his representative, Mr. Jones, present,
and very attentive and polite. Such letters are of
little value unless they come from one friend to
another, both greatly esteeming each other, or the
bearer has plenty of money. Letters of introduction, under other circumstances, will scarcely
procure the stranger a gratuitous dinner. If poor,

he will be sent up the state by other letters, and passed from house to house and town to town, for work.

3d.—In the evening, on horseback, with Mr. Wood, Mr. Jones, &c. I took a delightful airing to German's Town, along the romantic banks of the Schuylkill to its falls. Bridges of singular beauty, and roofed over, stretch across this pure, transparent river, on the banks of which birds have planted many cherry-trees, now of prodigious size, and from which we and others wantonly broke off large boughs, full of ripe cherries, and laid them across our saddles, that we might eat them as we rode along. In every direction, fruit is ready to fall into the mouths of passengers. At German's Town, I called upon and talked with an old countryman, long settled here, Mr. Pysley, once of my native Isle of Ely, who says that the day for emigration is gone by. " I," said he, " came here in the best of times, but I have had to work hard on my stall, and have known no rest, from the clamour of my awl, and my lapstone and hammer. Let those who will come, expect to work all their days, as I have done, and then only just live." He talked and thought kindly of all he left behind, but particularly of his dear native land, which he can never behold more.

Sunday, 4th.—Introduced to Mr. Maginnis, an Irish lecturer on elocution, and to an English gentleman, Mr. Hobson. Europeans, so far from home, meet and mix sweetly like milk and honey. Attended Dr. Storton's chapel, an immense, elegant rotundity, like Rowland Hill's in the Surrey road. The Doctor's pulpit was supplied by an American preacher of much saucy simplicity of manner. I visited a noble mansion-house in this city, erected purposely for and presented by the citizens to General Washington, which he refused, and which now stands a goodly monument of his unequalled magnanimity.

The negroes in this state and city, are all free and independent. A slave, thanks be given to William Penn! cannot live here. That they are free and happy, need not be told: it is known by only looking into their faces, and contemplating their erect statures, both of which here lose every thing negro-like but their colour, and acquire all the majesty of man.

5th.—Yesterday, being Sunday, the grand anniversary of Independence is necessarily celebrated on this day, which is brother Jonathan's immortal universal festival. Roaring cannon and merrily ringing bells salute the morn, and, until midnight, all is frolic and hilarity, from one end of this mighty empire to the other. At night, in Vauxhall Gardens, I saw a representation or effigy of the late General Washington, and heard an oration, in which that illustrious man was compared to Cincinnatus, and highly eulogized. I talked with citizen Fleming and Jerry Wardour, jun. Esq., both rich, and the latter particularly intelligent and communicative, having great experience in all matters touching emigrants and emigration, as many thousands of persons and pounds are constantly passing through his office and hands to this country. He says that no body, who is living comfortably in England, should think of emigrating. But to those who resolve to do so, he recommends British settlement in Pennsylvania and the eastern states, in preference to Illinois and the western country; because the latter is sickly, being exposed, in a high degree, to bilious fever; is supplied with only bad water; and is so far from, or rather altogether without a market for produce. He had never heard of any persons, excepting visitors, returning; but of many, the most unfit, settling down comfortably there, from Bond-street an Holborn, London. Mr. Birkbeck still lives in a log cabin, doing little or no business. The Flowers and he are irreconcileable enemies. Grand-children will reap the benefits of emigration thither, but fathers and mothers, although they cannot starve, must sacrifice themselves. Two long years must pass before any thing can be made from the land, which must be cleared at a cost of 22 dollars, or 4*l*. 19*s*. an acre. It is therefore better to give 9*l*. for cleared land, or uncleared, with house and good farm buildings on it, than 2*l*. an acre in Illinois, where there is no market, no house, no convenience, yet land capable of raising

provisions sufficient for Great Britain's great and
many wants. New Orleans is their only market for produce, which, being perishable, must
be sold, even for freight down the river, which it
is sometimes insufficient to pay. There are several
fine states nearer to that general market than
Illinois and Birkbeck's settlement; of which I
have (says Mr Wardour) reported unfavourably,
and thereby offended Mr. Birkbeck, who, by the
bye, has much misrepresented and spoken unjustly of the eastern states, and that without ever
having seen them. In these only, however, can
an English farmer flourish; for here, indeed, when
you buy, you get either the land or the building
on it for nothing. In order to do business well,
a man must privately look about him; he must
have his eyes in his head, and see who must sell;
thus making a difference in the cost of 50*l.* to
nearly 100*l.* per cent. This and next year offer
fine chances for buying, so great and pressing is
the want of money. There are many of your
countrymen who think of coming, and do come,
quite unfit for this country, bringing with them
little variety of knowledge in different kinds of
labour, but all their old prejudices, the worst ware
they can bring; while the native American knows
every thing, and hates or fears nothing. The
Englishman thinks nothing good or right but what
is English, both in theory and practice. He thinks
his system and mode of farming must be best, but

H

he would do well to try it only on a small scale,
and not rashly lay aside what is American, and well
tried; for those who have long lived on the soil,
must certainly know what is the best.   In the
state of Ohio, though so flourishing, there are
none born in it who are 20 years old.   It is of no
use travelling down rivers to see and know countries, or get information about them; you must ride
through them to and fro, and often stop.   There
recently came, in one of my ships, an English
bricklayer, wife, and family, but their unfitness
for this land was quite ludicrous.   They thought
they were to be nobles here, although sent from
your country by their parish officers.   And then,
who would ever have thought of seeing librarians
from Bond Street come here, to start circulating
libraries, in the wilderness of Illinois.   Your
friend John Ingle, however, now in Indiana, is a
good fit fellow, knowing what he is about."

6th.—At noon I left the good city of William
Penn.   I am now swiftly gliding down the Delaware in a superb steam-boat, 60 yards long, 14
broad, with 36 beds for gentlemen, and 20 for
ladies, all in the cabin; moving from 10 to 12
miles an hour.

At six, p. m., we quitted the boat and river, and
entered three coaches, which conveyed us through
Newcastle, 40 miles to French-town, on the Chesa-
peake bay; where another huge boat received us
to supper and bed, *en masse*.   It landed us to

breakfast at the city of Baltimore, 120 miles in 12 hours; fare six dollars.

7th.—In this city, put up at Gadsby's hotel (the best) containing 150 beds, fine warm and cold baths, and a well stored reading-room, with files of all domestic and foreign papers. Here I saw my letter on negro-killing, copied into a paper, 1,500 miles from Charleston. At breakfast I found meats in abundance, besides a peck of eggs, and huge dishes of toast and rolls soaked in butter, and smothered with cream, to make the hard crust tender. I am now again in negro-land, and all the comforts of slavery surround me. In Philadelphia I seemed a man; but here, a god for negroes to worship. All is homage and black attention. The city, seen from the bay, might be mistaken for Rome, and the huge dome of the Exchange for that of Holy St. Peter's.

At ten, a. m., entered *Uncle Sam's* mail for Washington city, that is to be. During this long journey, I saw no good land, save the marshes on the banks of the Delaware. All seems exhausted, worn-out, rusty, and hung up to dry, or rather to bake in the sun.

At four, p. m., reached Washington, which, viewed from the Capitol hill, looks like a Roman village, for all is Roman or Grecian here. The streets are a mile or two in length, with houses a quarter of a mile apart, beautified by trees and swamps, and cows grazing between. At first view, a stranger might suppose that some convulsion of nature had swept away whole streets, and laid waste this far-famed metropolitan city.

At seven, p. m., I met, at a private table at the house of a friend and countryman, several exiles, to tea, or rather supper, where I was received and treated with all imaginable kindness. Here I was formally introduced to my countryman, Mr. Elliott, of the City Gazette. I visited Messrs. Coote and Dumbleton, good brewers of brown stout, on the banks of the great river Potowmac, late of Huntingdonshire, Old England. From the latter gentleman, I learn that nearly all the British emigrants feel disappointed. " It is not sufficient," says he, " that an Englishman lives; he expects to do better than live." Mr. D. seems to have done nothing for himself yet, but harm; having, together with his brother, spent all their money in mechanical pursuits. Constant work cannot be had, yet it is thought to be better than half a crown per day, constant, in England.

8th and 9th.—" Farming," say Messrs. C. and D., the brewers, " is more comfortable and profitable in England than here; for large and fine estates in Virginia do not keep families with necessaries. They send a little fire-wood to this market, for the sake of a few dollars, which some borrow one of another, for marketings daily. Neither is brewing so profitable as at home, although less capital will suffice, there being no public-houses to buy here; but all the malting barley must be bought at once. Some, however, are not able to do so. Porter is cheaper here than at home." My now generous host, it is said, is almost the only successful emigrant, doing more business, and better too, than any other merchant; and yet he came hither without capital. His superior talents have insured success, which will, and must follow him. He is deemed the *smartest*, and wisest Briton in the city. Still, there are several hundreds of fine young men here and in Philadelphia, all out of employment; men, who ought not to have left England's overstocked common and glutted market. English labourers, and first-rate mechanics, too, are seen working, at the Capitol, for the low price of half a dollar per day, or whatever the master-builder pleases. Many firms, too, are lessening and disappearing, through want of capital; they hold so much unnegociable paper, and must hold it until the indorser pleases to cash it.

10*th*.—My host, every where the public eulogist of America, says, " that England is the place for men of fortune, but this land for the industrious bees who cannot live there. Fools must not come, for Americans are nationally cold, jealous, suspicious, and knavish, have little or no sense of honour, believing every man a rogue, until they see the contrary; thinking imposition and extortion fair business, and all men, fair game: kind, obliging conduct is lost upon them. A bold, saucy, independent manner towards them is necessary. They love nobody but themselves, and seem incapable of due respect for the feelings of others. They have nothing original; all that is good or new, is done by foreigners, and by the British, and yet they boast eternally."

Such is the rough sketch of an admiring artist, once in a state of infatuation, but now getting sane and sober. The scales have left his eyes, and he begins to see, to his sorrow. I, too, fancy I see something like a strong and general feeling of disappointment, pervading almost all I meet, who have recently emigrated; and, on examination, I find that my observation does not deceive me. All have over-rated America. Hope told a flattering, lying tale, and they believed her to their own undoing. A visit to this country will increase an Englishman's love for his own, whether he can or cannot live in it. If he cannot, he comes here, cursing the cause, hating the change, and hoping to return, on some fair future day, which fate may yet have in store for him.

Sunday, 11*th*.—To-day, I received a long epistle from Joseph Lancaster, very eulogistic on my letter and conduct touching negro-killing, but not so honorable to Carolina. " On mentioning this affair," (says he,) " in a stage, it operated like an explosion on all present." Met the Rev. John Wright, who complimented me on having

dared to attack the beast in his temple, meaning
slavery in Carolina. He states, that Mr. Birkbeck, if he had taken good advice, had never
gone to Illinois to deceive himself and others,
and injure many. Introduced to Messrs. Matchem
and Shanks, two native citizens, one in the government, and both eloquent and ingenious men,
who openly accuse the English emigrants of shewing contempt for America, by odious comparisons,
and by not socially mixing with the natives. Both
parties in this matter err, and alike stand in need
of correction. The American, so called, although
his father or grandfather was perhaps a British
convict, despises all recent emigrants, because he
fancies, that they who know most, must despise
him. Fancy and jealousy then, must bear the
blame. There seems so little here to remind me
that it is Sunday, that I had almost forgotten it.
Religion, however, became the theme. There is
more intolerance here than in England. Metho-
dists predominate, and are brimful of bigotry ;
and the Catholics are very fiery and violent in all
spiritual matters, but, having no power, they cannot injure their fellow-citizens. All sects hate my
reverend friend, because he is an Unitarian, and
hates slavery, and therefore nothing good can be
in him or come out of him.

13th.—Met and talked with both Dumbletons,
who have failed in two distinct enterprizes. The
elder in a brewing concern in Philadelphia, through

uniting himself to a falling firm, at the head of which was a thief and swindler ; and the younger brother in a threshing machine, in the English fashion, to hire out at 16 dollars per day; but he was seldom able to get a job, the farmer not being able to spare the dollars. Eight horses or oxen, therefore, tread out the grain, 100 bushels a day. The machine was knocked to pieces, and the proprietor set off, a poor pedestrian, to New Orleans, walking to and fro, up and down the Ohio and Mississipi, and that, without spending any money save his earnings, of which he brought 10 dollars home. He thus travelled 4,000 miles, to see, hear, and know what he could of the western wilds, and their towns and cities, where he could earn only three dollars a week, (but slaves, six dollars,) and that not constantly. Slaves are preferred all over the west. While with his machine, he worked hard, many days with his shirt off, under a roasting sun. As I have his western journal, he may hereafter speak for himself. Both these young men, as well as the Chamberses, lived freely, and acted imprudently. They dressed in stile, and would have dinners, which cost four dollars a week. Much less beer is here made from the same quantity of malt than in England ; about one half less.

14th.—Met Mr. Cocken, late of Lincolnshire, who came to this city with money, and has increased it. " As good farms and farmers as any in England, are," he says, "to be found in this state of Maryland. My son a few years ago only, purchased and began with 500*l.*, and has now made it 5,000*l.* If I were a young man now, I would begin on the poor worn-out land round this city, which is to be bought low, and may soon be regenerated by plaster of Paris, one bushel to the acre, from the port of Alexandria, whence it is plentifully imported and prepared for sowing. The English system is wanted. I have seen fine red clover, two or three tons on an acre, foolishly spoiled by depasturing and stocking hard, whereas it ought to have been cut and used after the soiling mode." I conceive, as does Mr. Cocken, that English farmers, with skill and a little money, must do well, though not rise or fall so fast here as in England, things not being so changeable. What is here gotten is a man's own, it comes gradually, but surely. Dr. F. Dawes, and lady, late of Wisbeach, in the Isle of Ely, with whom I dined this day, wish, but are reluctant to return, seeming to stay here only to find fault with every thing. " No body," says he, " is getting, or is able to raise any money." The man of whom Mr. C. speaks in his letters, as " getting money as fast as he can count it," is unable to raise 2,000 dollars for a farm, which he wants to buy near his own ; and, if he were so rich, would he, think you, come to Washington, six or seven miles, with three lbs. of butter under his arm ? As to Mr. Long, from Lincolnshire, he has removed three times; is dissatisfied with all things, and thinks no man honest."

The history of a great number of emigrants in this country shews unprincipled looseness in morals, and but little or no real well founded integrity. Public offices and government clerkships are filled by men who really could be no longer tolerated in trade, many having cleared out, or as it is more commonly called, backed out, four times in a few years. Yet such are the most esteemed citizens, taking precedence of tradesmen, and ranking with the aristocracy of the city. Dirking, says my nameless friend, is a common unnoticed offence; a peccadillo which renders no man uncomfortable, but him whose body is the subject of it. We have too much liberty. Ours is a fine government in theory, but its laws are neither respected nor enforced. Military schools contain the seeds of death to American liberty. It is the pride and pleasure of Americans to get into debt, and then by avoiding payment, show how adroitly they can cheat and wrong each other. Few look upon knavery with disgust, but rather with a smile of approbation. It is indeed difficult to trade with the people in an old plain honest way. Knavery damns the North, and slavery the South. Free blacks without a certificate are here seized, put into our city gaol, advertised a month, and then sold for gaol fees, when they become slaves for life. Who would expect to find a certificate always in the pocket of a poor wandering African, who has become free ?

16th.—Introduced to Mr. Wm. Elliott of the Patent office, the contents of which constitute a splendid monument to the ingenuity and mechanical genius of this country. Many models appear which have never been copied. Mr. Elliott is an Englishman, descended from a noble family, and was a neighbour of, and known to Archdeacon Paley. He is, too, an eminent mathematician and astronomer, philosopher, and public orator. By him I was introduced to Mr. Adams, a learned, highly intelligent, and honourable Yankee. Republicans affect to be no respecters of persons merely, but they cannot conceal the effect and influence of property and authority.

I met again Mr. Adam Lyon, late of Chatteris, Isle of Ely, now a butcher in this city. He states, that farming at Honey, near his native town, is better than any here, although he knows of some farmers in Maryland who net great profits. A dollar in trade here is said to be equal to a guinea in England, but business not so easily or respectably managed. I received from Mr. Edw. Dumbleton, an experimental brewer, a statement of brewing porter in this country, by which it is clear to him, that by a capital of 1,400l. 700l. or 50l. per cent. is to be netted by the brewer, while the retailer or publican with little or no capital gains 100*l*. per cent.

17th.—With Messrs. T. Coote and Dumbleton I visited the navy-yard, where I saw several eminent mechanics, nearly all Englishmen, some of whom are receiving not above 1¾ dollar a day, although at home they received 3*l*. a week. The steam machinery is here " mighty fine," "superbly elegant," as a native would call it, and the new 100 gun ship of war is a most noble vessel, a floating battery worked and manned by 900 men, and altogether as good and gallant a ship as John Bull ever saw. Gouging still flourishes. His Excellency, Mr. Monroe, while a young man, constantly kept his hair closely shorn, in order that his head might be less exposed to this brutal practice.

Mr. J. D. is now retailing bottled porter at a net gain of 7*l*. sterling per month. Mr. Thomas Coote, the brewer, prefers his chance to any which he could take in England. So cheap is all butcher's meat, and so dear are all vegetables, that for some tables the latter cost more than the former. A fat lamb or sheep will scarcely buy one bushel of new potatoes; but four bushels of ripe peaches shovelled loose out of a waggon, will just do it, if a sixpence is added.

Sunday, 18*th*.—This being Sunday, I visited the white and black Methodist congregations at

George town, to the latter of which (the black) the white mayor of the town, a rich Englishman, of long and high standing, is minister. At half a mile distant, we could distinctly hear their devotional songs. We found a mighty assemblage of priests and priestesses, for all preached, prayed, and sung together. The pious prayers, and sensible, cheerful singing of the poor negroes, (who are, however, apt to rise into wild enthusiasm), are very honourable to black capabilities, and exonerate them from the charge of natural and moral inferiority.

19th.—Talked with the Reverend John Wright, Unitarian minister, proprietor of a critical review, and of a store in the city, and late an object of Episcopal prosecution at Liverpool. In England he was at the head of a forum, and occupied some space in the public mind. What he was there, he is here; often fearlessly speaking, writing, and inditing a good matter. He generally preaches but to a few, although on one occasion he had the honour of preaching in the speaker's chair before the President and Congress; a compliment for which he was indebted to the Honourable Thomas Law, the brother of the Right Reverend the Lord Bishop of Chester. In this matter the two brothers furnish a splendid contrast. Mr. Thomas Law received him in a strange land; paid him all the respect in his power; and subscribed 100*l.* towards building him a conventicle.

20th.—Edward Wilson, an eminent merchant of Philadelphia, an Englishman of unspotted name, and a Quaker, brother to Thomas Wilson, of Houghton, Hunts. says, " an emigrant recently came to me with 5,000*l.* sterling, which he put into my hands, and in confidence wished me to use it for him at my discretion. I did so, and returned it to him in two years, having made the 5,000*l.* into 8,000*l.* He seemed well pleased with my stewardship. He left in England a discarded son, for whom I prevailed on him to send. He came, and the old man gave him 200*l.* to start in business here, while he (the father) bought land in the western country. In less than three years the son was the richest man of the two. I said it would be so."

By mail I received this morning 150 dollars from Lorent and Wulf, which I acknowledged to Judge King, but which I lent to Jew Jones of Washington city, and which he spent at New York ; when I wanted it again he said he had never had it. He was sued for it, and, as defendant, gained his point, because he had not given me credit for it in his ledger. He is not an Israelite, indeed, in whom there is no guile. Two hundred and fifty emigrants arrived last week at Baltimore, and were unable to get employment there : what disappointment to the poor pennyless wretches ! I observed a venerable looking gentleman yesterday at meeting, of the name of Washington, a cousin of the late general, and much resembling him, it is said, in person. The memory of that unequalled man seems, however, little revered, and his family is not more respected than that of any other person. Mr. Savage, an emigrant from Downham in Norfolk, who married my townswoman Miss Blinkhorn, introduced himself this day to invite me down to Marlborough, where he is well settled as a shoemaker. His wife receives 150 dollars a year and has all the wood she wants for fuel or other purposes, a house, and four acres of land, with range for cows and sows; all for instructing two or three children belonging to a richer neighbour. He loves the country. The people are willing to give or lend him almost any thing. He states, that making shoes, and raising tobacco, are both good trades, a crop of the latter having been worth from 200 dollars to 300 dollars an acre; and costing only about 30 dollars; a fine profit.

21st.—I was formally introduced to Dr. Beattie of George-town, the young sprightly eloquent orator at the city forum, where he shines a public defender of duelling. My reverend heterodox friend joined us, and contended that the blacks have no claim to a common origin from our father Adam; the form and construction of their bones, and the difference of their colour, constituting so complete a contrast with all other nations, are held to be positive proofs that they spring from some

other and inferior source. This doctrine is very
palatable to America. I regret that it should be
espoused by an Englishman. White men here sell
their own yellow children in the ordinary course
of business; and free blacks also sell their immediate offspring, male and female.

Called on my townsfolk, Jack Bellcare and his
wife; both are disappointed; she would not have
left Sutton, could she have counted the cost and
sorrow of it, although they are getting a living, and
have disposed of their children. She keeps a little
store; he works and drinks heartily, but has not
yet spent all their Sutton money; Jack left a
comfortable home and dairy behind him, and now
works bare-headed on the road, cursing the hot
climate.

Almost every private family chariot in this city
is found daily on the stand as a hackney coach
for hire, to either whites or blacks; to all who can
pay.

22*d*.—I heard this evening America's unequalled
preacher, Doctor Storton of Philadelphia. He
has one unpardonable sin; he is an Englishman, a
refugee from the church of the late Reverend Samuel Pearce of Birmingham. He preaches well,
and prays earnestly and eloquently, and that too,
for all white men, and red men, and black men *in*
Africa, but not for the poor negroes of North America, who are here quite forgotten by the priests,

who, would they use it, have an influence that might work wonders in the black man's favour. But this would be treason in Maryland.

23*d.*—It is remarkable that the cows graze loose all over this huge metropolis, and come and go of themselves, night and morning, from and to their owners' houses and yards for milking, after which they are each fed with a quarter of a peck of corn meal.

Ignorance and love of animal indulgence, it is said, here frustrate and set at nought the system of representation. A good man, therefore, cannot get into Congress; but a bad man, not fit for a constable, often succeeds by the means of influential whiskey. Flatter vice and folly, and you are popular. I was here introduced by Mr. Elliott to the Hon. Thomas Law, (a well known republican, brother of the late Lord Ellenborough, Lord Chief Justice of England) who received me kindly, and on his courteous invitation I promised to visit him.

" Sun-flowers," says Mr. Elliott, " breathe each as much in one day as twelve men. I consider them as highly propitious to health, particularly in low and marshy situations; and I therefore surround my hermitage with them."

Sunday, 25*th.*—Young Rawlings, late of Chatteris, called to say that three of my simple-hearted countrymen from Gamlingay, Cambridgeshire, had

I

inquired for me, and represented me as a spy, but still thought and talked kindly of and wished to see me. By a spy, they did not mean a government spy in the common acceptation of that term. This young quaker is an assistant in a store at 300 dollars a year and board. He saves only 100 dollars, and, if he cannot become master of the concern, thinks of returning home, where he can do better. Yet he thinks 100 dollars here equal to 100*l*. sterling in England. Mrs. Stile, late of Sutton in the Isle, is ready to take the benefit of insolvency, but has disposed of her daughters in matrimony.

Mr. Gale, a worthy, feeling, meritorious Englishman from Yorkshire, and once dandled on the poetic knee of Montgomery, but now at the head of the government organ, *The National Intelligencer*, says, that British emigrants possess habits and prejudices which render them unfit to mix with the natives down to the second generation. They, therefore, should not attempt to associate with North Americans, but should form distinct settlements like the Germans. Such a step would insure them success and happiness in a new country; on coming into which they should depute a confidential agent of their own to apply at the National *Land Office* at Washington, where Mr. Elliott and other Englishmen, forming a society to instruct and guide emigrants, would point out to them the best sections of land and climate, with their local description, and that without the expense and labour of looking and wandering all over the empire to their ruin.

Mr. Cockin, an old experienced farmer from Lincolnshire, says, that on good land 50 bushels of Indian corn is raised at three quarters of a dollar, or one dollar per bushel; and that the English system, so far as is practicable, is much wanted here. The American mode of ploughing wears out the soil faster than the cropping. They just move and pulverize the surface, which in wet or dry weather either blows or washes away into the valleys. By the English mode, fresh soil would be raised, and the exhausted surface soil turned down to rest and replenish itself.

26th.—" A propensity to cheat and deceive," says a shrewd informant, " pervades all classes of this people, from the lowest mechanic and tradesman, or companies in trade, up to nearly the first officer of government. It is the boasted qualification of the *smart man.* Thieving is a characteristic feature of Maryland, which is peopled principally by Catholics, who correct all evil by absolution. The Carolinians keep and train up large dogs for hunting and finding runaway or concealed negroes, who are easily scented and found by them, if they be in the woods. The mode of training is thus: Set a young negro daily to strike a pup, and then run from it. This is dog-training. My cousin, Captain H. Rugeley, in my presence ordered a young negro to strike a half-grown cur, which immediately seized the boy, who was worried a little, for my amusement and instruction. Hence these dogs, though generally docile and gentle to well dressed whites, instantly seize on any strange black man who approaches the plantation, just as an English greyhound flies upon a hare.

I am told that Mr. Long, late of Lincolnshire, wrote his puffing letters to England, under feelings of great disappointment, and said that he would give 1,000 guineas to be reinstated in his farm in Lincolnshire. Letters from emigrants, I have proved to be at best but questionable and doubtful authority. Janson, author of *The Stranger in America*, it is here said, came and returned a stranger. Parkinson, too, the experienced farmer and brewer of Doncaster, returned and said, the land would not grow grass. This is not so great a misrepresentation as it at first sight appears. In many parts of Maryland and Virginia, the grass seems indeed dead, and all that survives is artificial grass.

28th.—When Mr. T. C. Wright first came to George-town, 17 years since, the forest approached his door, but now it has receded a mile and a half. The situation and prospect of things some years ago justified the statements now called *Puffs*.

Certain approaches to something like equality, and consequent familiarity of the rich with the poor, both of which classes profess to be no respec-

ters of persons, generate a manner highly repelling
to the aristocratical feelings of the well-bred English.   Dr. Dawes was waited on to-day by an
American proprietor of land, offering his farm at
six dollars an acre; the Doctor asked what had
been its greatest produce per acre? At one time
15 bushels of wheat, but now only eight bushels.
He said he had lost money by farming, through
not pursuing a proper mode; but could tell the
Doctor of a better mode if he would buy the farm
offered.   Land is frequently bought and sold, and
kept for many years, but never paid for, unless an
offer above the original cost is made and accepted.
Interest money is paid or payable on the purchase,
which is held like a mortgage, and in time it reverts
to the vendor or his heirs.

I visited the Catholic university at George-town,
to witness the ceremony, previous to the vacation,
something like the *Commencement*, at Cambridge.
I found a large and splendid assemblage of bishops,
doctors, priests, pupils, and spectators of all ranks
and religions.   The young gentlemen delivered
their orations, after which they received prizes and
degrees from the hands of the archbishop.   This
institution is said to be highly respectable, and is
open to all sects and parties in religion or politics;
it is therefore a nursery of great men for all sections of the empire.   Although Catholic, it professes not to make proselytes; yet many pupils
are induced to adopt this faith, and nearly all seem

to part and meet with their preceptors here as
with kind and indulgent parents.

Friend John Steed, a poor excommunicated
quaker, once of Earith and Wisbeach, introduced
himself to me this day. He feels grievously disappointed, and wants temporary employment as
an assistant in a store, He is nearly broken in
both spirit and pocket, and finds charity cold, and
friends few or none. He is kindly housed by the
ever friendly Dr. Dawes, and thinks of returning
soon if he cannot succeed. He would not have
come here if he could have formed, on the other
side of the water, a correct idea of the state of
things in this country.

The poor white, or white poor, in Maryland, it
is said, scarcely ever work, but send their children
to beg, and live on corn-meal and dried fish only.
Working is disgraceful in a slave state, where
blacks only work. " Will you work?" " What,
work? I'm no negro, I guess." Thanks be given
to slavery for all this.

30th.—His Excellency, James Monroe, Esq.,
President of the United States, when out of office,
is poor, not more than able to maintain himself
and family, never having had time to gain a fortune. Our late President Madison," (says friend
Jenny, to whom I was this day introduced by Dr.
Dawes,) " was, and is a poor man. He married a
poor quaker girl, one of a large family of girls,
raised in a boarding-house, but now all married to

Congress-men. While Madison was President, his wife, Dolly Madison, used frequently to visit our friend's meeting-house in George-town, though she was no longer a quaker."

I rode all day with friend Jenny, and slept at his house. He is a shrewd land-jobber, who has quickly enriched himself. His eyes are in his head, and he sees all points of the compass at one view. By him I was kindly accompanied to the beautiful mansion and plantation of —— Lough-borough, Esq., the most intelligent agriculturist (except Mr. Day, of Camden,) whom I have yet seen. This gentleman offers his beautiful much-improved farm and mansion at 200 dollars, or 45l. sterling an acre, just two miles from the city. This price was thought too high. Mr. Jenny says, that 100 acres of land is plenty for an industrious family, who will net 1,000 dollars a year, exclusive of maintenance. Land 15 miles N. W. of George town, and about Rockville, is better than it appears to be; for, out of cultivation, it has no face, never having been sown with grass seeds. Some time since it cost 7 dollars an acre, and is now offered at 15 dollars, with good buildings, fences, and other improvements.

Sunday, August 1st.—I heard the Rev. Dr. Allison, a judicious Gillite,* and chaplain to Congress ; and, in the evening, I attended an interest-

* Calvinists are here called Gillites, or disciples of the late Dr. John Gill.

ing conversation at the hospitable seat of T. C. Wright, where I met several native and adopted citizens. Emigration was the theme. It was agreed that emigrants should all come in the temper and spirit of the fathers, the first settlers; that, ultimately, such pioneers as Birkbeck and Flower in the wilderness, must benefit themselves, and that the last twenty years' history of emigrants furnishes encouragement still to emigrate. " The English," says Mr. Wright, " who have to live here by their own hands, make the most dissatisfied of labourers. They run all over the land in quest of the highest wages; and in so doing, lose half the week in finding wages for the other half, and part with the substance for a shadow.

Two or three of the English have this day and recently fallen dead at the city fountains, in consequence of drinking excessively of cold water, while they were in high perspiration, under a heat, by the therm. 98° and 100°, in the shade. To avoid this danger, it is only necessary to drink a wineglass half full of brandy first, and a pint of water immediately after. Thirst is thus safely quenched, with much less water than would be necessary without the spirits.

3rd.—Previous to a heavy thunder-storm this morning, a hurricane came on (a common precursor) and raised dense clouds of dust, which thickened and darkened the horizon, and made all look like London in a dark smoky fog in November;

but when the rain fell, the atmosphere resumed
its transparency.   During the continuance of the
storm, the heat was the greatest ever known here,
being 101½° in the shade.

Unnatural prematurity is here very common.
Boys look grave, and talk, act, and dress like
men, and expect and exact the same treatment as
men, though only 12 or 13 years old.

The poet Bloomfield, Author of *The Farmer's
Boy*, has a sister living at Alexandria; and in its
vicinity live two of the ancient family of Fairfax,
on immense estates, granted at an early period to
a branch of their house, but which, owing to want
of management and prudence, are found to be insufficient for the support of their several house-
holds.

5th.—That prominent want of respect for rule
and rulers apparent here, may I think be traced
to the disorderly economy of private families.
The children are rarely forbidden or punished for
wrong doing, being only kindly solicited to do
right; nor is strict discipline tolerated in schools.
Hence respect and obedience to parents, guard-
ians, masters, and governors, is never implanted,
or soon eradicated.   Authority, in consequence,
whether public or private, civil or religious, is neither feared, nor willingly obeyed, through any
period of life.

Sunday, 8th.—I heard this morning a Scotch-
man, Dr. Laurie, who at the end of every sen-

tence seems to have finished his oration. He appeared to me to be a man of but little talent. The psalms in use here would disgrace a school-boy's theme. My first impressions on the subject of religious worship in America are not removed. Religion still appears to me to be a matter little understood and much less regarded than in England.

Doctor Dawes and Friend Steed.—The former has bought a farm of 400 acres of poor land, and no buildings, seven miles from this city, at 10 dollars an acre. The latter (Steed) might engage himself at 300 or 400 dollars a year and board. What would they have more? Both, however, are eternally croaking, and write home unfavourable reports. They yet concede to me this fact; namely, that in this country lives a population of several millions, rapidly increasing in an unprecedented degree, and living (blacks excepted) as a whole, in a state of society and animal ease, greater than in any other country since the world began. My friend Wilson, of Houghton, Hunts. is much mistaken in his statements, in which he endeavours to prove a net annual loss of 146*l*. in cultivating 200 acres of land in America.

9th.—I this day visited Alexandria. When the British invaded it last war, they took away and freighted with flour, tobacco, bacon, and other provisions, 21 vessels from Bermuda and the West Indies. In this port, four miles from Washington, were seen young men of the British navy, all armed against their own fathers and brothers, emigrants quietly settled here.

John Steed's quaker brother, an emigrant in Pennsylvania, feels satisfied that he is away from England. I received this morning a pressing invitation by post, from John Ingle, my old school-fellow, settled in Indiana only 1,500 miles off me! He feels perfect satisfaction in a new and flourishing settlement. I accept it.

11*th*.—The attachment of goods here is common in the absence of the body. One state is a refuge for the debtors of another, and this circumstance constitutes a perpetual inducement to plunder and migration. The British are much addicted to these practices. They may be followed into other states, but so great is the expense and difficulty of suing such refugees, that it is rarely attempted. The peaches are very small this season, but Mr. Cocker, last year, saw them weighing from 12 to 14 oz. each.

The Cammucks of George-town, two brothers from Lincolnshire, came hither two years ago, unable to pay their passage: now, one is buying 10 acres of rich land for 800 dollars, paying down 500 dollars on account. The other began with a small school, and in three months was able to pay the captain for his passage, and keep himself well, and soon raised money enough to go to the Western country. Friend Steed engages himself to Jones and Co. and begins to repent of having

written such deplorable statements against this
country. Letters of emigrants and travellers
should not be rashly written, because they are
shown long after the writer becomes ashamed of
them. An emigrant, unable at New York and
Baltimore to get employment in his trade, and not
to be persuaded to try the towns near, paid his
passage this week for England, but first inquired
at the news offices for papers stating the number
out of employment, which amounts to 1500 families collected in New York city, all in distress
seeking a refuge in Canada. Mr. Perry offered
several stone-masons, willing and able to work, to
the Pennsylvanian farmers at half a dollar per day,
and to keep themselves, but none were wanted.
There is no money to pay them with.

14*th*.—Dined with Mr. Eno, late of Tyd, near
Wisbeach, a citizen of the world, a kind-hearted
man to emigrants generally, and who preserves
entire, for those who call at his tavern, all his
original English feelings mixed up with American
hospitality. He thinks that few emigrants ever
rise above their former stations, or meet with any
thing here which should induce them to quit their
homes in England; while the bulk of those who
come, both masters and labourers, remain miserably poor. " With respect to myself, (says he) if
I had a fortune I would live in England; as I have
not, I am better off here." I gathered from the
ground under a tree in his garden, plums half

roasted and too hot almost to hold in the hand or mouth, and eating like fruit half baked. Heat 96° in the shade.   This is a demoralizing climate, and to it may be traced that prominent want of industry and good habits invariably seen and felt in this dissolving warmth.

Sunday, 15*th.*—Killing in a duel was last month decided in a court at Halifax, to be no murder, provided the matter was fairly conducted. Thus it is that custom obtains a power superior to the law, which deems it murder. The law then, thus insulted, had better be expunged from the statute book of British America. Four grand duels have been fought this week near this metropolis by young men of the United States' navy and army, who are always practising, by shooting at targets and other marks. The President, for such crimes as these, has the power to break and disgrace any officer of either army or navy; but, such is the power of custom, that he cannot and dare not do it.

16*th.*—*Picture of the condition of the American people, agricultural and otherwise.* Low ease; a little avoidable want, but no dread of any want; little or no industry; little or no real capital, nor any effort to create any; no struggling, no luxury, and, perhaps, nothing like satisfaction or happiness; no real relish of life; living like store pigs in a wood, or fattening pigs in a stye. All their knowledge is confined to a newspaper, which they all love, and consists in knowing their natural, and some political rights, which rights in themselves they respect individually, but often violate towards others, being cold, selfish, gloomy, inert, and with but little or no feeling. The government is too weak and too like-minded to support and make the laws respected, or to teach the people justly to appreciate their excellent, but affronted constitution.—" There are amongst them," says Mr. Perry, " no materials or seeds of appreciation for it. It was by mere accident that they ever had a constitution ; it came not from wise choice or preference. In England only, exists such a preference and real love of liberty. She must continue to be the Great Nation in spite of all her enemies, foreign or domestic, while America, you see, is retrograding and quite unable of herself to achieve any thing grand. Whatever she does is by instruction and foreign aid, without which she cannot advance. If A, B, C, be taught her, she cannot teach herself D ; yet she possesses the boasting, vain-glorious egotism of all-knowing Europe, although of and in herself, knowing nothing. Almost all Americans are boys in every thing but vice and folly ! In their eyes *Uncle Sam* is a right slick, mighty fine, smart, big man."

Great evil results to emigrants from not coupling good and evil statements relating to America. Not half the number would come if they were but

properly informed and enlightened. Under such
impressions, those who would then come would
be generally of the right sort.

In October, at the fairs in Pennsylvania all is
fine, mighty fine, and dashy flashy. The Dutch
women then shine and look gay; but at home are
like slaves, living hard, and ploughing all day in
the hot field. " More robberies and murders,"
says Mr. Perry, "are committed in Virginia, than
in all England. Whole families are murdered at
once, and buried in a hole in the woods, and three
or four slaves are wantonly shot and buried at
once, when not useful nor marketable. But all
this seldom excites any notice, or is much known,
in or beyond the neighbourhood. It is indeed
good policy to conceal it, as the making it known,
it is said, might and does increase the evil. Human life is little valued in America."

In conformity with my resolution to give an
impartial account of all I meet with, I have mentioned Mr. Perry's statements and impressions,
which must, however, I am informed, be received
with much caution and qualification; because,
though capable of judging, he is not cool and
sober enough for unprejudiced, patient, and correct observation.

19th.—I visited the beautiful rural seat and
pleasure grounds of the late poet and minister,
Joel Barlow, on the heights of George-town. I
made many inquiries after this celebrated author

of the *Columbiad*, before I could learn when, where, and how he died and was buried; circumstances now scarcely known. He seemed almost forgotten. He died while minister from this country to the court of the Emperor Napoleon, and in pursuing him towards Russia, to obtain the removal of decrees against commerce. A tomb, into which I am now looking, was built for him on this estate, but it is still empty. His body was sought for, but, it is said, could not be found. A few graves mark these forlorn domains.

Visited Mr. Simpson, and viewed his English-like farm, about which I had heard much boasting, and much about his getting money as fast as he could count it. I saw, however, nothing in the English style but whitethorn quicks, or fences in the English form ; which, though old, were so thin and full of gaps that stock are not kept in without an inner fence of posts and rails. The climate is thought to be unpropitious to the growth of these beautiful and useful ornaments. This estate is the only one on which I have seen the experiment tried. Here is a low mean house and a garden in ruins, and a small barn, surrounded by little heaps, (not stacks); 60 acres of wheat, 30 of oats, 20 of rye, no sheep, about 15 cow-kine; wheat averages 10, oats 12 to 16, rye 10 to 12 bushels an acre. A large English barn would hold all the grain in the straw, although it is all mowed or cradled. The straw and hay all goes

to the city market for the horses of the President
and Foreign Ambassador, who pay well for it, and
therefore, as the straw is worth almost as much as
the grain, little or no manure is made, and the
land is of course starved. Turnips, except a
patch, are never grown. Such a system wears out
the land, and if introduced into England would
soon cause famine, or make us dependant on
other lands for bread. I saw here a fine *Spring
dairy;* that is to say, a dairy of stone built over
a spring of pure cold water continually flowing
through, and round it, so that the milk and cream-
vessels may stand in water to prevent the butter
from turning to stinking oil, which it soon does
when exposed to the common atmospheric air.
These spring-dairies, and smoke-houses for drying bacon, are indispensable appendages to an
American farm. In the evening I sat and smoked
segars till bed-time, with this good, kind-hearted
man, in a honeysuckle bower, about which were
buzzing several humming birds. " You see,"
said my host, " several large farms around you,
not able to maintain even their negroes from the
produce, so barbarous is their management; yet
none of the land is so poor as not to bear almost
spontaneously; plenty of peaches, cherries, apples,
and plums, wherever men or birds plant them."

21*st.*—In the navy-yard of this city is now living
a free black man, who, together with his wife and
a large family, all free, were stolen away from

K

their own house in the dead of the night, and sold into the distant state of Georgia. He alone managed to escape, but the rest have never since been seen or heard of. Such outrages on humanity and Christianity provoke no investigation, for Mammon, the supreme deity, must not be affronted. It is difficult to believe that a whole family of free-born people, living in the core of a free nation, the freest of the free, could thus fare in the nineteenth century.

By the papers to-day, I learn that travellers to the west were, last week, publicly assaulted and plundered by hordes of labourers at work on the great western road, who stopped the United States' mail, demanding dollars and guineas from all the travellers, and lifting up their axes to strike all those who refused to deliver up their cash. There is no redress, because on seeking justice, the parties complaining must be bound over to prosecute. But this is inconvenient, and summary justice cannot be had; and therefore the thief escapes with complete impunity.

The natural soil is never to be made so fruitful as in England, for except in river bottoms, (land, in the valleys of rivers,) it is water-proof, and incapable of saturation. The rain never soaks in, but runs off as from a duck's back. Dig a spit or two deep, and it is dry and dusty within a few inches of the surface. This dryness contributes to increase the great superabundant heat which is here felt; for the soil reflects and retains the sun's heat, which rises all night, and makes the common air like the breath of an oven; hence the thermometer falls not, but is stationary night and day in the shade; these things are not so where the earth can be saturated with rain. The plaster of Paris so much talked of does not enrich the soil; it only kills a destructive species of *animalcula*, and insects which prey on the roots of clover and grain.

The States of New York and Pennsylvania are best for an English farmer of any condition, who cannot live in England; but, if he can by any honest means make both ends meet, he ought to stay at home, or if he will emigrate, let it not be to the western wilderness of this country, nor to any of the southern states.

23rd.—In a long conversation with several emigrants, we decided that farms, whether small or great, near cities and good towns in the eastern states, are always to be preferred in point of interest to any in the wilderness or elsewhere. For in them, society is comparatively good, and markets for produce sure in all years, for all that can be raised; whereas in the west there is no market, except when England and Europe, (generally at peace with America,) are short of grain. No home market can be expected until they become thickly populated. The west is only fit for emigrants of very small means, and large work-

ing families; all workers. Those who, like Dr.
Dawes, come here to know that their evils at
home were comparatively imaginary and unreal,
cannot return too soon.

I visited and inspected the Doctor's farm, five
miles from the city, consisting of 400 acres all in
a wild, neglected, exhausted, and abandoned condition, but susceptible of regeneration by good
management. The soil is deep and of a brown
loamy sand, which sparkles like silver ore, or
with what the Doctor calls *mica*. It is so deeply
bedded or rooted with sharp sedgy grass, that a
yoke of six oxen seems necessary for heaving it
the first and second time. He determines on sowing it, when fit, with grass-seeds, tares, turnips,
and other green crops, but no corn or grain, until
he can double the quantity per acre grown by his
neighbours. The former proprietor was always
unable to support himself and his negroes on this
estate; and once, in a half-starved plight, went
for food to his neighbour, Mr. Simpson, who supplied him with corn-meal.

Farms and Farming in Maryland and Virginia.

Ten bushels an acre were here deemed a living
profit by some farmers. " For ten years," says
Mr. Cocker, " they resisted plaster of Paris and
good management, as an innovation by which they
conceived the land would be spoiled. At last
they were convinced by starvation, and by seeing,

under a better system, 20 or 30 bushels an acre, where once they raised only seven, eight, or ten, without plaster. Mr. Worsley, an English farmer from Lincolnshire, now a first-rate manager in Virginia, has in about 15 years gained 5,000*l.* by farming, although he began with only 500*l.* He says he has not introduced the English system, because it is not suited to the climate, which, at best, is unfavourable to agriculture, as instanced in washing rains and forcing heats. The former expose the roots of grain and rob them of the soil; and the latter draw the plants fast, and make them, particularly if thickly sown, very weak and long, before harvest. It is in consequence laid flat on the surface, and the produce and quality are not half so good and abundant as from a thin standing crop. One bushel and a half of wheat for seed is plenty. Three have been tried; but far from being any advantage, this additional quantity rather injures the crop. Although manure is not so necessary, nor so capable of being used to the same advantage as in England, it is here too much despised. To sell all the hay and straw, when a good price can be obtained, and to buy plaster, is held to be better than manuring, because the plaster is cheap, and there is no labour in using it, and by binding and stiffening loose, light, and hot soils, it protects them against the washing rains." Mr. W. thinks ten bushels of wheat per acre too little for the farmer. Even if

it sells at one dollar per bushel, it pays little more
than the cost. " Labour," says he, " is quite as
costly as in England, whether done by slaves, or
by hired whites, and it is also much more troublesome. Although much of it is not needed, yet
more than is done ought to be done. It would
pay well, and be money well spent. We give three
quarters of a dollar per day, all the year about, except in harvest, when it is 1½ dollar, or 6s. 9d. sterling and board. A year in some farming States, such
as Pennsylvania, is only of eight months duration,
four months being lost to the labourer, who is
turned away as an useless animal to starve on a
bare common, if he has not laid up for this evil
day. Mr. Worsley's land is worth 100 dollars
per acre, but has only dead fences and no quicks,
or green hedges ; all woven fences. The greatest
produce of wheat and corn averages, under the
best management, from 16 to 20 bushels of wheat—
20 to 30 of Indian corn—Rye, 16 to 20—and
barley less than wheat. The system of cropping
is, Indian corn or Red Clover, before wheat. The
clovers, both white and red, are very abundant,
running high up to the breast of a man, but are
laid flat by the rains and their own weight of head
and leaf, producing in hay two tons per acre. It
seems a highly profitable species of produce ; for
if depastured, it fattens all the cattle and pigs
without corn, before winter. Many sheep cannot
be kept in summer. Little mutton or wool is

wanted, and were they generally marketable, there
is no winter food for sheep. Turnips do not prosper; they cannot be raised so as to attain any
size, and if they could, even Swedish turnips, the
most hardy of all, would not endure the frosts.
All would rot, and the sheep, unless housed and
fed, must perish."

26th.—With a large party of ladies and gentlemen I visited the great falls of Potowmac, 15 miles
west of Washington. On my way thither I saw
no good farms nor farmers, but much land in
possession of people, who neither occupy nor
wish in anywise to improve it. They farm on a
swinish system, and raise from 10 to 15 bushels
of Indian corn, and eight to ten bushels of wheat
per acre. Poor, indolent farmers! Here I saw
plenty of peaches wild, and planted by birds.
About the rocky falls of this river all is wild,
romantic, savage, and sublime, to a degree beyond
my power to describe. Here are pits, or quarries
of marble, an infinite supply! When polished, it is
beautifully veined; a dark blue grey, red and
black. The capital here finds its majestic pillars.

Mr. Birkbeck's letter to emigrants landing in
the eastern ports, appeared this day in the city
Gazette. It contained little new; only wishing
them to examine and judge for themselves between his settlement in Illinois and those in
Pennsylvania, and elsewhere.

Mr. Worsley thinks that the west is the best
destination for poor industrious farmers, who will

there live well on their own good land, and encrease its value, but capital is best employed near cities and towns, where there is a certain market. " But," says Mr. Perry, in reply, " ten acres near New York or Philadelphia, or in such states, are infinitely better for a poor man than hundreds of acres in the west. I know of 60 acres at Feversham, in my native Kent, which average 200*l.* a year net profit, after immense taxes, tithes, and poor rates, are deducted. How much happier must a man be there than in the west, with 2,000 unprofitable acres. You talk of your wild turkeys and your game, but they are not there; game is more scarce than in England. No honest answer to inquiries can be had in the west, or elsewhere. All praise and lie, because all wish to sell, and think the inquirer wants to buy." Commodore Barney admits the truth of Perry's statements respecting the country generally.

30*th.*—Mr. Birkbeck (in this day's paper) accuses Mr. Cobbett of lending his active pen to eastern land speculators, who wish to see Illinois settlements in ruin and utterly discarded. Mr. Dunn, however, of this city, says the west is the only country for small capitals and large families, every branch of which shall there fructify, and in due time have each a farm of its own. Surplus produce is marketable enough in the shape of pigs, horses, beeves, and whiskey. The western people can better afford to sell at half, than the eastern can at whole price, because they grow double the quantity per acre, and there is a rapidly encreasing population. The western market is New Orleans, and that only. It is 1,500 miles from Illinois; the produce is sent down the Ohio and Mississipi. A supercargo, or the owner of it, must go with it to sell it, or the farmer is perhaps cheated out of all, or at best sells at an incalculable loss. A ship's cargo, or Yankee speculation to that city, is sometimes composed of iron coffins, or nests of coffins filled with shoes, so accommodating both the living and the dead.

Grasshoppers, so called, but in fact a species of locust about the length of my little finger, swarm in countless millions all over this and the contiguous states, where oats and other crops are sometimes cut unripe to prevent their being devoured by these almost worse than Egyptian locusts. They hop, jump, and fly from about six to ten feet from the ground, and devour every green thing above and below. A hat left in the field was devoured in a night. Their wings and trunks are beautifully colored. On their rising from the surface they frequently strike my nose. In all the plain round this city they leave scarcely a blade of grass. It now looks as rusty and dusty as a ploughed field, the grass being eaten down to the very roots. The intelligent Mr. Adams says, that when he was surveying the territory on the Michigan, and other Lakes, flies were seen falling in clouds, and lay dead and stinking on the land nearly knee-deep. What fine manure! But how offensive to the Pharaohs of the country! By the papers to-day, I see that Miss Courtney, the daughter of an emigrant in Mr. Birkbeck's settlement, was killed in a few hours by the bite of a huge spider, such as I saw in Carolina, scattering thousands of eggs in my path. It seized the unfortunate lady on her forehead; no cure could be had of the Indian, or other doctors. Her head swelled to an enormous size, and after her death was livid all over. The herb called the Plantago is said to be a remedy, if applied in time. The west country mail and travellers are now repeatedly stopped and robbed by parties of men at work on the Philadelphia road, who will not suffer any person to proceed until plundered.

3rd.—Lord Selkirk, while here, always deemed it expedient and politic to travel in the disguise of a poor man, to prevent his becoming a daily prey to tavern imposition and wild outlawed thieves. This mode is wise in any man moving in and through a wild country. His Lordship's settlement, so very near his heart, is said to be in ruins, and a constant prey to the Indians, excited against it by the north-west company, although he honourably paid the barbarians for their land. Murder, and acts amounting to civil war, have been committed on both sides and by all parties.

Sunday, 5th.—I left this city on an agricultural tour into the states of Maryland and Virginia. I

was accompanied by Mr. Dunn, the friendly ser-
jeant-at-arms to Congress, who felt kindly anxious
that I should see and know his list of friends. We
travelled on horseback, resting the first night at
Squire Simpson's. We visited Mr. Webb, who 26
years since came here a London mechanic, and
bought 500 acres of poor land, which he has but
little improved, getting only from six to ten bushels
of wheat per acre. He thinks plaster of Paris,
without manure, of no real service on poor, worn-
out land. Plaster is found to operate on land by
attracting dew. More dew is always seen in
plants and grain growing on plastered fields. The
dew palpably shews where the plaster has been
used, and the land is cooled by it. Mr. Webb, the
father of a family, feels well satisfied that America
is the country for a poor and industrious man.

Farming.—A gentleman of considerable property plastered and clovered three years successively, without either mowing or depasturing. The
whole produce of the land was suffered to grow
and rot, and at the end of the third year, it was
ploughed and sown with wheat, and yielded thirty-
five bushels per acre. This was a novelty in
farming, and too expensive an experiment for farmers. Droves of cattle are bred in the southern
and western back-settlements, and sold to the
graziers on the Potowmac at one dollar per head,
and in a year after to the butcher at from 10 to
15 dollars, who in his turn makes 30 dollars, so

gaining 100 per cent on the cost. I cannot but
doubt the correctness of this statement, although it
seems to come from good authority. It appears
improbable to an Englishman, who never sells a
calf at a week old, under 4 dollars or 5 dollars.
Webb and Simpson, both Englishmen, think that
10 bushels of wheat an acre, gives a living profit,
and feel well assured that estates with, or near
a market, are infinitely better than the western
country, which they contend is without a market.
" We saw," say they, " two men who had returned,
preferring 100 acres of poor land, like ours, to
500 in the west, where there was no market, nor
money to be had or made. Even in the east,
where land is far off a market, or inconveniently
situated, it is not worth half so much as it would
otherwise be. The produce cannot be carried to
market, when most wanted in the winter.

6th.—I reached and slept at Harper's Ferry,
where is *Uncle Sam*'s grand central depôt of arms
and ammunition. I visited the armoury, which is a
magnificent establishment, replete with all that is
necessary for the destruction of the human family.
Here also is a manufactory of arms, conducted
on the most scientific principles, and abounding
with almost every species of ingenious machinery,
worked by steam, and supplied by water running
from the mountains near, and carried to the top of
the buildings, which, together with the town on
the banks of the river, stand in a fortification of

rocks. The traveller enters Harper's Ferry by a steep declivity of two miles, so rugged, that I expected we should all break our necks. The southern bank opposite to the town is perpendicularly higher than the ball of St. Paul's cathedral, and on it are growing huge forest trees, which are cut and tumbled down this awful precipice, and floated down the Potowmac. The romantic and stupendous scenes of nature are here unrivalled. No traveller should return from America without seeing Harper's Ferry, which is very well sketched by the late president Jefferson in his *Notes on Virginia.* I ought to mention, that I dined this day with Mr. Marlow, a kind-hearted sociable gentleman, living out of society between two huge mountains, the Chotocton and the Blue Mountain, and losing the sun daily three quarters of an hour sooner than other places in the neighbourhood. He purchased his present estate, all of fine land, save the mountain land, 300 acres, at 20 dollars an acre, about three years since, and is now offered 60 dollars for it, but it is falling in value. It is all in a state of cultivation and enclosed, and is the third purchase on which he has lived awhile and improved for sale; having thus gained 25,000, or 30,000 dollars, without a cent to begin with. He thinks highly of Illinois and the western states generally, but considers Missouri to be the best, and to be pre-

ferred, as being the richest soil, and a land of negroes.—"There," says he, "the market is good
and certain, and produce may be taken down the
Mississipi, to New Orleans and the eastern parts,
as cheaply as I can get mine to Washington, Baltimore, or Philadelphia, for I have to pay half a
dollar a barrel for 80 miles only, and the farmers
of the west can send it 2,000 miles for six dollars."
Mr. Marlow gains nothing by cultivation merely,
but by making improvements, and by the encreased value of land, one third of which he always keeps in wood, or rather uncleared, and
deems that part the most valuable.

7th.—I visited and spent the night with Mr.
Worsley, a first-rate practical farmer and grazier,
late of Lincolnshire. He owns a fine farm,
in a Maryland valley, of 350 acres, which 13
years ago he bought at 20 dollars an acre, but
which is now worth 60 dollars. It has averaged
yearly, exclusive of a good living, a net gain of
600 dollars by cultivation only. He finds 40
miles from a market of no importance, as the
carrying is done when men and horses have
nothing else to do. He is also paid for the carriage, and brings in return plaster, for which he
must otherwise have gone empty; or if he preferred it, he might sell his grain to a neighbouring
miller at a city price, only allowing the miller for
the carriage to the city:—" My expenses," says

he, " on an acre of wheat, amount to 12 dollars, and it has always averaged 22 dollars, or
23 dollars at market, so netting near 100 per
cent. I have always 150 acres in grain and corn,
100 in clover, and 100 in wood, the latter of
which is worth, to sell, 150 dollars an acre, but
that must remain as indispensable to a farm without any green hedges. I consider green clover
crops in value equal to grain, when fattening
beasts and pigs pays well. This dry year, the
four-years old beasts, which cost in, as stores, 35
dollars a-head, will sell out only for the same
money; a sad loss. All my time, keep, and
labour are wasted on them." I saw his herd of
swine, 100 in number; some fat, others only half
fat, all fed in clover only, and generally fat
enough for market in the autumn, but never fit for
his own use; corn being necessary to make them
firm and fit for smoking into hams. This herd
seems now just fat enough for London porkers;
the citizens not desiring it thoroughly fat. Viewed
and examined the threshing floor, where 50 bushels
a day of wheat are trodden out by five or six oxen,
and a horse amongst them, and three or four men
to brush them up and shake off the straw, and
keep on a supply of fresh grain. The men drink,
and "muzzle not the ox which treadeth out the
corn."

Both man and beast seem to know and do their

business well. Mr. Worsley keeps five male negroes all the year round, and in harvest five extra hands, a fortnight only. Clover sown in wheat or rye in March, is frequently mown in great abundance after the grain is off: such is the richness of the soil and climate, that two tons an acre are often thus gotten. It runs up high as the waist of a man, and pigs are fattened on it besides; thus are two crops, one of wheat, and the other of clover, both gathered from the same field in the same year. Mr. Worsley says, " I would not have Dr. Dawes's land as a gift, if I must be confined to live on and out of it. Mr. Simpson has saved but little money, not half so much as he ought; on good land, with his industry and skill, he must have been worth ten times as much money as he is." But he is hospitable, and keeps open house to all, and he is never without visitors. When the British burned the city, the ladies fled to him.

Mr. Worsley began with 100*l.*—borrowed 900*l.*, had some with his wife, and is now worth 30,000 dollars. He was always a working, economical man, spending nothing, selling every thing, and turning all to some good account. Dr. Franklin's theory is Worsley's practice:

> " Get what you can, and what you get hold;
> That is the stone which turns lead into gold."

Cost of one acre of Cropping on Mr. Worsley's
good farm :—

	Dollars.	Cents.
Rent	2	
Taxes	0	9
Seed Wheat	1	50
Ploughing by *hire*	3	
Reaping or cradling . . .	2	
Carting and threshing . . .	2	50
Carting to mill near home . .	1	
1½ bushel of plaster, at 60 cents	1	
	13	9

The average price and quantity 18 bushels at
1 dollar 25 cents.

Dollars.	Cents.
22	50
13	9
9	41

Net profit on one acre of wheat which is raised
without a year's naked fallow.

Got 500 dollars by pigs last year, and sometimes more.

Proved a net gain of 130*l.* a-year, and a good
living for family, during 13 years.

The first cost of the farm, 360 acres, and stocking 9,300 dollars.

Present stock and cash 6,000.

3,000 capital for seven years. ⎱ employed.
3,000 ditto for six years.   ⎰

8th.—I moved on to the seat and pleasant farm-house of —— Johnson, Esq. a young gentleman married to a delicate young lady of taste and amiable manners. Mr. Johnson lives in capital style in a house of stone, the labour only of which cost 3,000 dollars, on a large estate near the Sugar-loaf mountain. It was left him by his father, and contains mines of iron and a foundry, very profitable. " I travelled," said he, " through the western country by Kentucky, Ohio, and Tenessee, seven years since, but saw nothing to induce me to leave the eastern states. It is there impossible to turn produce into cash when wanted: no market but distant Orleans. Produce is surrendered to enterprizing men, as they are called, on the rivers, but who frequently prove to be thieves; for if the boat is *stove in*, or markets are bad or dull, there are no returns; you hear no more of either produce or the boat-men. Companies and steam-boats' folks are safer to entrust it with. To go yourself to market is impossible, for while selling one crop, you would lose the time for raising another. This impediment to the success of capitalists in the west, is likely long to continue, or to remove only slowly. The west is only fit at present for a father who has many sons whom he wishes to settle on estates of their own, and who will be able to live there, but not in eastern comfort and respectability. I know many men of capital tempted to sell out in the east and purchase largely and settle down in the west, but who continued there only a short time, being right glad to sell out with loss and re-purchase their old eastern estates, or others at a considerable advance."

Mr. Johnson thinks these are good arguments in favour of the east, with which he is satisfied, and that satisfaction he gained by seeing the west. Mr. Johnson, now only 32, was then gay and young, and the west has been ever since improving; several farmers having made fortunes trebling and quadrupling their first capitals by purchasing.

" West country hospitality," says Mr. Johnson, " is most abundant, and is well exemplified in the conduct of many of the most respectable settlers, towards a stranger who was waylaid and robbed of 3,000 dollars. On making it known, colonels, majors, captains, and lieutenants, all as one man, instantly armed without fee or reward, and scouring the country round for many miles, overtook and seized the robber, and recovered all the cash for the overjoyed stranger."

I noticed to-day, that at lone houses a little out of society, the children all rushed to the doors to gaze upon us, and with a fixed, wild, staring eye, seemed to say: We have never seen such strangers before in this world.

9th.—Being now in the neighbourhood of his excellency the president's country seat, or farmhouse, the patrimony of his family, I find that his neighbours are rejoicing because his excellency, on coming here last week, was arrested three times in one week by neighbours whom he ought to have paid long ago; the debts being money borrowed on his estates. He has long been under private pecuniary embarrassments, and offered all his estates for sale in order to discharge the demands of his creditors.

I reached the elegant farm mansion and table of Colonel Thomas, to dine. Here I found many interesting sons and daughters, who, together with their sire and mother, seemed full of good-will and generous hospitality to me, a stranger. The colonel has two farms, one of 600, and the other of 300 acres; bought 30 years since at two guineas an acre, all fine land, which averages from 20 to 25 bushels of wheat per acre: one dollar a bushel is a fair price if mechanics were reasonable in their charges. Some of them soon get fortunes:—" On my farm of 300 acres," says he, " I give to my steward one sixth of the produce raised, which to him is from 500 to 600 dollars annually, besides land for hemp and flax, a cow, and all the poultry he likes to raise. I think farming a slow way of getting money, except where the family are all workers, and live economically on bacon, potatoes, and sour skim milk, as do many farmers of Dutch extraction. But the children so raised, when they get the property into their own hands, generally spend it faster than

it was gotten. I feel myself but little richer by
the boasted increased value of land while I keep
it. It maintained me at first, it only does so now:
housekeeping expenses for a genteel family have
increased in proportion, and, indeed, more than
either land or produce. I however prefer farming, because it is a certain independence. I think
highly of plaster of Paris and management, and
plough my land more than once for wheat."

The colonel has relatives in Illinois doing well,
and well pleased, and who took good capitals, and
workmen, and mechanics, and implements for
building first-rate houses. He thinks the west
the best country; the land there increases so fast
in value. " My store-bill," says he, " is here
6,000 dollars a year."

I bade farewell to the colonel, who desired
that I would visit his western friends, and report
of them, and re-visit him on my return.

10th.—Supped and slept at New Town with
Mr. M'Gill, a venerable and highly respectable
merchant, who knows that farmers have made
large fortunes quickly, where disposed to economy
and industry. Still, many of the Virginians have
spent all as fast as it came, indulging in all manner
of luxury and excess; giving their children most
expensive educations, which never turned to any
account, as they afterwards all sat down on small
plantations. Colonel Thomas (says he) has saved
much and spent liberally too, although he talks

to you of money being made slowly by farming. Bacon, potatoe, and bonny claber farmers (Germans) have become invariably rich by cultivating. On farms of 300 acres each, 100 is in wood, 100 in corn and rye, for the support of the farm and establishment, and 100 is in wheat, clear gain, which might be put into the pocket every year. Twenty-three thousand dollars capital is necessary for every farm of 300 acres in this fruitful valley, and about 10 per cent. profit on such capital is realized where good management exists. He thinks highly of the west, and feels anxious for the success of Mr. Birkbeck's settlement. He must enrich himself, family, and followers by the increasing value of land, and that without cultivating an acre, if he does but retain the title-deeds in his own hands. He feels sure that land on the Miami of the lakes is fine and desirable for settlers, especially when the canal from New York thence shall be finished, and deems settlements on the Missouri flourishing and inviting. Mr. M'Gill is of Scotch extraction, and is a kind-hearted, well-informed man.

11*th.*—I dined, supped, and slept with **Mr. T. Hillery**, a water-miller and planter of the most complete kind, occupying two large plantations, one rich, and the other poor, worn-out land. On the former he gets from 35 to 40 bushels of wheat an acre; on the latter poor land from two to five bushels: he averages 25. He is satisfied with five bushels for the first few years. The poor land he bought at six dollars an acre, but is sure of greatly increasing its value, although he shall gain nothing but rather lose by cultivation, for on 500 acres he could not support his family. Mr. Hillery is a man of large capital, enterprizing habits, and great industry; being always in the mill or the field, at work from sun-rise to sun-set. He is one of a large family of sons, who are all settled in a similar way: their father, in great agricultural riches and eminence, is still living. A poor man, (he says,) must never buy poor land; he must go to the west; but he is convinced that the east is the best for the present employment of capital, which cannot be invested with advantage in the west, unless the farmer is a trader also. Then he may succeed, but not by cultivating alone; there being no market there except New Orleans, where, if produce can be sold, it is found not to be worth raising. He has seen several who have returned, preferring the eastern states: he never felt any desire to emigrate, but means to visit the west for the purpose of seeing and judging, and buying estates for each of his children, in such parts as are likely to become the most inviting to, and lie in the channel of emigration. The poor man, if any body, must be the pioneer in the western regions. He showed me what he called his fine large ears of wheat, which are of the white and red bearded species, not half the length of the English, nor so fine and large in the kernel and

quality. Mr. Hillery thinks well of plaster, but
by experience proves that it will not act bene-
ficially on poor, worn-out land without manure.
Its good effects are evident enough in suitable
land, so as to discover to an inch where it is
sown. On clover the cattle will eat the pasture
bare where plaster has been sown; but if a spot
has been missed, they leave that untasted, and
never touch it. It is seen to produce abundant
dew, and is thought to contain alum and to stiffen
the soil, so as in time to destroy all vegetative
power. It is suitable only for light, warm soil.
He thinks that ten per cent on capital or four per
cent in addition to common interest is not generally made by cultivation, even on good land with
good management; but if liberal housekeeping is
taken into account on such improved soils, which
it is not customary to do, that a profit of 15 per
cent has been, is, or may be obtained. Wheat is
now only 36 cents or less than eighteen pence sterling a bushel, and unsaleable at that or any other
price at Buffalo state, New York. The distance
from market makes it so.

Milling and Millers.—Mr. Hillery, who owns
a most complete grist and saw-mill, worked by
water, buys no wheat, but has more of his own
and of his neighbours', than he can grind.—He
takes the tenth for toll. He finds it almost impossible to get a careful, faithful miller at 500
dollars, or 112*l.* a year!

Sunday, 12*th.*—Last evening I re-appeared in the
Federal City, after spending a week in that beautiful fruitful vale, 40 miles long, and seven broad,
partly in Maryland and partly in Virginia, and the
only fertile spot, north of Carolina, which I have
yet seen. Here I found much information, real
hospitality, honesty, great good will, genuine ur-
banity, and friendship, accompanied by wealth and
independence. I was pressed to return and revisit
these squires and farmers on some future day, and
spend weeks with them. For this kindness I am
indebted to my friend Mr. Dunn, to whom it
would give me pleasure, if this page should bear
my grateful remembrances.

I saw a fine apple-tree, full of fruit, evidently
planted, as are many other choice trees, by the
hand of nature.

14*th.*—"Aristocrats," says my friend Mr. Elliott,
"are breeding fast in America: no men in the world
are more aristocratical than the heads of departments; they spurn, and cannot even speak to,
common men, unless it be to purchase popularity
cheaply. Four ranks variegate this demoralizing
country, (i. e.) the heads of departments, clerks
in office, merchants and traders, and the lower
orders. The third named are considered much
below the first, yet above the second, and are
therefore treated with more respect than the clerks
under government, who are mere slaves, dependent
and removable at pleasure without explanation.

There are already nobility in existence in the
Cincinnati society and military schools."

" Our great orator, Randolph, is an orator of
nature," says Mr. Jones, " and half an Indian.
He was once sneered at in the house on account
of his pedigree. He smartly replied, and boasted
of being descended, by his mother's side, from an
Indian princess and a Mr. Smith, an English
gentleman, an early settler in Virginia, who was
taken prisoner by the Indians, and about to be
offered up a sacrifice to their gods; but at the
moment when the fatal tomahawk was raised to
destroy him, this princess stepped forward and
prevented the dreadful blow. He immediately
married his preserver."

15th.—In the Michigan territory, on the borders
of the lakes, in July last, flies, thick as swarms
of bees on a bough, covered the face of the earth,
and for six days darkened the sun, moon, and
stars, making the air noisome and pestilential.
The sides and ends of houses on which the sun
shone not, were blackened by them. They seemed
to lose their skin daily and die by millions every
minute : cattle, swine, and the Indians, feed on
them luxuriously. Their length is three inches,
with the feelers which protrude from both head
and tail. Corn fields and large boughs of trees
were broken down by their weight. Mr. Adams,
two years before, saw the same phenomenon.
They are nondescripts in natural history, but

called by the French settlers of the neighbourhood *Mosquito Hawks,* as they feed upon mosquitoes and drive them away.

Intending on the morrow to leave this city, on
a tour through some of the northern states bordering on the lakes, and from thence by the falls of
the Niagara to the western country, I advertised
in the National Intelligencer for a travelling companion, but not finding any offers agreeable to me,
I determined on starting unaccompanied. Two
or three kind introductory letters were put into
my hands by Messrs. Adams, Elliott, and Dunn,
to his Excellency Jonathan Jennings, governor of
the state of Indiana, Major Hooper of Hamilton,
N. Y., and Jacob Lowndes, Esq., the prison philanthropist, the Howard of America.

16*th.*—At six, a. m., 1 started for Philadelphia
and New York ; and in the Delaware river, passed
a packet-ship from London, brimful of emigrants.

18*th.*—I passed king Joseph Bonaparte's palace
on the banks of the Delaware on the Jersey side,
and many other delightful farms, houses, villas,
and villages, with fruitful and extensive salt and
fresh marshes, and meadows full of hay-stacks,
just such as are seen in Lincolnshire and Norfolk,
having the sea ready to burst in and over them,
and inclosed by water ditches, as in the fens of
England. At noon I landed for the first time at
the beautiful and justly famed city of New York.

Elegant hackney coaches were in attendance on

the wharfs, and took us to the Washington Hall, the second best hotel in this city, where we dined at a long public table, groaning under the weight of luxuries. The company seemed of the first and best grade, principally boarders and visitors from the southern states. All seemed hungry and thirsty, and as if living only to eat and drink.

After dinner I took a hasty walk about the city, which seemed all bustle and confusion. It was like Michaelmas or Lady-day in England; at every door, in almost every street, carts and waggons were seen lading or laden, removing furniture, merchandize, and men from the city to the country. Stores and offices, and firms were closed, or only doing business as if by stealth. But why all this? The yellow fever was raging and turning citizens out of doors into the grave; and on discovering that one gentleman lay sick of it at our Hall, we determined on quitting the city and repairing to Philadelphia next morning.

I saw the once celebrated Aaron Burr, a little lean, pale, withered, shabby looking, decayed, grey-headed old gentleman, whose name is too well known in transatlantic history to need my notice. I saw also in court, but very indistinctly, Mr. Emmett, the distinguished lawyer, and long-persecuted Irish refugee, the companion of Sampson, whose life and sorrows have been recently written in this city. All our plans were disconcerted by this dreadful fever, and we therefore left this at six in the morning after a stay of only nineteen hours in this great mart for all America.

20th.—This day, I dined at Judd's hotel, Philadelphia. I talked long with friend Edward Wilson, a rich English quaker and one of the best men I have seen in Pennsylvania. He was a refugee from Northamptonshire, and by trading in the importation of British goods, has become opulent. I was twice invited to dine with him, but could not.

" Though there is some distress here," says he, " there is room for all, masters and labourers, in agriculture ; but I cannot advise people, who are comfortable in England, to come here, unless they can appreciate the advantages arising to their children and posterity generally. Fathers and mothers should expect to sacrifice themselves for their children. The rage for speculation has ruined many, farmers not excepted, who purchased lands now not worth half the cost. The banks are the sources of that ruin ; but as they are nuisances fast removing, trade, though as bad, or worse than in England, will soon become better. Those farmers and merchants who have been prudent, are either rich or well to do. There are not above four houses in Philadelphia able to import goods into it. I am declining the business myself, it being far better to do no business than to do it unsafely. As to slave states, if I were blind, I could tell when I was entering any of them. I can smell them ; the moral air is putrid. Ma-

nagement and every thing else tells a slave state.
The beautiful small rich favourite farms with complete houses and offices on them, all of stone,
with the mail road and river Delaware in front,
sold this summer at 85 dollars an acre, though
worth 100 dollars. They average 25 bushels of
wheat per acre, and sometimes produce 40 bushels.
Your Mr. Long from Lincolnshire, and others,
have bought excellent lands in Pennsylvania
within 40 miles of this city, and nearer other markets, with all improvements, cleared and inclosed,
having complete house and buildings, at only 15 and
18 dollars an acre, the cost only of the buildings,
or perhaps only of the fence, but which land three
years ago sold at 60 dollars an acre. One dollar
a bushel here is a living profit, and better than two
in England. Mr. Long, though of an unsettled
turn, has bought his land well and must do well.
He has waited long, though not in vain. There
is much fine land in and all over the eastern states,
particularly in this state, and in New York, to be
bought well (as much must be sold by the sheriff)
and with a fine market for every kind of produce,
and not in a slave state. The western-country
labourers return here, unable to get paid in any
way for their work, it being impossible to sell, any
where or at any price, the wheat which they receive in lieu of cash. One poor fellow, after threshing a month, returned quite unable to sell his
share or bring it away ; and if the farmer has 20

miles to carry it to the river, it is not worth his
while to grow it, for no money can be had for it,
but goods only, which he must receive at the
vendor's own price, and in like manner his produce. All is done by barter. I know several
whom I advised not to go westward, now repenting and unable to raise ten dollars. They have
lost much by lending, and by the reduction of
their lands, which are now, though much improved,
unsaleable, or if saleable, at immense loss. My
partner's father (an Englishman) had 17,000 dollars, when a few years since he went into the wilderness, but now is he indeed a repenting man,
unable to raise or borrow ten dollars on or from
his estate."

22nd.—"Young men in trade," says Mr. Wardour, "and clerks from England, had better stay
at home, or if here, return home immediately."
Fifty passengers returned last week from this city
to England and Ireland. He conceives that no
accurate calculations have yet been made to prove
what are the profits in agriculture. He knows
that the rent of his purchase does not net above
three per cent. on the capital employed, though
situated so near to Philadelphia and with a mansion upon it. Both Wardour and Wilson have
great numbers of emigrants passing through their
hands, and establish many well. They send labourers to masters, and advise them to begin a job
without a bargain; for, if good for any thing and

steady, they are sure to be remunerated in the east, and treated with more respect and equality than people coming from old countries can form an idea of. It is true that many men labour during the winter for their food, lodging, washing, &c.

I met a Pennsylvanian farmer in the steam-boat, who states that plenty of labourers were to be had, all the harvest, at half a dollar per day and board. There were many more than could be employed. Much distress is therefore expected in the coming winter through excess of labourers. Messieurs Price, Krugg, Wardour, and Wilson, all distinct firms and personages, agree in opinion and evidence that the eastern states are the best for the employment of capital; yet they partially admit that New Orleans will or may be a market, a grand emporium for the western wilderness. Ships go there to buy produce; but, Mr. Wardour says, why should men of capital go to settle there, while fine cleared and improved land in the east, with every possible advantage can be bought any where, for the money it costs in fencing and enclosing. Western land must be enclosed and cleared, and at a much greater expense than the eastern, and then after all be without a market for surplus produce, or purchasers for the land and its improvements. Lands, even in the old and thickly settled state of Kentucky, are so depressed in price and so unsaleable, that a dollar cannot be raised upon or from them. Living is uncommonly cheap;

fowls 9s. sterling per dozen, and every thing in proportion. Housekeeping is cheaper by 100 per cent., and 30 per cent. for a genteel family, than at Philadelphia. Mr. R. Flower, in a recent letter, says that female servants and others are much wanted, as well as mechanics of all sorts. The females of every description have nearly all got married or engaged.

24th.—I returned to Washington city this day, after a journey of about 700 miles, during which I saw many situations inviting to emigrants both in Pennsylvania and in other states on the banks of rivers; but little or no good land elsewhere.

I feel some regret on quitting the purer air, the fairer scenes and better tables of Pennsylvania and New York, where, at almost every meal, rich and precious fruits garnished the ever tempting table, and sharpened the failing appetite. At Philadelphia I thought the roasted beef equal to that of Old England, and every thing at Judd's good hotel, fair, sweet, and cleanly, just what an Englishman loves, and deems indispensable to his comfort.

I am forcibly struck every where with the prominent boldness and forwardness of American children, who seem unabashed, manly, and conversable, because they are always, from early life, introduced to all strangers at home or abroad. They fear nothing, care for nothing, and never blush,

but think themselves to be all-knowing men and
women, never to be slighted or affronted with impunity.

Sunday, October 3rd.—By mutual agreement, a
band of philosophers, last evening, met to smoke
me off to the western wilderness; and smoke
we did till one o'clock this morning, when they
escorted me to, and saw me safely packed in
Uncle Sam's western mail, and bade me a hearty
farewell for three months. Thus, with some regret, left I city, summer, and civilization behind
me, as much from a wish to be faithful to my
promise, as to see, hear, and know. My eyes
and ears, indeed, begin to feel something akin to
satiety; but I had engaged, and solemnly vowed,
to the faithful patriarch, that I would travel 3,000
miles to visit his well-beloved son in Indiana, if
he, the father, would continue my steward at
White Hall during my absence. Three thousand
miles is nothing of a journey here; and now seated
and well shaken together with one of *Uncle Sam*'s
high sheriffs, a gentlemanly colonel, and other
passengers, all very sociable, I move along gaily.
At noon, we passed through Frederick-town, a
very long promising place, quite English in its
appearance, and well situated in a fine rich valley,
which yields the finest Indian corn yet seen, and is
the best wheat land in America, being a part of,
or bordering on, the extensive fertile valley before
mentioned, which stretches through Virginia,

Maryland, and Pennsylvania, and shows the best farms and farmers in the land. My agreeable companion, the colonel, says that no land is here selling by forced sales, nor any under 100 dollars an acre, and that few or no persons within his knowledge complain of hard times, but those whose pride or imprudent speculations have involved them. We supped and slept at Hager's-town, a market town, with three Dutch gothic churches, adorned with tall spires, and a good court house. This town is highly delightful, and almost surrounded by small mountains; the scenery is beautiful, and both in and around an air of grandeur prevails; except, indeed, at our tavern, where, though it is Sunday, all is smoke and fire, and Bacchus is the god.

4th.—Early this morning we commenced a perilous journey, ascending and descending the Allegany mountains all day. All here is wild, awfully precipitous, and darkly umbrageous, high as the heavens, or low as perdition. I almost resolved on not returning this way by mail, which carries and keeps one in constant alarm, unless the traveller has nerves of iron or brass. Such, however, is the expertness of the drivers here, that there is no ground for real apprehension.

—— Kennedy, Esq. and the high sheriff, both highly intelligent men, deem the western country the best for the employment of capital, because, say they, we, if there, could send our surplus produce to New Orleans, at a less expense than the Hager's-town people can send theirs to Baltimore. We think that in time to come, when merchants of capital settle in Orleans, all western produce will find a good market there; and that good land at reduced prices is not to be had generally in the eastern states, for when a forced sale is made, creditors commonly take good care it shall make about its value, or sufficient to cover the debts. Where there are no creditors, it may sometimes, but not often, be otherwise.

5th. — We rode this day over our English General Braddock's grave. To prevent the Indians, then in pursuit, from discovering his body, he ordered it to be buried in the midst of the road, at the foot of the Allegany mountains, in 1756.

I slept at Cumberland, on the Monongahela, where are the remains of a British fort once used against the Indians.

6th.—Off, an hour before day-light, along the banks of the Monongahela. Just as we were starting, up came a Mr. Morgan and six negroes, requesting of the gentlemen passengers that he and his negroes might be graciously permitted to share the stage with us: we consented. My companions' compliance, indeed, surprised me a little, and in came Morgan and his black cattle. He had been round the country jobbing, like a pig-jobber in England, and had bought half a score; but they, feeling themselves in a free state, snuffed up free air, and took the liberty to escape. He was unable to recover more than six; four were lost and most reluctantly abandoned. He bought them, he said, for a gentleman planter, in the distant territory of Missouri, to which they were going down the Ohio river. Within two miles east of Washington, Pennsylvania, we found that the strap, which confined our luggage, had given way, and scattered Morgan's trunks and money a few miles behind. We sent men and horses back, and to our surprise found all safe. On leaving Washington, several other gentlemen entered our stage, but would not permit Mr. Morgan and his negroes to enter.—" What?" said they, " ride with negroes ?"—Much strife now ensued, and a battle was intended ; but to quiet the angry passions of both sides, a stage was provided for the refusing party. Our ride, for the last three hours of our journey, was fearfully romantic, amongst huge rocks which hung over on both sides and seemed ready to fall upon us, the effect of which was greatly heightened by the moon-light.

Between twelve and one o'clock we reached Wheeling, Virginia, on the Ohio, and went supperless to bed. I shared mine with a young student, Mr. Paul, of Washington Academy, now bound to his father's house at Maddison Ville, Indiana, who is there a Banker, or Bank Director.

7th.—We found the Ohio river nearly dry, so droughty has been the summer. It is now fed

only by mountain springs.   Here I unexpectedly
met my friend Mr. Edney and lady from the Isle
of Wight, a branch of the Pittiss family of that
Isle. I dined with him at his boarding-house, and
agreed to visit his recently hired farm. I received
an invitation from a learned Doctor to ride 800
miles down the Ohio with him and his Excellency
Governor Miller, just chosen king of and going to
the Arkansaw territory. I waited five days for
his Excellency and his aquatic suite, but lack of
water prevented his arrival.

8th.—I crossed the Ohio with Mr. Edney, to
view and examine his farm, on mountainous
banks, down to the margin of the river. It consists of 500 acres, hill and dale, or river-bottom
and mountain land, the best and richest in the
state of Ohio, seven miles from Wheeling and
other good markets. Two hundred acres have
been cleared and cultivated twenty years. Two
hundred and fifty are in wood, mountain land, too
high and steep for the plough, and which, if
ploughed, would all wash away. Eighty acres
are in pasture, natural pasture, the richest, finest,
and most luxuriant I ever saw. So thick and
matted is it, with fine natural grass and white
clover, that it is with difficulty I can force my foot
through it to the soil, which is a sandy loam, and
has been crowded with cattle all this summer,
the dryest ever remembered. But all river-bottoms are cool, rich, and inexhaustible. The arable

land has been cropped fifteen years successively, yet still the wheat-stubble and corn-stalks are strong, thick, and rank, and the land on which the wheat grew is well laid down, or seeded with natural grass and white clover, a smothering plant of both, and all done by the hand of provident nature. So complete is it, that an English farmer would say, " What a fool have you been, thus to waste your grass seeds." It is now, two months after harvest, a complete fattening pasture, and, but for the stubble staring in it, might be mistaken for an old home-stall poisoned with manure, and too rich and rank, or sour, for use, and therefore to be broken up. This bottom land, however, may well be rich, for it has been robbing the mountains from time immemorial. Amongst the corn still standing, although well horse-hoed six weeks ago, are seen rank weeds, tall as the tall corn. The sun makes every inch a hot-bed. Ploughing seems shamefully performed, not half the land is turned over or downwards. It seems, (as we say at Somersham) as though it was ploughed with a ram's horn, or the snout of a hog, hungry after grubs and roots.

The mountain land is good, and well stored, and enriched with huge sugar trees, which are tapped every spring, and many cwts. made therefrom; but much of this land is too steep for cattle to climb up it, and the timber is of little or no worth save for the uses of the farm and fire. Mr.

Edney has this estate, on lease of 14 years, from Squire Zain, the head man of Wheeling. The rent for the first three years, is 400 dollars; the next three years, 500 dollars; the remaining eight years, 600 dollars. Three years' notice to be given if he wishes, or is wished to leave before the expiration of the lease. The cost of necessary farm-buildings to be deducted from the rent. This land was, this year, bought by Mr. Zain, at 18 dollars an acre, but thought to be worth not above 12 dollars, because received in lieu of a debt. Mr. Edney is, it is thought, cheated; the good opinion of the neighbourhood is against his bargain. " What he will thus expend would have bought a better farm.—The landlord would have been glad of him rent free." The farm, however, is very good, and susceptible of great improvement. Nature has here done all she can, and art little or nothing.

9th.—A miserably wet (and as sailors say) dirty day. I fell sick of Wheeling, imprisoned by a high and almost inaccessible mountain, to the top of which I climbed yesterday. I revisited Mr. Edney, who has wrangled and parted with his father-in-law, once my hospitable host at the Isle of Wight. He with his family have settled down on wood-land, all in wood, 40 miles in the state of Ohio. One son is to be planted there, and the rest, with himself, in better Missouri; but he is very undecided, and finds that America is not *Newport*, in England. He lost all his horses, cows, dogs, and men and maids brought over as hired servants. The animals were stolen, or they strayed and died, while his servants snuffed up free air and fled, except one female who fell in love, while on board, with the black steward, and who, on landing, went to a magistrate, at Baltimore, for marriage; but his worship said that it was contrary to custom and the law of the land, for a white woman to marry a negro, and he could not and should not allow it.

Sunday, 10*th*.—By free and frequent conversations with intelligent residents and travellers here, I find that public opinion is favourable to location in the western country, which they say has never yet lacked a market for surplus produce; and as men of capital only can raise produce, and as their number is comparatively few, it is unlikely that the surplus produce will ever greatly exceed the demand. Much of what is raised will necessarily be consumed by those who raise none; and some will always be wanted at New Orleans and other river towns, cities, and new settlements. This, in part, is true. Society, say they, in the west is almost as cheaply attainable to farmers as in the east, for in both he must seek it in towns and distant cities, save what his own family affords. Mellish, in a recent publication, says, " the flower of the east is seen moving west." I think so too, for what finer men can I expect to meet than those whom I have seen moving from

thence westward? I called on Mr. Yandal, a
gentleman whose ancestors accompanied William
Penn to this country. He seems proud of his
English origin; and introduced me to an English
brewer, who (the people here say) is to gain 100
per cent. on his capital employed. He has bought
a brewery from a Wheeling gentleman, who is
fitting up another brewhouse in opposition, contrary to stipulations. Mr. Edney yesterday bought
two horses at 50 dollars, his own price, but not
worth above 25 dollars each. All in the neighbourhood know that my green and liberal friend
has English money, and all conspire against it.

11*th.*—Waggons (not many) are daily arriving
with goods and emigrants for the river, down
which, when the waters rise, they are to float in
flat boats called arks, two and two of many living
creeping things, occasionally anchoring on the
banks and surveying the promised land. A gentleman recently called at the Cincinnati bank for
specie, or good negotiable paper. " No," was
the answer, " we, sir, have neither." The paper
of that city, the pride of the west, is negotiable
only in the city for necessaries, and there only at
30 and 40 per centum below par, or United States'
paper. The best mode of dealing here is, on
your arrival, to go to the Cincinnati broker and
sell just so much of the United States' paper as
will get you enough of their paper for expenses at
the tavern or elsewhere; all must be spent here,

none taken away, for out of the city it is mere
waste paper. Such are banks, banking, and
bankers; let therefore the traveller hereafter not
depend on them, but take with him either hard
dollars or notes of the United States' bank or its
branches.

12th.—I left Wheeling at eight this morning;
the tavern bill three and a half dollars per week for
board merely. I crossed the Ohio into the state
so called, and passed briskly through St. Clair's
Ville and Morris-town, and a hilly country; all
fine land in grain, corn, and pasture, with a beautiful clover face, white as with a shower of sleet;
and abundance of flourishing orchards full, above
and below, of excellent fruit, although sixteen
years ago all was wild, and a complete forest. In
almost every orchard is seen a cider press, and
under every tree large apples, so thick that at
every step you must tread upon them, while the
boughs above are breaking down with their over-
laden weight. It is here no crime for either man
or beast to rob orchards. Land is worth from
15 to 30 dollars an acre, with all improvements
included, and a market, as yet, for all surplus
produce. At 30 miles' end, I rested for the night
at a homely but comfortable stage-house on the
road, with a young Irishman, Robert G. Ormsby,
Esq. of Louisville, Kentucky, aged 21, of fine
person and manners, and a fellow student of the
celebrated Irish orator, Charles Phillips, Esq.

He has been four years in this country with rich
uncles ; is a favourite with the ladies, and is now
on his way to Pittsburgh, to marry a beautiful
American with many thousands of dollars. " So
general," says he, "in Kentucky is the intercourse
between white men and black and yellow women,
that soon it will indeed be difficult to know and
distinguish who is who."

13th.—I started alone at three this morning,
well pleased with Mr. Ormsby, who mounted his
stage for the east, and I mine for the west. In
consequence of thus meeting with this gentleman,
I determined for the future, on always breaking
through the custom of waiting for introductions
before entering into conversation.

At four this morning, on the driver getting
down to lock the wheel, the horses started, and
instantly struck a stump of a tree, and upset the
mail with a crashing fall, which bruised my side,
cut my face, and blackened my eyes ; the two
leaders escaped into the forest, and we saw them
no more. The driver went in pursuit of them,
and left me to guard and sleep one hour and a
half in the damaged vehicle, now nearly bottom
upwards. When I awoke it was daylight, and
I walked up to a farm log-house, the people of
which put their heads out of the window and
thus addressed me,—" Stranger, come *into* the
fire !" and I went in, without being burned. At
five, the driver returned, and with two horses

only, we got under weigh, and moved on through Cambridge and Washington to breakfast, and at sun-set reached our inn at Zainsville, where I determined on resting a few days to repair the damages of the past day.

My inn is a good one, stored with newspapers, and full of good things, and visitors to devour them; and the town of Zainsville is very flourishing, and likely to become a city. It is now a county seat and a fountain of law and justice, situated on the banks of the fair Muskingham river, 84 miles from Wheeling; eighteen years old, with 3,000 inhabitants; good land 20 dollars an acre; plenty of coal and excellent water, being well supplied by springs and the river, and affording good society; many strangers continually passing to and fro. Here is kept a folio register, in which travellers write their names, from whence they come, and whither they are bound, with any news which they bring with them. The bank paper of this town is 20 or 30 per cent. below par. The supreme court of assize is now sitting, and the supreme judge, Wilson, who lodges at my quarters, is now to be my nightly companion in table-talk. His lordship calls me " stranger," and guesses me to be an Irishman. He is surprised that I speak so well, and wonders how many " dialects," we have in England. " I saw," says he, " lately, a lady from your country, who wondered at hearing the English language so well spoken here."—"We seem, sir," said I, "a wonder unto each other! In this western country you see emigrants only of an uneducated class, a low grade, full of provincialisms in their talk." Judge Wilson is intimately known to and acquainted with several nations of Indians. "Several persons," says he, "have in my time voluntarily turned Indians; one, a child taken from Virginia, is now a squaw, but more delicate in her conduct: she of course retains her original colour, and seems the better for her civilized origin."

14th.—Rambling round and through the town I saw a glass-house, and several fine mills, having at command all the water of the river, which might be made to work mills without number, and machinery of an infinite variety. I wandered in the fields shooting pigeons, which is here fine sport; they fly and alight around you on every tree, in immense flocks, and loving to be shot. They are rather smaller than English pigeons, and have a lilac breast; but in other respects are blue, or blue grey. They breed in the woods, and seem to court death by the gun, the sound of which appears to call them together, instead of scaring them away; a fowling-piece well charged with dust shot might bring down a bushel of these willing game dead at your feet.

At noon, I roamed into the supreme court, where I saw my new friend, the supreme judge, Wilson, on the bench, in the midst of three rustic, dirty-looking associate judges, all robeless, and dressed in coarse drab, domestic, homespun coats, dark silk handkerchiefs round their necks, and otherwise not superior in outward appearance to our low fen-farmers in England. Thus they sat, presiding with ease and ability over a bar of plain talkative lawyers, all robeless, very funny and conversational in their speeches, manners, and conduct; dressed in plain box-coats, and sitting with their feet and knees higher than their noses, and pointing obliquely to the bench of judges; thus making their speeches, and examining and cross-examining evidence at a plain long table, with a brown earthen jug of cold water before them, for occasionally wetting their whistles, and washing their quid-stained lips: all, judges, jury, counsel, witnesses, and prisoners, seemed free, easy, and happy. The supreme judge is only distinguished from the rest by a shabby blue threadbare coat, dirty trowsers, and unblacked shoes. Thus sat all their lordships, freely and frequently chewing tobacco, and appearing as uninterested as could be. Judge Wilson is, however, a smart intelligent man, rather jocular, and, I think, kind-hearted.

15th.—Talked with a farmer from Pennsylvania, who, ten years ago, bought his land near this town at two dollars uncleared, and the best, he calls it, in Ohio. The first crop of wheat was 35 bushels per acre, but never so much after; it now averages 20 to 25 bushels per acre, at 63 cents per bushel, about 2*s*. 10*d*. sterling; then, not half that price : 40 bushels of oats, per acre, at 20 cents, about 9*d*. sterling; but will be worth 60 cents, or 2*s*. 4*d*. per bushel. He gave, this year, three dollars for clearing land, 50 per cent. above the cost price of fee simple. Clearing, means simply grubbing up small surface-roots in the way of the plough, and cutting down a few large trees within about three feet of the ground, and deadening or girdling the rest, which is done by cutting out about three feet of bark all round the body of the hugest trunks, which then, root and branch, begin to die. What are cut down, together with the lop, are rolled by levers into heaps and burnt. He has lived on it, and can now sell his estate, with all improvements, at only ten dollars an acre. He always found a market for produce, at some price. He believes the land about Frederick and Hager's towns much better than this, because there it is limestone land, and therefore more enduring. " I would leave Ohio," says he, " if I could sell out well here, and return to the land of fish and good oysters, my dear native Pennsylvania. Plaster is never used here, but if the land were fallowed, as in some parts of the east, we could grow 40 bushels per acre."

16*th*.—At three this morning, I left Zainsville, so called in honour of Mr. Zain, of Wheeling, who has here a large estate given him by the state, for cutting a road from Wheeling to this town. On changing horses, I spoke to a potatoe farmer, who raises only 100 bushels per acre on rich land, and sells them at half a dollar per bushel; just 300 less in quantity per acre, and 100 per cent. more in price than in England. " I guess," says he, " that we Ohio folks do not manage potatoes so well as they do in Ireland and England."—" No, sir, if I may judge by your quantity, you do not indeed." " No, I guess not." Quantity of acres of produce is here thought to be of much greater importance than quantity per acre. The great object is to have as many acres as possible cleared, ploughed, set, sown, planted, and managed by as few hands as possible; there being little capital, and therefore little or none to spare for hired labour. Instead of five acres well-managed, they must have 20 acres badly managed. It is not how much corn can be raised on an acre, but how much from one hand or man, the land being nothing in comparison with labour. Eight hundred dollars per hand is, and has been made from one slave annually.

I passed all this day through a fine rich landed country, full of the natural means of living well by the sweat of the brow. The poor complain of want of money, and others of a scarcity of it; but none of want of common necessaries, such as bread, meat, and whiskey. At my inn for the night, I met and spent the evening with Mr. Chi-

chester, a polished, gay, and interesting American
gentleman, travelling together with his mother and
sister, in their family carriage, attended by a
negro, from Kentucky to Virginia. I found them
very communicable and free with me on discovering that I was an Englishman, bound to their
Illinois friends, the Flower family; "who," they
say, "are very happy and content in their log
cabin, where balls and good society are often
found." "This family," says Mr. Chichester,
"is very popular, and of great benefit to all kinds
of settlers in the neighbourhood, disposed to build
and settle down. Mr. Flower must enrich himself and family by the increasing value of land
bought; the only way now of making money any
where. Land generally in the west is fallen 50
per cent., and farming there is slow money-making,
but farmers can live." "And what more," said I,
"can they do in the east?" He believes that raising and grazing cattle and pigs, is here a more certain game than agriculture, and, for a small family
with capital, he thinks that the east is to be preferred, especially as land improved can be now
purchased there at a low price, with the certainty
of a convenient market. He thinks that Ohio and
Kentucky do not average above 20 bushels of
wheat per acre; nor even that, because the management is so bad. "There is more ignorance,
sir, in the state of Ohio than in any other part of
the union. Not many are able to write their

names, and in the thinly settled parts of Kentucky, ten dollars will procure you the life and blood of any man.　Negroes, you see, are here in Ohio equal, and placed at the same table with whites. I knew a party of whites who last year in Kentucky roasted to death, before a large log fire, one of their friends, because he refused to drink. They did it thus :—Three or four of them shoved and held him up to the fire until they themselves could stand it no longer ; and he died in 20 hours after. No legal inquiry took place, nor, indeed, ever takes place amongst *Rowdies*, as the Back-woodsmen are called."

" In America," says Mr. Chichester, " gentlemen seek not to marry young ladies with fortunes : they are too high minded to have it said that they marry for money ; but, if the lady's father has money, they expect that he will give her some, either during his life or at his death.　Children, though you, sir, think differently, are very kind and dutiful to their parents."

Sunday, 17th. — At Chilicothé to breakfast, where I rest for the day and night.　This town is situated on the beautiful Sciota river, in a rich valley of plantations. Its population is 3,000, and its age 20 years.　Many houses and town cots are deserted for migration further west. The American has always something better in his eye, further west ; he therefore lives and dies on hope, a

mere gypsey in this particular. The land is here
very fine, of a dark, loamy, rich soil, inexhaustible,
and apparently alluvial. The pasture, even during
drought, is full of clover. It is worth 20 dollars
an acre generally, if improved, that is, cleared.
It costs ten dollars an acre to clear and enclose it,
if all the trees are cut down and burnt, or otherwise removed. Log heaving, that is, rolling trees
together for burning, is done by the neighbours in
a body, invited for the purpose, as if to a feast or
frolic. This custom is beneficial and fraternal,
and none refuse their laborious attentions. Nine
tenths of the adult population here own and cultivate land. A market, therefore, is not now so
certain, nor will it be in days to come, as in the
east, though some price is generally to be had for
produce (says my informant), at New Orleans;
but when much land becomes cleared and pro-
ductive, the market every where, without foreign
demand, must be glutted. This evil, however, will
check itself; less produce will be raised when it
cannot be sold. But as the farmers have little
capital to employ in cultivation, the surplus produce will never be very superabundant. If, however, they had more capital they would not employ it in raising unmarketable commodities, but
turn it, if possible, into other channels.

Fat fowls are here one dollar per dozen; pork
and beef four cents, or two pence per pound; ba-

con, 10 to 12 cents per pound, 50 per cent. being gained by smoking and drying. Two years old steers, fat and good, for 12 dollars each.

The qualifications for voting at an election in Ohio are, that the voter must be a citizen, resident two years in the state, one year in the county, and 21 years of age. Sometimes he is known to vote from three to six times at one and the same election, and sometimes strangers are brought in to vote.

Corn and wheat are here prodigiously cheap; the first is 10*d*., and the latter 2*s*. 3*d*. sterling per bushel. Seventy-five bushels of corn per acre cost only six and a quarter cents, three pence half-penny per bushel. Three men and three horses here raise 100 acres, if they will, or 30 acres commonly. Nothing is reckoned for land; land is nothing; labour every thing. In England it was almost vice versâ, ten years since.

I saw an ancient mound of huge circumference and great altitude, and a large bricked house (a rare thing here) split, and its position altered by the earthquake which visited Ohio in 1815. The buildings generally vibrated from four to five inches. Sugar loaves and tin vessels suspended from the ceilings of shops and stores, violently struck each other, and palpably shewed the exact vibration. " It shook people," says my friend, the Chilicothé squire, " out of their beds, knocked down brick chimneys, and made the old log houses crack and rattle; and on the Ohio banks, the earth and trees rolled down in immense masses into the bed of the river. On the Mississipi too, the convulsive motion of the water was truly awful, running and rising mountains high, and in one part of that river a stream of fire rushed from and divided the water, while the solid land on the high mountainous banks was seen in an undulating agitation, like the waves of the sea. New Madrid sunk down several feet, without the earth opening her mouth to swallow. The land, however, in many parts round this town, is covered with water. It is frequently visited with a shock."

18th.—At nine this morning I left sweet Chilicothé and the squire, who called to take his leave of me, and who seemed to part from me with regret, and I with him, on account of his intelligent and communicative spirit.

A genteel young man was boarding here and had a room to himself. " Who is it?" " Why, it is Judge Grimpe." A gentlemanly man, seeming, a recluse, of unsociable and steady studious habits, with a salary of 1,000 dollars a year, which surely cannot compensate such a man for such services.

The road from Wheeling in Virginia, through this town, to Louisville, Kentucky, 360 miles, was cut entirely by the father of the present Squire Zain, a rich citizen, to whom I was introduced, and who for such signal services had the power of choosing the best land all along this road. Hence he became very rich. Mr. Zain is friendly to liberty, it is said, in the best sense of the word, and is destined to leave behind him a town, Zainsville, as a monument to the Zain family for ever.

My landlord at Chilicothé, the first who has demeaned himself so much as to say at parting and paying, " I am much obliged to you, sir," states, that he recently bought 75 acres of good land in Ohio, at the small price of 75 cents, or 3s. 4½d. per acre. It was at a forced sale, and the land has since been privately resold at three dollars an acre, a profit of 350 per cent. Mr. Cowen of Danville, Kentucky, one of the twelve fine men in the stage, over the mountains, joined me again to-day. He states, that Indians willingly sell their lands and territories, as soon as white settlers begin to approach and encroach upon them, or when game and skins become scarce. A few weeks since, a party of them passing quietly through Ohio, from the lakes, were wantonly shot at by a white man, when a pregnant squaw was wounded and nearly killed. The offender was instantly taken and put in jail for trial; the neighbourhood shewed them every kindness, and the civil authority lost no time in procuring them justice. This was good policy. But the Indians, if the squaw dies, insist on two white lives. An eye for an eye; a tooth for a tooth; exact retaliation is their law.

Six miles west of Chilicothé, the land is remarkably rich. Here I met and passed General M'Carty, to whom my friend nodded and said, " How do, General." The General looks dirty and butcher-like, and very unlike a soldier in appearance, seeming half savage, and dressed as a back-woodsman. " Like General Jackson," says my friend, " he is fit only for hard knocks ánd Indian warfare." We passed his seat, very little bigger and no' better than my kitchen at Somersham. " It is not now exactly what it was. During the last war it was in part burnt down, and he contents himself with just what the fire left him—a mere apology for a house. It stands on an eminence close to the road, in the centre of a large, uncultivated, but rich domain. I passed plenty of sugar-trees, and troughs to hold the sap or juice, and abundance of tall iron-weed five feet high, in full flower; all sure indications of fine land, and seen throughout the western country, and always noted by land-hunters. I saw at Chilicothé, and elsewhere, to-day, many ancient mounds, and one regular extensive fortification now defaced by the plough. Many such are found over these wild regions. They are evidently the handiwork of an unknown and distant age and people, whose history, and every relic by which they might perhaps have been identified, have perished.

I had fine wild venison at dinner to-day, good and fat as ever fell to the lot of a lord. There is plenty of it in this section of the country; but what is strange, no mutton, nor beef that is good, where it ought to be the best. Every thing, though wild, is generally good, except beef, which is best tame, and fed on cultivated, instead of wild vegetables, which make it ill-flavoured, dark, and tough. Found iron-weed all day, and fine extensive peach orchards of several acres each, having nearly half the trees spoiled, by hurricanes breaking down their boughs when heavily laden with fruit. These dead arms, or boughs, hang on from year to year, until they rot and drop of themselves, and the sight is singularly desolate and ruinous: all this for the want of a pruning knife and hatchet.

At eight, p. m. I reached a poor log-house, to lodge in, full of mean company, who must be treated with as much respect as the highest, and so I treat them, and receive much coarse kindness in return. Kindness begets kindness; nor is it lost upon them. An Irish emigrant, said my landlord at Chilicothé, recently rode in the greatest possible haste all one night, to the land office here, to make an entry of a section of land uncleared, which pleased his eye. He foolishly thought there would be twenty other competitors

for it. He bought it, began clearing and fencing
it, by hired hands, determined to have it all in
cultivation immediately, as though it was the
only spot to be bought and farmed in this empire of unnumbered acres, glutted and smothered
in superabundance. Poor Pat was mistaken!

19*th.*—I started this morning at four o'clock in
frightful darkness, darkness which might be felt,
and over a horrid road; but with an expert driver,
and good horses, we move on to daylight and a
breakfast fifteen miles off. Here we met, at breakfast, the high sheriff of the county, a grey-headed,
rustic, dirty-looking old man, meaner than a village constable in England, but a man of good
understanding.

The uncle of my friend Cowen, one of the first
settlers in Kentucky, during the Indian war, met
a hostile Indian in the woods: both had rifles,
and fired at each other at the same moment, but
both missed. It was a war of extermination.
The red man then threw his fearful tomahawk,
which also missed. They then came to close
quarters, rolling over each other, and struggling
for the Indian's huge hog-knife, which had grazed
along the throat of Mr. Cowen's uncle, who at
length got the knife, thrust it into the belly of his
antagonist, and leaving it in up to its hilt, set off
to the fort for a party to despatch the dying
warrior. To have fled from a pursuing enemy,
like him, would have been certain death, so swift

and sure-scented are they to track and find a white man.

Three months since, a duel was agreed on in Lexington city, K. Y. The party challenged begged and obtained three months' time, for " settling his worldly affairs, and making his peace with God." But as the party so challenged has the liberty of choosing weapons, and mode of fighting, he fixed on muskets charged with grape-shot and two balls; the distance to be five paces. The pert braggadocio, who had sent the challenge, and whom the neighbourhood wished to see killed, refused the mode and terms thus offered, and so this affair of *honour* ended. The barbarous base-ness and cruelty of public opinion, dooms young men, when challenged, to fight. They must fight, kill or be killed, and that for some petty offence beneath the notice of the law. Established names only (says Mr. Cowen) may refuse to fight, but that is rarely done; to refuse is a stain and high dishonour.

I now pass many farm log-houses along the road; miserable holes, having one room only, and in that one miserable room, all cook, eat, sleep, breed, and die, males and females, all together. When I see and know more, I will describe a log-house minutely.

We passed through pleasant Maisville, in Ken-tucky, on the banks of the Ohio, which we had first to cross on a large team-boat, worked by eight horses, on to which we drove, stage and all, without quitting the stage. We have now travelled 220 miles from the last crossing of this noble river, which here runs through and waters a valley of fine orchards and plantations of unequalled fertility; river-bottom land, just such as must fascinate a Lincolnshire farmer, who seeks for pleasure and profit united. Here I lost my gay, graceful, jovial fellow-traveller, who, tired of his journey, wanted to luxuriate awhile in all-accommodating Maisville. At six o'clock, p. m., we stopped to rest, sup, and sleep, at Washington, K. Y., having a population of 1,000 souls, but little or no good land to sell, by forced or other sales yet. It is generally cleared and enclosed, and worth, with all improvements, from 40 to 50 dollars an acre, in a fine country.

This is the third or fourth town of Washington which I have passed since I quitted the metropolis of *Uncle Sam*.

20th.—Welcomed to breakfast fifteen miles from Washington, by a sensible, shrewd, old rustic landlord, and farmer, who knows of little or no land to sell, by forced sales yet; the improved value is from 30 to 40 dollars an acre. He has hitherto been always able to sell produce at some price. The only market is Orleans, which is attended with difficulty, some expense, and much risk of health, and loss of time, as some one or two of the farmers must go with the produce.

Here was on a sick bed a stranger farmer, out
of funds, returning from New Orleans and Natches,
on foot. In the dismal swamps of the Mississipi,
he caught the bilious fever, and then the jaundice
and ague. " I left," said he, " the folks of the
two latter cities, dying faster than graves could
be dug to receive them. No papers have been
received from either city for some weeks past.
The printing-offices and presses, it is supposed,
are stopped, because the cities are deserted. No
animal food is allowed to be brought in or sold."
This sick moneyless stranger is, it appears, on his
way back to Chilicothé, and is very humanely
sent on by the stage, free of all expense, and is
received and fed at every tavern with gratuitous
kindness. Even my driver gave him, this day, a
dollar. This humanity and hospitality seem national in the west.

I rode over an extent of hills, 20 miles, so flinty
and barren, that the plough never could and never
will touch it. The hogs that grunt and roam
over it look lean, hungry, and starved. The few
inhabitants live by hunting and shooting squirrels
and good wild ducks. I saw a fresh-water turtle
on the edge of the creek. On these stony, flinty
hills, the first settlers of Kentucky fell, being most
of them destroyed by battling with the Indians,
who considered themselves invaded. They fired
from ambushes. The bones of the unfortunate
Kentuckyans still remain above ground, bleaching

in considerable numbers, at the bottom of a deep hollow of the mountains, into which their bodies were thrown in heaps, for want of earth and industry to bury them.

Wheat, in this state, is fine in quality, and in quantity averaging about 25 bushels an acre; but where the land is fallowed, from 40 to 50 are frequently had. Fallow means corn land, or land planted first with Indian corn, then with oats the second year, and with wheat the next, which is generally more abundant than when sown immediately after, or amongst the corn at the last horse-hoeing; for the land gets a good ploughing for the oats, and another for the wheat. What a curious idea of fallowing does this seem to an English farmer, who knows of no fallow, positively so, except a naked fallow!

After passing the hills of stone and human bones, all the land, which conducts to the city of Lexington, is rich, cultivated, cleared, and well settled or located; and, with the exception of wooden worm fences, looks much like the best districts of Old England, only that the soil of Kentucky is better. Here are fair green pastures for cattle, and could green hawthorn fences be by magic thrown around them, while I slept an hour, I should, on awaking, fancy myself in Leicestershire. At five this evening I entered the city, the far-famed metropolis of *old Kentuck*.

21*st*.—Rambled through and round the city of

Lexington, seated in the fairest, richest plain of
Kentucky.   None of the streets are yet filled up ;
the outline, is large, and resembling Philadelphia,
particularly in the form and construction of the
market, which is built over a small rivulet, now
quite dry, and concealed by the market, sheds, and
structures.   Unfortunately for this city there is
no navigable river nearer than the Kentucky river,
ten miles distant, which empties itself into the
Ohio.   Every edifice, saving the college, a beautiful building, seems filthy, neglected, and in ruins,
particularly the court-house, the temple of justice, in the best square, which, with its broken
windows, rotten window-frames, rotten broken
doors, all ruined and spoiled for lack of paint and
a nail, looks like an old abandoned bagnio, not fit
to be compared with any workhouse in England.
This city, it is here said, is retrograding, but in it
are many comfortable abodes, and the best society
of Kentucky.

Called at the seat of Squire Lidiard, a rich English emigrant, who with his lady and two elegant
daughters, came to this western country and city
in consequence of having read and credited Birkbeck's notes and letters, and having known and
visited the Flower family in England. Mr. Lidiard
was well known on 'Change; had a counting-house
in London, and a house at Blackheath.   When I
first called upon him, he was from home.   I left a
message for him, saying, that an old countryman,

known to his friend Wardour of Philadelphia, had called, and was at the stage-house. On his return home to dinner he soon came down to me and said I should accompany him to pot-luck. I did so. The sight of an English face was mutually refreshing, and a sufficient introduction to each other. Mr. Lidiard scarcely knows what induced him to emigrate, having a fortune enabling himself and family to live in ease any where. " One thing, however, which weighed with me, was the probability of seeing my children well married in America. I must, however, complain much of American roguery. Hardly any body cares about poor honesty and punctuality. If a man can, or is disposed to pay, he pays; if not so disposed, or not able, he smiles, and tells you to your face, he shall not pay. I saw an execution defeated lately by that boasted spirit, which they call liberty, or independence. The property, under execution, was put up to sale, when the eldest son appeared with a huge Herculean club, and said, " Gentlemen, you may bid for and buy these bricks and things, which *were* my father's, but, by God, no man living shall come on to this ground with horse and cart to fetch them away. The land is mine, and if the buyer takes any thing away, it shall be on his back." The father had transferred the land, and all on it, to the son, in order to cheat the law. Nobody was, therefore, found to bid or buy. I, therefore," continues Mr. L., " decline all transactions

with Americans, it being impossible with safety
to buy or sell any thing of importance under their
present paper system.   I keep my money in the
funds.   Housekeeping is very cheap; 100lbs. of
fine flour costs only two dollars; a fine fat sheep,
two dollars; beef equally cheap, three or four
cents, two-pence per pound, the hide and tallow
being thought the most valuable; one dozen of fat
fowls from three quarters to one dollar.   Land
here gives a man no importance; store-keepers
and clerks rank much above farmers, who are
never seen in genteel parties and circles.   Yet,
here is the finest arable and pasture land in the
known world, on which grass, the most luxuriant,
is seen rotting for want of cattle.   Just kill a few of
the large trees (where there is no underwood) and
you have a beautiful clover-field and other grass
intermixed, as ever art elsewhere produced.   There
is no laying down here; it is all done by nature
as if by magic.   The land is full of all useful
grass seeds, which only want sun and air to call
them into a smothering superabundance.   But
what is land, however rich, without population to
cultivate it or a market to consume its produce,
which is here bought much under what either I
or you could raise it for.   Farmers are consequently men of no importance.   They live, it is
true, and will always live, but I much doubt if
ever the important English farmer could be satisfied with such living and farming.   I feel great

o

difficulty in advising any friends on the subject of emigration. I mean to wait two years longer before I do it. Liberty and independence, of which you and I thought so much and so highly, while on the other side of the Atlantic, sink and fade in value on a nearer view. Nobody here properly appreciates, but almost all abuse, this boasted liberty. Liberty here means to do each as he pleases; to care for nothing and nobody, and cheat every body. If I buy an estate, and advance money before I get a title, it is ten to one but I lose it, and never get a title that is worth having. My garden cost me, this summer only, 50 dollars, and all the produce was stolen by boys and young men, who professed to think they had the liberty to do so. If you complain to their friends and superiors, the answer is, 'Oh, it is only a boyish trick, not worth notice.' And again, I tell the gentlemen, that if I wished to be social and get drunk with them, I dare not; for they would take the *liberty* to scratch me like a tiger, and gouge, and dirk me. I cannot part with my nose and eyes. The friendly equality and intercourse, however, which can be had with all ranks and grades, and the impossibility of coming to absolute poverty, are the finest features of this country. You are going to Birkbeck's settlement?" "I am, sir." "I visited both Birkbeck and Flower in June last. Birkbeck is a fine man, in a bad cause. He was worth about 10,000*l.* sterling, but has deceived himself and others.

Both his, and Flower's settlement (which are all one), *is all a humbug*. They are all in the mire and cannot get out; and they, therefore, by all manner of means and arts, endeavour to make the best of it. Birkbeck tells me, the reason why he does not cultivate his land is, because he can buy produce cheaper at Harmony, much cheaper than he can raise it, although its price is double what I am giving at Lexington market. The Harmonites all work, and pay nothing for labour. Mr. Birkbeck, in June last, was the proprietor of 10,000 acres, and forfeited his first deposit, ten cents an acre, on 30,000 acres, which prove to be, as is his settlement generally, the worst land in Illinois. Nobody now cares to buy of, or settle down, with either him or Flower. I like Flower the least; I would prefer Birkbeck for a neighbour, dressed up, as he is, in a little mean chip hat, and coarse domestic clothes from Harmony, living in a little log-house, smoking segars, and drinking bad whiskey, just as I found him, rough as he was. Mr. G. Flower is inducing mechanics to come from all parts to settle, although there is no employment for them, nor any market now, nor in future, at New Orleans or elsewhere, for produce, unless a war comes, which may require America to supply other nations in want. Sometimes I think Birkbeck is right. But still I think that both he and Flower will get rid of all their dollars, and never raise more; dollars and they will part for ever. They

will live, but not as they did, and might have lived
in England or in the eastern states. Labour costs
more than double what it does in the east. The
west is fit only for poor men, who are the only
proper pioneers of the wilderness. I do not believe
that land will improve in value, but that much
money will be wasted in improvements. Slavery,
sir, is not so bad as we thought it to be, provided
the slaves are not hired out like pack-horses, but
kept by their own proper owners. They would
then be gentlemen-servants. You know that we
never prize a pack-horse, nor treat it so kindly as
one of our own."

22nd.—After breakfast this morning I visited
the seat and pleasure-grounds of Mr. Speaker
Clay, who concluded the peace of Ghent, now
gone to his chair in Congress. The house is
pleasantly situated on fine land about two miles
from the city, but is far inferior to the old house
of my matrimonial cousin, G. Thompson, Esq.
of Somersham, Hants. The windows are broken,
and the frames and doors are rotten for want of
paint or tar; the gardens in a piggish state, full
of weeds, the walks gullied by heavy rains; the
grass borders and lawn, wild, dirty, and unmown,
and every thing else inelegant; although the soil
is rich to excess, and almost all kinds of vegetables spring spontaneously and grow luxuriantly,
and the house is brimful of negroes, who might
keep all in the neatest order. I saw in one en-

closure near the house, the finest after-grass and
the coarsest hay in the world. The grass is so
tough and old before it is mown that it is little
better than dry straw after. Mr. Clay is the pride
and glory of Kentucky, whose inhabitants think
their state monopolizes talent and intelligence.
They are gay and voluptuous to a proverb, and
seem, it is said, better abroad than they are at
home.

Cheap living.—Visited the market. Beef, best
cuts, six cents—common cuts, three cents per lb.;
a whole fat mutton, for two and a half dollars, one
hundred pounds weight. Fowls, fat, three quarters of a dollar per dozen. Good nag horses fit for
any man, from 80 to 100 dollars. No money
is now to be had or raised on mortgage of land or
houses, however good, nor from any thing else but
negroes; nothing but black flesh and blood can
command money. A fine English family from
Lincolnshire passed yesterday through this city
on their return from Birkbeck's settlement, with
which they seem quite disgusted, and fully satisfied and assured that it would not, could not do.
They were quite out of funds, pennyless strangers
in a strange land; but they were able to borrow
some money from the United States' branch bank
to enable them to proceed on to Philadelphia.

23rd.—At nine this morning I left the city of
the plains, which will continue to flourish when
other cities fade and die. It has now a popu-

lation of 6,000 white souls. How many blacks I know not.

At three, p. m., I ended this day's journey at Frankfort, the seat of government, and metropolis of Old Kentucky. This pleasant town stands in a fine valley, roomy enough to contain it, and but little to spare. Nature has fortified and shut it in with inaccessible rocks and hills all around, but the rocks are neither rough nor broken. The town boasts a good state, or parliament house, and prison, and a church or two, and altogether displays more taste and cleanliness than Lexington city. It is seated on the Kentucky river, navigable to the Ohio, and has the best inn or tavern which I have yet seen in the state. Here is all the accommodation I need. The rocks and hills, which now hang over me, seem as perpendicular as walls in some parts, and as though they were formed by art. I ought to mention passing through two neat and interesting baby towns, called Paris-town and George-town. The land hereabouts, though there are few forced sales, is selling at one quarter its former price and value.

Sunday, 24*th.*—I left pleasant Frankfort at nine, a. m., and reached Shelbyville at four, p. m., a good-looking, youthful town, so named in honor of the governor of Kentucky.

General Jackson, (says my intelligent fellow traveller) although thought to be irritable and quarrelsome, is one of the warmest of friends and neighbours, and to visitors most frank, generous, and hospitable. During his late eastern visits, his conduct to all persons and parties was kind and conciliating, insomuch that those who once thought they hated the warrior despot, were compelled to love the man. If private humble citizens invited the General to dinner, he invariably went there in preference to a public dinner. He is of unalterable determination, but very slow, thoughtful, and cautious in coming to it. His manners are mild, simple, and plain. He lives in an old loghouse, which, though another and better house is building, he determines on never quitting but for the grave. " I cannot," (says the hero of the wilderness) " I cannot desert an old friend."

During the last conversation, I passed in the forest the lone grave of an unfortunate stranger and traveller. A ridge of logs or trees was laid over it to mark the spot where he died and was buried. He was found dead with a gold watch in his pocket, and his horse grazing at a short distance from him ; both horse and rider were of elegant appearance. He had been robbed of 3,000 dollars, and from some unknown hand had received a rifle ball, which entered the back of his head and came through and out between his eyes; he evidently never saw the hand which fired, nor felt the ball. A fellow living near, who was seen to follow the traveller with a rifle, was suspected, apprehended, and tried for the murder, but as no-

thing, save circumstantial evidence, could be produced against him, (which, however strong, will
not convict here) he was acquitted. Public
opinion, however, condemned him, and unmer-
cifully pulled down his house about his ears,
which we passed in ruins; and he accordingly fled,
blackened and blasted, to another distant refuge
in the wilderness.

I saw this day a party at cricket, and one man
in a barn threshing with a flail, an odd sight here.
Yesterday a gentleman, drunk, in the stage, drew
his dirk, the common appendage of a Kentuckian.
He had the stage stopped, jumped out and fought
the other passengers, myself excepted. They dressed him soundly, disarmed him, and with the unanimous consent of the screaming ladies, left him
behind, on the road, to fight with and spit fire at
the trees.

25th.—A fine fat buck crossed our road this
morning, the first I had yet seen. In the evening I
reached flourishing Louisville, a grand river-town
and port of Kentucky, on the banks of and opposite the big rocky falls of the Ohio, here a mile
broad; 700 miles by water and 360 miles by land
from Wheeling, Virginia; and about midway
between Washington city and New Orleans. The
land here, and all round this town, and in the
valley, to Shelbyville, is excessively rich and the
finest in the state, but I fear is sickly to its inhabitants. Louisville must become a place of high

importance, if pestilence prevent not. Our hotel, called Union-hall, is very capacious and full of company, composed of polished military and mercantile gentlemen of New Orleans, many of whom are waiting for the troubling or rising of the waters, and consequent movement of the steamboats. Board here, with five in a bed-room, is two and a quarter dollars per day, a shameful piece of extortion, when it is remembered that provisions of all kinds here, cost a mere trifle; yet in the hall, an immense dining-table seems crowded with good company. Notices, however, are posted in several rooms, by the landlord, stating, that unless gentlemen-boarders pay up, further credit will be discontinued.

26th.—I rode in a hackney coach to Shippingport, a sort of hamlet of Louisville, standing on the margin of the river, opposite to a flourishing new town on the other side, called Albion, in Indiana. Counted from twelve to sixteen elegant steam-boats aground, waiting for water. Boarded and examined the *Post-boy*, which cost 50,000 dollars, and is intended only for passengers up and down the Ohio and Mississipi waters, containing fifty births or beds, a separate dining-room, a ladies' room, and state room, with a fine promenade at top, having three decks, with all necessary and elegant appurtenances. The boat called the *United States*, is much superior to the Post-boy, being of 700 tons burthen, a complete

floating hotel, little less than the London Tavern.
The passage down from hence to Orleans is 75
dollars, a price which competition, and the unnecessary number of boats built, will greatly reduce.
Entered and dined at a low (but the best) tavern
in Shipping-port, intending, if I liked it, to board
and wait here for the troubling of the waters; but
owing to the meanness of the company and provisions, I soon left, and returned to head-quarters
at Louisville. The traveller, who must necessarily
often mix with the very dregs of society in this
country, should be prepared with plain clothes, or
the dress of a mechanic; a gentlemanly appearance only exciting unfriendly or curious feelings,
which defeat his object, and make his superiority
painful.

The American, considered as an animal, is
filthy, bordering on the beastly; as a man, he
seems a being of superior capabilities; his attention to his teeth, which are generally very white,
is a fine exception to his general habits. All his
vices and imperfections seem natural; those of
the semi-barbarian. He is ashamed of none of
them. Labourers and mechanics are here rather
scarce, although so many are said to have returned
home to England from New York; the former
receive one and a half dollars to two dollars a day,
and the latter, two and a half dollars, with provisions very cheap. Emigrants, of this description,
should never linger about eastern cities, and sup-

pose that, because there is no employment there, none is to be found in America.

The new steam-ship, now at New York, cost 120,000 dollars, is intended only for passengers, and to run from New York to Charleston, Savannah, and New Orleans, twelve times a-year, taking, in the year, 5,000 passengers, at 200 dollars each, the voyage. The steam-boat, *Vesuvius*, from New Orleans to Louisville, freighted, in one trip, 47,000 dollars, and cleared half, that is 23,500 dollars net profit. Sixty or seventy of these fine boats are now on the Ohio and Mississipi rivers.

27*th*—At sun-rise I left Louisville, in Colonel Johnson's carriage and pair, for Vincennes, in Indiana, well pleased to turn my back on all the spitting, gouging, dirking, duelling, swearing, and staring, of old Kentucky.

I crossed the Ohio at Portland, and landed at New Albion, a young rising village, to breakfast, where, for the first time in America, I found fine, *sweet*, white, home-baked bread. The staff of life is generally sour, and, though light and spongy, very ill-flavoured, either from bad leaven, or the flour sweating and turning sour in the barrel.

At eleven, a. m., I rested, and baited at a farm log-house, having one room only ; the farmer came to it ten years ago, and has settled on two quarter sections of land. He has a good horse-mill at work, night and day, to which people come with grist, from 10 to 15 miles, working it with their own horses, four in number, and leaving him (the miller) an eighth for his toll. " My land" (says he) " is good, but not like that of old Kentuck. I get from 40 to 60 bushels of corn, and wheat, 25 to 30 bushels per acre, and a market at my door, in supplying gentlemen-travellers, and emigrants." The first house is, for five or six years, a miserable hole, with one room only, after which, rises a better, and the old one remains for a kitchen. This man seems full of money, and knows all things; he damns the state government for deny-ing him the privilege of slavery, and of using his Kentucky negroes, who, in consequence, (he says) are hired and exposed to cruelty. " I was raised under a monarchy government, in Virginia, where every man did as he pleased. This Indiana a free state, and yet not at liberty to use its own property! You tell me to quit it, I guess, if I do not like it." " Yes, I do." " Well then, the government, d—n it, has the power, it seems, to drive me out." This strange man was very civil and coarsely kind to me, and whispered aside to my driver, that he knew I was a very large pro-prietor in this state.

I travelled till sun-set, 32 miles from the Ohio, and slept at Mrs. Moore's farm-log-house tavern, with three rooms, and a broken window in each; all moderately comfortable, until the pitiless, pelt-ing storms of winter come, when it will snow and blow upon the beds. My hostess would, in England, pass for a witch, having a singularly long, yellow, haggish, dirty, face and complexion. She has three fine sons, but no servants. They do all the household work, and that on the farm, themselves, hiring none. They clear five or six acres every year, have cleared 60 acres, and mean that the other 60 of their quarter section should remain in wood. They located themselves here eight years since, and find good land, good crops, and a market at the door. Two of the young Moores mounted their horses, and, with five dogs, set off hunting at bed-time, until midnight, after racoons, foxes, wolves, bears, and wild cats. I saw a skin of the latter animal, much like a tame cat, only bigger, and its tail shorter; they live on partridges and young pigs, and poultry when they can get them; they never mew and call out like the domestic cat. Here is a pet bear, which took an ear of Indian corn out of my hand. One of these pets recently broke its chain, and came into the house, where lay a sick and bed-ridden man, and an infant child on the floor, with which the bear, much pleased, marched off. The poor old man, not knowing, till then, that he was able to turn himself in bed, suddenly acquired supernatural strength, sprung out, and running after the bear, threw him down, rescued the screaming babe, unhugged and unhurt, and then jumped into bed again.

28th.—Now quite out of society; every thing and every body, with some few exceptions, looks wild, and half savage. To his honor Judge Chambers's, to breakfast. His log-tavern is comfortable; he farms two and a half quarter sections, and raises from 40 to 60 bushels of corn an acre. Nearly all the good land on this road is *entered.* " I had," says he, " hard work for the first two or three years." The judge is a smart man of about 40, and not only a judge, but a senator also, and what is more, the best horse-jockey in the state. He seems very active, prudent, cautious, and industrious, and, like all the rest of the people on this road, kind-hearted. He fills the two-fold station of waiter and ostler in part; I say in part, for, as he has no servant, the drudgery must be done by the traveller himself, if he have a horse or horses. His honor left my driver to do all, and hastily rode off to a distant mill for his grist, now much wanted, and with which he returned in about two hours, while her honor, Mrs. Judge, and the six Miss Judges, prepared my good breakfast. These ladies do all the work of the house, and some of the field; every thing seems comfortable and easy to them, although the blue sky and the broad sun stare and peep through cracks and crevices in the roof of their house. While I sat at breakfast, his honor's mother, a fine smart young woman of four-score, came briskly riding up, and alighted at the door;

as good a horsewoman as ever mounted a side-
saddle.   She had been to pay a distant visit, and
seemed as though her strength and youth were
renewed, like the eagle's.   She reminded me of
Moses, " with his eye not dim, nor his natural
force abated."

At noon, I stopped at another log-house, quarter-section farmer's, with two fine healthy boys,
much civilized, who, of themselves, have cleared
forty acres of heavily timbered land, such as is
seldom seen, and cropped it twice in eighteen
months.   What prodigious industry !   It is, they
say, worth ten dollars an acre clearing.   It is;
and an Englishman would, indeed, think so, and
demand double and treble that sum, for that
quantity of excessive labour.   They, however,
now wish to sell out their improved quarter
section, and remove further from the road.   These
young men drink spring water, and like it better
than whiskey, and look heartier and healthier than
any settlers I have yet seen in the wilds.

I rested all night at another quarter-section
farmer's, who, together with his brother and wife,
has cleared thirty acres in eighteen months, without hired hands, and is now rearing a second
log-house.   They find a market at their door for
all they can raise, and ten times as much, if they
could raise it.   They burn all the logs and trees
rolled together in immense heaps, and prefer the
wood-land to the barrens, the latter being thinly

timbered with dwarfish trees and shrubs. The
wife, husband, brother, and three wild children,
sleep in one room, together with three or four travellers, all on the floor, bedless, but wrapt up in
blankets. I, being a mighty fine man, was put into
the new house, which, though without either doors
or windows, was distinguished by one bed on a
bedstead, both home-made, and as soft as straw
and wood could be. Into this bed was I honourably put, and at midnight favoured with a bed-
fellow, a stranger Yankee man whom I had seen
on the mountains; and at my feet, on the floor,
slept two Irish, and one poor sick American, all
pedestrians, who had wandered here in quest of
employment. Thus housed and bedded, we were
faithfully watched and guarded by several huge
hunting dogs, lying around the entrance of our
bed-room, barking and growling to the howling
wolves, bears, foxes, and wild cats, now roam-
ing around, and seeming ready to devour us.
Our hostess hung on the cook-all, and gave us
fowls, ill-flavoured bacon, and wild beef, all stewed
down to rags like hotch-potch, together with coffee
and home-made sugar, for supper and breakfast.
All was coarse, wild, and ill-flavoured.

29th.—At sunrise I passed two waggons and
herds of cattle and people, very wild-looking and
Indian-like, rising from camp, having *camped* out
all night after the fashion of English gypsies.
Stopped at a wretched cabin, having only one

room, and that brimful of great dirty boys and girls, all very ragged and half naked; and again at the house of a Mr. Lewis, from Virginia, where every thing presented a fine contrast; clean, healthy, civilized children.

Breakfasted at an infant ville, Hindostan, on the falls of the White River, a broad crystal stream, running navigable to the Ohio, over a bed of sand and stone, smooth and white as a floor of marble. This baby ville is flourishing; much building is in progress, and it promises to become a pleasant, healthy, large town, before I see it again. The land, too, is rich and inviting. I now crossed, in my chariot, White River, and in two hours after stopped at a quarter-section farmer's, who has never cleared nor inclosed any of his land, because sick or idle; being, however, well enough to hunt daily, a sport which, as he can live by it, he likes better than farming; " and besides," says he, " we had at first so many wild beasts about us, that we could not keep pigs, poultry, sheep, nor any thing else." Called on another quarter-section man, sick, and who therefore has done but little himself; two young boys have cleared five or six acres. The tavern keeps them all; a tavern, with one miserable hole of a room.

I stopped again at a two quarter-section farmer's, who said; " I am an old man, and have only my boys; we cannot hire, but we do all the labour, and get 60 bushels of corn per acre, but

P

no wheat of any consequence yet. We can always
sell all the produce we raise from the land to travellers like you, and others, new comers." " But,"
said I, " what will you do when your said new
comers and neighbours have as much to spare and
sell as you have ?" " O, then we'll give it to cattle and pigs, which can travel to a market somewhere. I see no fear of a market in some shape
or other." This was a shrewd old fellow.

I met and passed five or six huge waggons laden
with goods, chattels, and children, and families,
attended by horsemen, cattle, and footmen, and
many negroes, all returning from the Missouri
territory to their native home and state of Kentucky, which they had rashly left only two months
since. Having sold out there in good times at 30
dollars an acre, and being now scared out of
Missouri by sickness, they are returning to repur-
chase their former homes in Kentucky at 15 dollars an acre; or perhaps, says my informant, they
may return to the Missouri, when the fear of sickness subsides. They have left their father behind,
as a pledge of returning; but still 100 acres in
Old Kentuck are worth 300 in Missouri, except in
river-bottoms, that is, valleys of rivers.

Passed another Washington, a young county
seat (or town) and several fine neighbourhoods of
rich land, full of iron-weed, but not so rank as in
Kentucky, yet bearing plenty of huge sugar-trees.
Every state in this mighty Union seems emulous of

building towns, monumental piles of immortality to General Washington.

Rested for the night at a good bricked house tavern on the White-river ferry, but without one glass window in it. It is getting old and wearing out before it is finished. Here I found a good supper of buck venison, fowls, whiskey, and coffee. My hostess, the owner, was lately a rich widow, and might have remained so, but for a Yankee soldier with a knapsack at his back, whose lot it was to call at her house. They are now married, and he is lord of the tavern, land and all. My host had a large party of distant neighbours assembled to effect a corn shucking, something like an English hawkey, or harvest home. All, gentle and simple, here work hard till eleven at night. Corn shucking means plucking the ears of Indian corn from the stalk, and then housing it in cribs, purposely made to keep it in, for winter use. The stalk is left in the field; the leaves, while half green, are stripped off, and tied up in bundles, as hay for horses and cattle, and good food it is, much resembling in form the flags in English marshes. After I had retired to bed the hawkey supper commenced; all seemed fun, created by omnipotent whiskey, with which they plentifully supplied me, although in bed. "The Doctor, the Squire, the Colonel," said they, "shall drink and lack no good thing." I was consequently pressed to rise and join them, about one o'clock. I refused

" Then," said they, " Doctor, you shall drink in bed." My charioteer had foolishly called me Doctor, Squire, Colonel, and what not, during the whole of this wilderness journey; hence, I was here applied to as an eminent physician.

30th.—Travelled 12 miles to breakfast on fine buck venison at three farthings per pound, or one dollar for the buck, at the house of a shrewd old kind-hearted Pennsylvanian, now nearly worn out and ready to sleep, either with or without, his fathers. " I have," says he, " lately lost my son, and my farms are running fast to ruin. I have 200 acres, some of which I hire out, and I have just finished what my son began, a good new log-house. This Indiana is the best country in the world for young men. Were I a young man I would live no where else in all the universal world." " Although," says he, " many hundreds of waggons, with droves of men and beasts, four or five hundred in a drove, and at least 5,000 souls from Kentucky have passed my house since last harvest, all bound for the Missouri."

At eleven, p. m., I reached Old Vincennes, the first and oldest town in this state, situated in a fine woodless *Prairie* on the banks of the big Wabash, a fine broad, clear, and generally deep stream, running to the Ohio by Shawneese town, but when its waters are low, weeds rise from the bottom, and grow, and rot, and impregnate the air with pestilence. On passing through this place, a farmer

said that last spring he lost seven cows, and that
hundreds were poisoned by some unknown herb
found growing in their pastures on river-bottom
land. A medical botanist was here much wanted.
An immense quantity of land in the neighbouring
state of Illinois, is here, I see, posted up in this town
for sale or lease, for a term of years, at one peck
of corn per acre, per annum. But who will hire,
when nearly all can buy? I passed away my 20
dollar note of the rotten bank of Harmony, Pennsylvania, for five dollars only! so losing 3*l.* 7*s.* 6*d.*
sterling. I was indebted five dollars to my faithful driver, who was now to leave me behind and
press on to St. Louis, Missouri. I said, " Now,
driver, which will you have; five silver dollars, or
the 20 dollar note; or what more than your demand will you give for the said note?" " Nothing." " Then take it, and bless banks and banking for ever." Bank paper is here an especial
nuisance, an ever fruitful source of evil, and ever
very unfriendly to honesty, peace, and good will
amongst hosts and travellers, who meet and part,
cheating and cheated, cursed and cursing, continually. My landlord here is very obliging, and
puts me into the best room and bed in the Vincennes hotel, where I am sleeping with a sick
traveller from St. Louis, who states that many die
daily, and his doctor there had 150 patients to
visit every day, or oftener. So much for the
healthiness of the ever-tempting Missouri.

Sunday, 31st.—The town of Vincennes is more than 200 years old; older than Philadelphia; but being of French origin, and in the neighbourhood of the Indians, ever hostile to the inhabitants and settlers round it, has grown but slowly, and is an antique lump of deformity. Although long the capital and mother town of the state, it looks like an old, worn out, dirty village of wooden frame houses, which a fire might much improve, for improvement generally has to travel through flames. Here is no church, save the Catholic church, the inhabitants being principally French Canadians, and the rest the refuse of the east, whose crimes have driven them hither, or dissipated young men unable to live at home. Hence Sunday is only a day of frolic and recreation, which commences on the Saturday evening, when every preparation is devoutly made for the Sabbath, and off they start in large parties on foot and on horseback, all riflemen, and cunning hunters, into the deep recesses of the forest, camping out all night in readiness for sabbath sacrifices, the bucks, the bears, the squirrels, and the turkeys, ready to be offered up by peep of day. This holy day is consequently ushered in by guns, which continue to roar in and around the town all day until sunset. The stranger might think it was closely besieged, or that an enemy was approaching. The steam flour-mill, a large grinding establishment of extortion, giving only 30lbs. of flour for one bushel of wheat, weigh-

ing 60lbs. is in operation all this day, and on
other days, day and night, and blacksmiths' shops
are in high bustle, blazing, blowing, and hammer-
ing in direct opposition to a law against Sunday
business and pleasure, but which is never feared,
because never enforced. The refuse, rather than
the flower of the east, seems, with some exceptions, to be here. But still good is coming out of
evil. The east is thus disencumbered, and the
west is peopled. Posterity will shew a better face.
Such is the process of empire.

I rambled round the town to the court-house,
or shire-hall, really externally an elegant building,
but decaying before finished, as though the state
were unable to finish what it had so well begun
before counting the cost. The State Seminary, a
very respectable edifice, but in little better plight,
was built by *Uncle Sam*, and endowed with an
ample township in the state. It is, however, only
a nominal seminary, because the trustees are not
empowered to sell any of its land for raising funds,
but must derive them from hiring and leasing it
out in farms. But while plenty of uncleared or
cleared farms can be bought at two dollars an
acre, who will ever think of hiring?

I saw two Indian graves on the eastern banks
of the Wabash. Each hillock is carefully arched
over with broad stripes of bark, each three feet
wide, with logs and sticks, or bands across. The
bodies are buried from one to two feet deep only.

Visited the house of J. Lowndes, Esq., the prison philanthropist and Howard of America, but did not see him. He was gone, as an Indian ambassador, to the government in Washington city assembled, and I passed him unconsciously on Thursday last, when I saw and noted in a handsome chariot, a venerable, gentlemanly, dignified countenance. It was that of this good and honourable man. I presented his lady, once the widow of the late Judge Vanderburgh, with my introductory letter to her husband, which I had brought from one of my friends at Washington city. She regretted the absence of her spouse, and received me graciously. This generous man is gone a third time to the President on behalf of the Indian chiefs who call him their father, having appointed and chosen him as the only honest American whom they have ever known; all with whom they before had dealt or treated, tricked them out of their lands. Mr. Lowndes knows their language, and has a speech always put into his mouth by these barbarian grandees. " Go," said they, " go, father, and tell our great father, the President, how we are deviled and cheated, and if he does not do us justice, go, tell him he is a hog, and that we would burn up the land if we could." Mr. L. replied, " that this was an undutiful speech for children to send to their father;" but in great rage they rejoined in their own tongue, " He is only a man." The chiefs, whom Mr. Lowndes represents, are of the Delaware tribe, the posterity of those from whom William Penn so honourably bought Pennsylvania, and who traditionally revere his memory down to this day.

November 1st.—During the last month the weather has been cold and dry, but generally clear and without fogs, and in the night frosty, shewing ice half an inch thick. Summer and I parted on the last of September, at Washington city, where she lingers until Christmas. Late last evening my host returned from his Sunday hunt, heavily laden with his share of the game, namely, two wild ducks, one wild turkey, seven squirrels, and one fine fat buck of 130lbs. weight. Hunting seems the everlasting delight of this town. When I went to bed last night the prairie and forest were both enveloped in a wide-spreading, sky-reddening blaze, which the hunters had kindled to drive out and start the game.

I met this morning Mr. Baker of Philadelphia, an intelligent traveller, who knows my friend J. Ingle, living eighty miles further west of this place, and who has kindly borrowed a horse for me, and agrees to pilot me thither to-morrow. I saw a large party of Miami Indian hunters, accompanied by their ugly squaws, all on horseback, and all astride, with their tomahawks and frightful knives girdled round them, dressed in blankets and turbans, and painted red, green, black, and white; every feature having a different shade of

colour, and all, save the squaws, apparently half
drunk, having their bottle of fire-water, or whiskey,
with them, which, after drinking from it themselves, they stopped and handed to me and my
friend Baker. We took it and applied it to our
lips, it being considered the perfection of rudeness
and barbarism, and little short of enmity, to refuse
any thing so kindly offered. This tribe had approached the town for the purpose of selling their
venison. Each horse carried two or three quarters,
fat and fine, ready skinned, and hanging down its
sides. The price was only a quarter dollar for
30lbs., not an English halfpenny per pound.

Although Vincennes is an old mother town,
abounding in rich land, it is uncultivated, and
there is occasionally a scarcity of necessaries,
particularly of milk and butter, which, with the
worst tea, are dealt out very sparingly; no lump
sugar, no brandy, no segars, no spitoons are seen
at this hotel.

All persons here, and all whom I have met,
hitherto, during this western pilgrimage, whether
they have or have not visited Birkbeck, think very
meanly of both him and his settlement. The
English emigrants particularly, (says Mr. ———)
deem themselves deceived and injured by his books
and mis-statements.

2nd.—Yesterday at noon came on a heavy gale,
which filled the atmosphere for the remainder of
the day and night, with a strange mixture of hot

smoke, ashes, and dusty sand, to the density and
hue of a London fog in December. The sun was
completely shorn of his beams, and the whole horizon, for unknown miles in circumference, filled
with a blinding commotion, like a gale in the great
desert; and at night to the N. W. the sky blazed
and reddened over a great extent, while the big
Wabash blushed, and the whole atmosphere became illuminated, as though it was the kindling
up of the last universal conflagration.

At ten this morning I left old Vincennes for
Prince-town. The horse which my friend Baker
had borrowed for me was mean and mis-shapen,
but covered with buffalo skins, which hide all
defects. The horses here are nearly all mean,
wild, deformed, half grown, dwarfish things, and
much in taste and tune with their riders. The
pigs, every where in great abundance, seem more
than half wild, and at the approach of man fly,
or run like deer at the sight of an Indian rifle.
Throughout the western regions they look starved
to death. This, however, is a bad season for them,
there being little *mast*, that is, acorns, nuts, and
other wild fruit and herbage. I passed over an
extensive, sandy, black, burning prairie, the cause
of yesterday's and to-day's thick hazy atmosphere,
the sun looking more like the moon, and as if
turned into blood. At noon, I rode through a
large rich river-bottom valley, on the banks of the

White River, and which, in winter, is as yet over-
flowed, from six to ten feet of water above the surface, as the trees prove by circles round their
trunks, and by their boughs dipping and catching
the scum of the surf. This land, of course, is the
finest for meadow, if it were wanted, but as the
prairies are all meadow, it is of no value. In it
stand such enormous trees as are seldom seen
elsewhere, having trunks like towers. Here, too,
flourishes, the long and far-famed, ever-green mis-
tletoe, planted by birds, or propagated only by
seed or berries, which are sown or deposited on
decayed branches and arms of oak and other trees,
to beautify the desolation of the winter forest.
Excessive drinking seems the all-pervading, easily-
besetting sin of this wild hunting country. Plenty
of coal is found on the Wabash banks, and there
are salt-springs in this state, but sad Yankee tricks
are played off in the working and making salt from
them. Grease and fat are used, to make it retain
a large portion of water, which assists in filling
the bushel with deception. Although fat is so
abundant, yet it is sold at 20 cents, or 10d. per lb.
and candles at 37$\frac{1}{2}$ cents, or 19d. per lb. Milk,
too, in a land which might flow with milk and
honey, is 12$\frac{1}{2}$ cents, or 6d. per quart, and not a
constant supply at that price, nor at any other
price, unless a cow is kept. Butter, bad, at 25
cents per lb. Beef, six cents per lb. by the quarter,
which lies on the ground all day at the tavern doors,

as if brought for dog's meat. Tavern doors are here never closed.

Saving two comfortable plantations, with neat log-houses and flourishing orchards, just planted, and which sprout and grow like osiers in England, I saw nothing between Vincennes and Princeton, a ride of forty miles, but miserable log holes, and a mean ville of eight or ten huts or cabins, sad neglected farms, and indolent, dirty, sickly, wild-looking inhabitants. Soap is no where seen or found in any of the taverns, east or west. Hence dirty hands, heads, and faces every where. Here is nothing clean but wild beasts and birds, nothing industrious generally, except pigs, which are so of necessity. Work or starve is the order of the day with them. Nothing happy but squirrels; their life seems all play, and that of the hogs all work. I reached Princeton at sun-set.

3rd.—I looked round Princeton, a four-year old town and county-seat. Here I found and called on my countryman Mr. Phillips, who came a visitor from Somersetshire, but fixed on a pleasant good farm of 300 acres close to the town, which he bought with some improvements, such as a small log-house, and a few acres cleared by art and nature, at 20 dollars an acre; " the only farm (says he) which I would have in this state of Indiana, but which I mean to improve and re-sell, and then return to England. I hate the prairies, all of them; insomuch that I would not have any

of them of a gift, if I must be compelled to live on
them. They are all without water, except what is
too muddy and distant for use. I am much per-
plexed with labourers; both the English and natives are good for nothing; they know nothing,
and it is impossible to get any kind of business
well done, either with or without money. Money
cannot be gained by cultivation. There is no certain good market; farm produce may, perhaps, be
sold at some price, but you cannot get your money
of the cheats and scum of society who live here.
I think that Birkbeck is right in not cultivating
his land, though wrong and mortified in having
written so hastily and prematurely. He and
Flower are both sinking and scattering money,
which they will never see more or gather again.
They cannot even hope to gain or increase their
capital, but by the contingent increase in the value
of their land, which is not the best of its kind.
With hired labour and a market, I should prefer
the western country, but here, though there is no
visible want, yet is there poverty indeed, and but
little or no friendship. No sharing things in
common; idleness, poverty, and cheating, are the
order and temper of the day."

Mr. Phillips and his wife both looked very
shabby, wild, and dirty. He apologized to me
for his dishabille, and said, " Sir, if a stranger
like you had found me in this plight in England,
and I could have seen you coming up to my door,

I should have hid myself. Here, however, no
shame is felt, but pleasure, at a visit from one of
my countrymen, whom I shall be happy to meet
again." He keeps an housemaid only, his wife
doing nearly all the drudgery herself, although in
England, a lady, unaccustomed to soil her hands,
or let her feet stray from the parlour carpet.

I had a long and interesting conversation with
a young lawyer, the supreme Judge Hart, living
in this town, but proscribed and suspended for
sending a challenge to three agents of his estates
in Kentucky, who, after injuring him, caricatured
him, and then refused to fight. The judge says
that English labourers know nothing, and are
worth nothing in agriculture here; hewing, splitting, clearing, grubbing, and ploughing among
roots, being a business which they do not, and
wish not, to understand. It is true that they are
handy with the spade, and that only. They feel
too free to work in earnest, or at all, above two
or three days in a week. Every English body
here is above work, except the good little farmer,
like your friend, John Ingle, and old Phillips,
the former of whom is likely to kill himself with
hard work. He was sick twice in consequence,
and once nearly unto death. Mrs. Ingle and her
husband gain and deserve a good name, and feel
happy and contented on a good farm, which is
too near the road. They bought a log-house,
town lot, pro tempore, at Princeton, at a forced

sale, for 300 dollars; which they now let for
forty dollars a year, to Mr. and Miss Fordham,
Flower's nephew and niece, who were sick of
the prairie of Illinois, where health could not
attend them.   Your friend, J. Ingle, lost his
horses for three weeks.   He is expecting more of
his English friends to follow him.   Mr. Birkbeck
is disappointed and unhappy; I know him well.
He has not cultivated nor raised, as yet, any thing
from his land, although the Harmonites refused
to sell him produce, because they thought it was
his duty to raise it himself, and plainly told him
so.   He will never make a farmer, nor money by
farming there.   It is idle to attempt to import
English labourers for the use of yourselves exclusively, for Birkbeck and Flower lost all.   The
same, says Mr. Pittiss, late of the Isle of Wight.
Women and girls, too, are here above assisting in
the house, at a price per day or week.   Wives
and daughters must do all themselves.   The girl,
or white servant, if one can now and then be had,
at one dollar per week and board, is pert and
proud as her mistress, and has her parasol at six
dollars, and bonnet at ten or twelve dollars,
and other articles in character, which, as dress
generally does with all grades, seduces them from
a virtuous regard for their duties, says this young
and sprightly lawyer.   People here, though poor
and idle, feel above thieving, the facility of living
without, and the certainty of exposure and sum-

mary punishment, seem to conquer the propensity, where it may happen to exist.

I feel convinced that none but working farmers, like John Ingle, ought to come to this western land. Water is bad, white, or milky, at Princeton; but beds are good, with the bed-room doors next the street, unlocked all night, in order that ingress and egress may be free, which is the more necessary, as there are, as is very generally the case here, none of those accommodations, either within or without doors, which an Englishman looks upon as quite indispensable.

I met and talked with old Squire M'Intosh, who, although he has lived 35 years here, away from his dear native Scotland, still regrets it. " I now live," says the squire, " on the grand rapids of the big Wabash, a mile above the White River ferry; call and spend a night with me on your way to Birkbeck's settlement, which is the reverse of every thing which he has written of it, and described it to be. The neighbourhood, however, do not think he intended to misrepresent and deceive, but that he wrote too soon, and without knowing the real state of things, and understanding his subject, or knowing where to find the best land. He ought to have examined, in company with one of *Uncle Sam*'s surveyors; he would not then have entered land in the lump, or mass, a great deal of which is not good, nor ever can be, being wet, swampy, cold prairies, something

Q

like undrained marshes in England. **Mr. Birk-**
beck entered much at the land-office, but sold
little, only such half sections as he ought to have
bought and kept for himself and friends. **Mr.**
Phillips, on whom you have just called, say the
gentlemen round me, is the slave of his own
English notions and passions; he is, therefore,
always hesitating and undecided; sometimes, when
things run crossly and crooked, he is seen and
heard heartily execrating this country and people;
and, at other times, he is well pleased. He is an
odd man, surrounded with eight fierce dogs, and
has a fine, never-failing mill spring, running a mile
through his farm, which, one year ago, cost 20
dollars, but is now worth only ten dollars an
acre, with all improvements. This is turning a
penny quickly! Despatch is the life and soul of
business."

4th.—The Supreme Judge, Hart, is a gay young
man of twenty-five, full of wit and humorous eloquence, mixing with all companies at this tavern,
where he seems neither above nor below any, dressed in an old white beaver hat, coarse threadbare
coat and trowsers of the same cloth (domestic,)
and yellow striped waistcoat, with his coat out at
the elbows; yet very cleanly in his person, and refined in his language. What can be the inducement for a young man, like him, equal to all
things, to live thus, and here?

Judge Hart deems *merchandizing* to be the most

profitable pursuit in the west, and the liberal professions the last and worst.

Mr. Nicholls, a cunning Caledonian, says, that
farming, except near the rivers, cannot answer;
but raising and feeding cattle and pigs may.
Store-keeping is here evidently the best of all em-
ployments, if cents and dollars enter into the estimate.   Money spent in improving land is seldom
more than returned with interest, and often lost by
reselling or selling out, especially if the labour is
not all done by the farmer; and if it is done by
his own instead of hired hands, he is not more than
fairly paid for his time and labour, which are both
money.   It is therefore best for the mere capitalist
to buy rather than make all the improvements, as
he certainly buys them much cheaper than he can
create them.   He should confine himself to the
east.

Mr. Phillips, the English gentleman on whom
I called yesterday, returned my call this evening.
He seems a mass of contradiction, and states that
this western country is the best he knows, but
that it costs more to live in it than in London; that
it is idle for a farmer to raise more produce than
he can use himself; but that there are farmers
making money as fast as they can count it, by raising large quantities of farm produce in this and the
neighbouring state of Illinois; that others might
do the same; that there is now a market better
than in the east, and that in five or seven years the

market at New Orleans down the river will be good and great; yet that the parties to whom you must sell are all d——d rogues. Feeding beef and pork he deems a good trade, especially when the land shall come to be clovered and sown with other grass seeds. He thinks there is little or no good beef in the wilderness, because it is raised and fed on natural wild vegetables, many of which are ill-flavoured and poisonous. Beasts often die suddenly in the fall of the year in consequence of being confined to such food. The natural white clover, in the month of June, salivates cattle and horses, which, however, still devour it greedily, and seem to thrive thereon.

Our party this evening were all agreed in this particular; that the western country is only fit for the little hard-working farmer with a small capital. He must live, and better than he could elsewhere, on and from the productions of his own hands and lands. He can retail his produce, and be gardener and farmer both; vegetables every where being scarce and dear, because people are too idle to raise them. Wholesale farmers from England expecting to cultivate from 300 to 1,000 acres, and sell the farm produce in lumps, will come here only to be disappointed. Small retailing farmers only are wanted here. Mr. Phillips deems that Birkbeck, Flower, and Mr. Dunlop of London, who have bought so many thousands of acres, and the latter of whom pays *treble* tax as a non-resident, will greatly benefit at some future time by capital so employed, although they may never cultivate an acre, or touch the land. The capital seems to be idle and sleeps, but it will one day, he thinks, awake, and find itself gigantically augmented. Mr. Phillips, whose opinion is not respected here, was never a farmer until he came here. His improvements do honour to his intuition.

General Evans, who this day formed one of our circle, is in part the owner of this town of Princeton, and of Evansville, which bears his name. He is a pleasant, rustic, middle-aged man, living here in a little log-house, together with his lady and daughter, who, having no servant, do all the work of their establishment themselves. Servants are not to be had. The same may be said of all the rest of the inhabitants. Envy and invidious comparisons have, therefore, no place at Princeton.

General Boon, during the last war, (says the General) lost two sons killed; and his favourite daughter and her friend were stolen by the Indians, who marched the fair captives two days without resting, and intended marrying them, but were overtaken by the colonel and his son, and a lover of the lady. The young couple, previous to this event, were on the point of marriage, and are now living as husband and wife in Kentucky. The captives cunningly indented the ground all the way from the Colonel's house with their high-heeled shoes, so that they might be tracked; and when they saw their brave deliverers coming up full speed, they fell flat on the earth, while the firing of rifles commenced on the Indians, who tried in vain to kill their fair prisoners by throwing their knives and tomahawks at them; but the pursuers triumphed, and all were recovered and restored unhurt. General Boon now lives in solitude 600 miles up the remote Missouri. He is 80 years old, very active, very poor, a hunter and a recluse by choice, and trains up his sons in the same path, feeling more happiness than he possibly could in society, where he would have lived and died, if he had willed it, full of scars, and honours, and days. His parents were always poor; his disposition is kind and hospitable; his manners simple and gentle; preferring to live meanly and rudely as a hardy hunter and squatter, wanting nothing but what nature gives him, and his own hands get him. He sleeps on a bear-skin, and clothes himself in dressed deer-skin, and though shy, is kind to intruding strangers. The western country is indebted to him, as he leads the way into the best spots of the wilderness. He was the first white man in Old Kentucky, and the wide, wild west is full of his licks. A flourishing settlement always rises wherever he has once squatted, and whenever any settlers begin to approach near his location, he quits it for ever, and moves on further west; and the place, which he thus abandons, is called Boon's

Lick. He never wants much land ; only a spot sufficient for the supply of his household.

I saw a man this day with his face sadly disfigured. He had lost his nose, bitten off close down to its root, in a fight with a nose-loving neighbour.

Judge Hart deems it foolish policy in Englishmen wishing to form English settlements and neighbourhoods, and thereby to perpetuate English distinctions and prejudices, so offensive to their adopted country, and so unprofitable to themselves. Nothing is good with them but what is English, whereas they should rather endeavour to forget the name, which ever kindles unfriendly feelings.

I saw a fine fat buck, fat as a Lincolnshire wether sheep, and weighing, when dressed and with the head off, 140lbs. It sold for two dollars, less than three farthings per pound.

Politeness, in manner and address, is more necessary here than in Bond-street, for here you invariably receive it, and to give it in return is justly due. The titles, " Sir" and " Madam," (not Ma'am) are pleasant to and expected by all; for however mean may be the exterior of a citizen of this free, equal country, there is a spirit and an intelligence, and often sprightliness about him, which decorate any thing and make even rags respectable.

Two months ago the High Sheriff of Chilicothé, Ohio, went to jail for want of bail. He had seized,

personally, on the funds of the United States'
branch bank. This was hard!

Birkbeck, (say my companions) complained at
first of our slovenly state of things, and the indo-
lence of farmers and labourers, and boasted of
what might be done, and what he should do, but
has, at the end of four years, done nothing but
talk of doing. The facility of a living for all, and
the consequent difficulty of procuring labour, even
for money, together with the sickly, relaxing
warmth of the climate, are obstacles which over-
whelm all industry. The principal care is how
to live easy. Time, and not man, effectually clears
and improves land in this country. Time here
changes his character, and preserves and reple-
nishes, while man destroys and wears out what he
can.

The reason (says Judge Hart) why Scotchmen
always get money, in this and all other lands to
which they wander, is, because they leave no
means untried.

The season, called *the Indian summer*, which
here commences in October, by a dark blue hazy
atmosphere, is caused by millions of acres, for
thousands of miles round, being in a wide-spreading, flaming, blazing, smoking fire, rising up
through wood and prairie, hill and dale, to the
tops of low shrubs and high trees, which are
kindled by the coarse, thick, long, prairie grass,
and dying leaves, at every point of the compass,

and far beyond the foot of civilization, darkening the air, heavens and earth, over the whole extent of the northern and part of the southern continent, from the Atlantic to the Pacific, and in neighbourhoods contiguous to the all-devouring conflagration, filling the whole horizon with yellow, palpable, tangible smoke, ashes, and vapour, which affect the eyes of man and beast, and obscure the sun, moon, and stars, for many days, or until the winter rains descend to quench the fire and purge the thick ropy air, which is seen, tasted, handled, and felt.

So much for an Indian summer, which partakes of the vulgar idea of the infernal. Why called Indian? Because these fires seem to have originated with the native tribes, and are now perpetuated by the White Hunters, who by these means start, disturb, and pen up the game, and destroy the dens of both man and beast, and all this with impunity.

To-morrow, through floods and flames, I shall endeavour to make good my desperate way to the retreat of my good friend, John Ingle, in Indiana.

6th.—At nine, a. m. I left Princeton on a horse carrying double, me and my guide, through the wilderness, to my friend John Ingle's, who had sent the said horse and boy twenty-five miles for my accommodation. The little town just quitted, and at which I paid the extravagant price of two dollars a day for board, has nineteen streets, and about one hundred and five houses, one prison, and one meeting-house, or church, all of wood; one supreme judge, and four other judges; and in the unpeopled county are another quorum of judges, and three generals. It is called Princeton, in honour of its living founder, Judge Prince.

We rode all day through thick smoke and fire, which sometimes met in pillar-like arches across the road, and compelled us to wait awhile, or turn aside. We passed only one comfortable abode, and three or four filthy one-room log-holes, surrounded by small patches, cleared samples of the bulk, which seems good land. I called at one of the three, a tavern, to beg for bread, but got none; only some whiskey. I saw a deer-lick, at which I dismounted and took a lick. The earth thus licked and excavated by many tongues, is of the colour of *fuller's earth*, not ill-flavoured, but a little salt and saponaceous, always attractive to the beasts of the forest.

At five o'clock, p. m., I reached the welcome abode of my Huntingdonshire friends, Mr. and Mrs. John Ingle, who, together with their English maid-servant, Rebecca, and six children, rushed out to embrace and welcome their old friend, school-fellow, neighbour, and fellow-countryman, and great was the joy of our meeting.

Here I found good sweet bread, like the English, and hot corn-cake, and supped, on what I sup-

posed fine pork steaks. "This meat (said I to
Mr. Ingle) is most delicious." "Well then, you
like it, do you?" "I do indeed." "What do you
think it is?" "Why, pork to be sure." "Well,
we thought we would not tell you until after supper, lest you should fancy it was not good and
refuse to eat *Bear*." "Oh," said I, "if this be
bear, give me bear for ever."

My friend's log-house, as a first, is one of the
best I have seen, having one large room and a
chamber over it, to which you climb by a ladder.
It has, at present, no windows, but when the
doors are shut the crevices between the rough
logs admit light and air enough, above and below. It is five yards square and twenty feet high.
At a little distance stand a stable for two horses,
a corn crib, a pig-stye, and a store; for store-
keeping is his intention, and it is a good one. Two
beds in the room below, and one above, lodge us
in the following manner; myself and Mr. Ingle
in one bed; in the second, by our side, sleep six
fine but dirty children; and in the chamber, Mrs.
Ingle and a valuable English maid. Thus, on
my account, husband and wife are divided. It is
not unusual for a male and female to sleep in the
same room uncurtained, holding conversation
while in bed. In a yard adjoining the house are
three sows and pigs half starved, and several cows,
calves, and horses, very poor, having no grass,
no pasture, but with bells about their necks,

eternally ringing. Shame, or rather what is called false shame, or delicacy, does not exist here. Males dress and undress before the females, and nothing is thought of it. Here is no servant. The maid is equal to the master. No boy, or man-servant. No water, but at half a mile distant. Mr. Ingle does all the jobs, and more than half the hewing, splitting, and ploughing. He is all economy, all dirty-handed industry. No wood is cut in readiness for morning fires. He and the axe procure it, and provender for the poor hungry cattle, pigs, and horses. His time is continually occupied, and the young boys just breeched are made useful in every possible way.

Nothing is English here but friendship and good-will. American labourers here, as usual, are very villainous; one, a preacher, took a piece of land to clear for my friend, and received, before he began, forty dollars on account, but refused to perform his contract. To sue him was idle. My friend, in the presence of the fellow's son, called him a right reverend rascal and thief. " Call him so again," said the son, doubling his fist ready to strike. My friend repeated it, and taking up an axe, said. " Now strike, but if you do, as I was never yet afraid of a man, I'll chop you into rails." Money rarely procures its value in labour. He deems that as much money is to be made from 200 acres of land here, as in England, while here the land is made your own.

To do that in England, is the top of a farmer's
ambition.   Here, a man can make all that he
cultivates his own.   He says that he shall live and
gain money this first year, though only sixteen
acres are in cultivation.   Mrs. Ingle, maid, and
children, suffered much in crossing the sea and
mountains.   They slept on the floor, in a hole, with
waggoners, and other male blackguards, where
the stench, both by sea and land, was little short
of pestilential.

Sunday, 7th.—More than half last night, Mr.
and Mrs. Ingle, and maid, were out in the woods
extinguishing the wide spreading fires, which
threatened to consume their fences, houses, and
corn-fields.   The whole horizon was brilliantly
illuminated.   These fires, if not arrested, or watched, sweep away houses, stacks of corn and hay,
and every thing within reach.   So fared Mr. Grant,
late of Chatteris, who is now dead.   The sound of
the axe, splitting fire-wood, salutes the ear every
morning, instead of the birds' song.   I was smoked
to death all night: our friends rested all day absent
from meeting, but still the knees of all present were
bent to the God of their good fathers.   Sunday
passes unnoticed in the English prairie, except
by hunting and cricket matches.

The bears, during the summer, are lean and
hungry, and seize the hogs and eat them alive.
It is no uncommon thing to see hogs escape home

with the loss of a pound or two of living flesh.
These creatures sleep all the winter quite fat.
Rattle-snakes abound here.   Mr. Ingle killed four
or five beautiful snakes of this species this summer,
and one or two vipers.

8th.—I accompanied J. Ingle, and water-cart,
to the spring, half a mile off, on the farm of Major
Hooker, a hunter, who sold us half a fat buck at
three cents a pound ; thus killing and selling from
four to six per week, besides turkeys, pheasants,
rabbits, racoons, squirrels, and bears.   This half
buck, weighing 70 pounds, Mr. Ingle carried
home on a shoulder-stick.   The major's, and other
families here, raise cotton for domestic uses, which,
in warm and dry seasons, flourishes well.   What
I saw in pods, and that which the women were
spinning, seemed of excellent quality.   The seed
of this plant was, in slave states, thought nutri-
tious enough, when boiled, for the support of
negroes; but as many died in using it, it was
abandoned.

The China leaf, or tea-plant, has been propá-
gated at Princeton, in Mr. Devan's garden, and
at Harmony, from seed brought from China.   It
is said to grow luxuriantly, yielding more leaf
than is used, and making a useful decoction,
similar in flavour, though not so pleasant, as that
procured from the imported plant.   It is manufactured by sweating it in an oven, and when

taken out, it cools and curls up, and becomes fit
for use. The indigo also is a little cultivated.
The woods abound with medical herbs. The Ching
Sang and Ipecacuanha are found, for emetics. The
vine is very luxuriant, and cultivated at Harmony
with success; while the trees are full of gum.
The Dogwood Bark is also found as efficient as
the Peruvian, and the Sassafras tea is in general
use for two or three months.

Great idleness prevails in the Illinois; little or
no produce is yet raised. G. Flower had contracted with the American hunters, to raise and
cultivate 500 acres of corn and grain; he finding
land and seed, and they all the labour of raising
and getting it fit for market, at nine dollars an
acre. This bargain became void.

9th.--A doctor, of little or no skill, lives twelve
miles distant, and this little settlement of Sandersville has no school for the children, who remain
at home pestering their parents, and retrograding
into barbarism. Mrs. Ingle dreads their mixing
and associating with the race of children who
surround them. A schoolmaster here would be
welcomed with a salary of from 400 to 500 dollars a year, although not one of the first grade,
but he must be content to live in a wilderness.

I feel, every day, more and more convinced that
the western country is suited only to working
families, like those of J. Ingle; where Mrs. Ingle,
(delicately bred) and all turn out to work, as to-

day, and the other night to put out the approaching fires.

The bears and wolves have devoured several sows while farrowing; they are then weak and defenceless, and therefore an easy prey. Never did I behold such ghostly pigs as here. Soap, candles, sugar, cotton, leather, and woollen clothes, of a good quality, are here all made from the land, but not without the most formidable, unremitting industry on the part of the females. Filth and rags, however, are often preferred. Imperious necessity alone commands extraordinary exertion. Yesterday, a settler passed our door with a bushel of corn-meal on his back, for which he had travelled twenty miles, on foot, to the nearest horse-mill, and carried it ten miles, paying 75 cents for it. This said corn is invaluable to both man and beast; black and white men both profess to think they should starve on wheat meal without corn.

The everlasting sound of falling trees, which, being undermined by the fires, are falling around almost every hour, night and day, produces a sound loud and jarring as the discharge of ordnance, and is a relief to the dreary silence of these wilds, only broken by the axe, the gun, or the howlings of wild beasts.

Retrograding and barbarizing is an easy process. Far from the laws and restraints of society, and having no servants to do that for us which

was once daily done, we become too idle in time
to do any thing, but that which nature and necessity require; pride and all stimuli forsake us,
for we find ourselves surrounded only by men
of similar manners; hence, the face is seldom
shaved, or washed, or the linen changed except
on washing-days. The shoes are cleaned, perhaps, never; for if, indeed, a servant, from England, is kept, he, or she, is on a happy equality,
rising up last and lying down first, and eating
freely at the same time and table. None here
permit themselves to have a master, but negroes.

A voyage in the stinking steerage of a ship, and
then a journey over the mountains in waggons,
sometimes camping out all night, or sleeping, like
pigs, as did Mrs. Ingle and six children and maid,
on the dirty floor of a bar-room, amongst blackguards, and then floating in a little stinking ark,
full of unclean things, will prepare the mind and
body for barbarizing in a little log-hole, like that
in which I dined yesterday, belonging to Mr. Ferrel, who, with his family, some adults, male and
female, in all ten souls, sleep in one room, fifteen feet by ten, only half floored, and in three
beds, standing on a dirt floor. The table, or
thing so called, is formed by two blocks and a
broad board laid on them, and covered with a
cloth, and seats or forms, in like manner, on each
side of the table, which is only knee-high. Proper
chairs and tables, they have none. When it rains,

boards are laid over the chimney-top, (which I can reach with my hand) to prevent the rain putting the fires out. This good-natured man has thus settled and removed, eight times, from one degree of barbarism to another. The victuals are served up in a hand-bason; and thus one room serves for parlour, kitchen, hall, bed-room, and pantry. The settlers, too, here, are without implements, but such as they can patch and form together of themselves; they are too distant and expensive to buy. What they have must cost nothing, like their houses, which are raised in a day by the neighbours all meeting together, so going in turn to serve each other, as we did yesterday.

10th.—Mr. Peck, late of Chatteris, introduced himself to me this day. Born and bred a labourer, he at length became a little farmer, on the dearest land in Chatteris, from which he brought a wife, four daughters, one son, a man, and 500*l*.; all, the perfection of British industry. Feeling themselves likely to lose all, they came here to two quarter sections, costing 145*l*. to be paid, in three years, by instalments; so leaving 355*l*. for stock, seed corn, and housekeeping, until they shall have cleared twenty acres, and raised produce. He begged I would come and dine with him, so that I might hear particulars of his former state, present condition and prospects, and be able to tell his old neighbours of his comforts and satisfaction. " Now," says he, " I feel I can live, and live well, by working, and without fretting and working, seventeen, out of the twenty-four hours, all the year round, as I used to do at Chatteris. And what is sweeter than all, I feel I am now the owner of 300 acres of land, all paid for, and free from all poor-rates, parsons, and tax-gatherers, and that I shall be able to give and leave each of my children, 100 acres of good land to work upon, instead of the highway, or Chatteris work-house. No fear of their committees now, nor of Ely jail."

It was pleasant to witness the boasting satis-faction of this good, honest fellow, and his family of young Pecks.

I saw an old, dirty, stinking Irishman, very well to do, settled on a quarter section here, but who says, were it not for his family, he could do better in Ireland; and therefore, for the sake of his fa-mily, he is content to live a little longer, and die here. They will be better off. He came to break-fast with us, and borrowed a razor to shave his beard, for once, instead of clipping it off.

Meeting Mr. Hornbrook, the first settler here, I said to him, " How is it, that you, and others, can do with such houses here, when you had such comfortable ones in England." " Oh," said he, " after our voyage and journey, we are glad to get into any hole, although we know, that in

England, they would think them not good enough
for stables."

On the eve of this day, a heavy battering rain
came, and put out the fires, and cleared the air,
and poured water down upon our beds. Great
lumps of the clay, or daubing, stuffed between
the logs, also kept falling on our heads, and into
our beds, while it rained. We needed an umbrella.

Mrs. Ingle, a woman of superior sense and feeling, states that the prospect of seeing herself, husband, and children dependant on grandfathers
and grandmothers, and uncles and aunts, and
thereby lessening the resources of two distinct
and worthy families, impelled them to emigrate.
It ceased almost to be matter of choice. Still, love
of country, former friends and comforts, from which
they tore themselves, is inextinguishable, and frequently a source of painful thought. Such a good,
proud feeling is very honourable, for with fair play
in England, it would have kept them there, and
increased rather than diminished the resources of
grandfathers, &c.

11th.—By a conversation with old Ferrel, I
find he began, thirty years ago, with nothing but
his own hands. Striking each hand, he said,
" This is all I had to begin with ;" and it seems,
that excepting his children, he has little more
now, merely a quarter section just entered, and a

log raised on it.   All seem very improvident and
extravagant, the family sometimes eating four or
five pounds of butter a-day, the produce of all their
cows.   Thus, with the corn-cake and bacon, a part
of the year, (for they are almost always destitute
of fresh meat, tea and sugar) is their table supplied.

Ferrel is a man of experience and discernment,
and states that he would not fetch corn from
Princeton, twenty miles off, of a gift, if he could
grow it, nor would he carry it to the Ohio for sale,
because it would not pay carriage and expenses.
When (if ever) they shall have surplus produce,
he will give it to pigs and cattle, which will walk
to market.   He always, and every where, had a
market at the door, and he always expects it, because of the number of idle people who do not,
or cannot raise produce.   He says, that as Mr.
Ingle was no judge of the quality of land here, he
has chosen that which is not lasting, namely black
oak land.   It is kind and useful, but after three
crops, he will see and believe, though he does not
now, that his old American neighbours know and
have got the best land.   He thinks that a slave
state, with negroes, well chosen, is the best for
capitalists, who need not, or cannot work themselves.   He still thinks that hiring when you can,
in a free state in the west, may sometimes pay, but
as nearly all feel themselves masters instead of
labourers, it is impossible to be regularly sup-

plied with hands. Kindness, equality, persuasion, and good pay will sometimes effect it. He says, that a man is seldom more than paid for improvements.

Supped with a Mr. Maidlow, a most intelligent and respectable Hampshire farmer, a neighbour of Cobbett's, who left England and his large farm, at about 16*s.* an acre, because, from a fair trial, he found it impossible to farm without losing money, although his wheat-land averaged six quarters an acre, and his landlord, —— Jervis, Esq., had lowered the rent 20 per cent. He brought a considerable capital and English habits and feelings, the best in the world, into the neatest and cleanest log-cabin that I have seen, and is building already a second, larger and better, for the preservation of all that is comfortable and respectable in the English character, being determined that neither himself nor family shall barbarize. This is impossible: all barbarize here. He has bought six quarter sections, and hopes not to do more than keep his property, get land for his family, and live and die comfortably. Riches he thinks out of the question, and it is his wish that the settlement should feel and act towards each other as one family; the reverse of Illinois, in which he intended to settle, and to which he was attracted by the books of Mr. Birkbeck, who refused him land, except at an advanced price, although he had

30,000 acres retained for people in England, who never came; while those who applied, many and respectable practical farmers, were denied.

The settlers here being all out of wheat-flour and Indian corn-meal, Mr. Ingle, self, a boy, and two children began, at noon, to gather and shell ears of corn for grinding into meal, and finished two bushels by night, ready for the mill, ten miles off, next day; when a boy on a horse started with it early, expecting to return on the following Sunday morning, if not lost in the woods.

12th.—Visited Mr. Potts's cabin and farm, 400 acres of good land, on which he lives, without a woman, but has a good man from Stockport in Cheshire, where they both came from, and thus they alone manage both the house and the field. They have dug a well, many feet through the solid rock, without finding water. I saw here an experiment which I little expected to see; the eighth of an acre of upland rice; three quarts were sown on it in May, in drills, eighteen inches asunder, and the increase is three bushels. The straw is like barley straw, and the stubble rank and stout, and not to be known from oat stubble, on rich fen land, only brighter.

Saw a poor Englishman, who some time since broke his leg, which from want of skill in the doctor, was not properly set; he is therefore now a cripple for life. This is an evil to which all are exposed. Many are now dying at Evansville of a bilious disorder; the doctor employed has lost nearly all who applied.

River banks are here always unhealthy. A family from Lincolnshire, attracted by fine land, on one of the prairie creeks, where no American would live on any terms, all fell sick, one died, and the farmer and his wife both lay unable to help themselves, or get help, except from one of their little boys, who escaped the contagion. Birkbeck strongly remonstrated with them against settling there.

The farmers (Americans) indebted to the store-keepers, are now forced to sell all their corn at one dollar a barrel, and buy it again for their spring and summer use at five dollars, a fine profit for the monied merchant. Forty bushels per acre of corn pays better (says the old farmer) than wheat, with only twenty to twenty-five. The land here, though good, is not first rate, or of the most durable quality.

A pigeon roost is a singular sight in thinly set-tled states, particularly in Tenessee in the fall of the year, when the roost extends over either a portion of woodland or barrens, from four to six miles in circumference. The screaming noise they make when thus roosting is heard at a distance of six miles; and when the beech-nuts are ripe, they fly 200 miles to dinner, in immense flocks, hiding the sun and darkening the air like a thick passing cloud. They thus travel 400 miles daily. They roost on the high forest trees, which they cover in the same manner as bees in swarms cover a bush, being piled one on the other, from the lowest to the topmost boughs, which so laden, are seen continually bending and falling with their crashing weight, and presenting a scene of confusion and destruction, too strange to describe, and too dangerous to be approached by either man or beast. While the living birds are gone to their distant dinner, it is common for man and animals to gather up or devour the dead, then found in cartloads. When the roost is among the saplings, on which the pigeons alight without breaking them down, only bending them to the ground, the self-slaughter is not so great; and at night, men, with lanterns and poles, approach and beat them to death without much personal danger. But the grand mode of taking them is by setting fire to the high dead grass, leaves, and shrubs underneath, in a wide blazing circle, fired at different parts, at the same time, so as soon to meet. Then down rush the pigeons in immense numbers, and indescribable confusion, to be roasted alive, and gathered up dead next day from heaps two feet deep.

13th.—Major Hooker frequently shoots, and then cooks and eats the huge wild cats, while Mr. Birkbeck and his family eat the rattle-snake, the flesh of which, says Mr. Ingle, is fine, sweet, and white, as an eel. Pigs also eat them voraciously. Armstrong, a hunting farmer, this day shot four deer, while he is too idle to inclose his corn-field, which is devoured by cattle and horses, save when a boy watches it to keep them off. This man and family then, though with plenty of land, must buy corn, and depend upon wild meat for the support of his idle family, who have either a feast or a famine. They keep several cows, but as calves are constantly with them (having no separate inclosure) and as the family eat 5lbs. of butter a day, for three days in the week, which consumes all the dairy at once, they go without during the remainder of the week. They never sell any, though it is 25 cents per pound. No fear of surplus produce from such farmers.

The hope, it seemed, of preserving and increasing his property, was amongst Mr. Birkbeck's ruling motives for emigration. To those to whom he is known, he is very hearty and sociable. To J. Ingle he said, " There are so many thousand dollars in that drawer; they are of no use to me: go, and take what you like." He is very careless and improvident, like the rest of his literary fraternity, and unconscious of what his powerful pen and high reputation were effecting by exciting a strong feeling in favour of emigration, at a moment when the people of England were despairing; so strong, indeed, that what he did and wrote, burst in upon them like a discovery. Unconscious of all this, he left undone all which he ought in common policy to

have done. The weakest head could see that
after purchasing land and alluring settlers, he
ought to have guarded against a famine by pro-
viding for their accommodation, building a few
log-houses, store-houses, and a tavern, and cultivating corn, so that the numerous callers in this
inhospitable waste might have found food, and a
shelter, and a person to shew the land, which he
had to resell. Whereas a stable, a covered waggon, and prairie-grass, formed their only shelter
and bed ; and not having food sufficient for himself,
there was little or none for strangers, and no person to shew the land, nor did he know himself
where it lay. He idly thought that if they wished
land they would find it themselves; and being
in expectation of many such families from England, he thought he had no land to spare, so that the
real practical farmers of both worlds who called,
turned away disgusted to other and better neighbourhoods, the Kaskasky, and Missouri, and Red
River, where more important settlements are rising.
He, therefore, as the rich families did not come,
has no real farmers in his settlement, and hoped J.
Ingle, being one, would come and make one solitary farmer amongst them. Trusting too, to his
own judgment, he has settled down on and entered
indiscriminately good and bad land, much of
which will never be worth any thing, being wet,
marshy, spongy, on a stratum of unporous clay,
over which pestilential fogs rise and hang conti-

nually. A United States' surveyor would, for a
few dollars, have prevented such a choice. Common policy and prudence, too, ought to have induced him to reduce his fine farming theory into
practice, otherwise it seemed as if intended merely
to deceive others. Even if he should, (as he now
says) lose by it, or could buy produce cheaper
than he could raise it, he still ought not so to buy
it, but set an example of farming. For of what
use is land, if it is not worth cultivating?

As a proof of his improvident conduct, and bad
management, his thirteen horses were all miserably poor and unfit for use, and when any were
wanted, he would say to a hunter, " Here's five
dollars for you, if you find and drive up the
horses;" for he had no inclosure. The man knew
where they were, and soon found them and received the fee; none then were fit for use. " Oh!
don't tease me about horses."

This evening, J. Ingle sat down by the fire, and
cleaned the shoes of all the family, which he does
every week.

Sunday, 14*th.*—Called on a Caledonian Yankee
farmer, busy at work in his garden, who said he
had no Sunday in his week, but would buy one if
he could. He is a quarter-section man, without
wife or child, shoes or hose.

After a meeting of 16 persons of this little settlement, in the log-house of my friend, who read a
sermon and prayed for all present, I visited Mr.

Hornbrook's, a respectable English family from Devonshire, on a good quantity of land, living in two or three log-cabins.

Amongst the inducements of the Flower family to emigrate, may be reckoned the probability of their wasting all their property by farming their own estate, about 500 or 600 acres at Marsden. It was badly farmed, and the Merino trade failed, which was Mr. Flower's hobby-horse; and seeing his favourite son was determined to live in America, emigration now ceased to be a matter of choice. They intended to settle in the east. G. Flower, who brought a letter from the celebrated Marquis de la Fayette to Mr. Jefferson, whom he visited, bought an estate of 500 acres at 10 dollars an acre, near Jefferson's, where they were to have lived; but, as Mr. Birkbeck could not approve it, on account of slavery, it was abandoned.

15th.—The English settlement in Indiana, up to this time, contains 12,800 acres entered, and in possession of actual settlers, 53 families having capital to the amount of 80,000 dollars.

Dolls. Cents.

Expenses of clearing and inclosing an acre of land, ready for planting, 6½ dollars; ditto of planting, with four ploughings and four hoeings, and harvesting, and stacking for market, at your own door, six dollars an acre; so making, the first year, an acre cost 12 50

	Dol. Cent.	Dol. Cent.
Brought up		12 50
Second year, wheat 1½ bushel seed	1 50	
Ploughing once, 75 cents ; clearing dead timber, breaking up stumps, and hoeing sprouts, one dollar 50 cents	2 25	
Reaping 1½ bushel an acre, or in cash	1 0	
Carting, threshing, &c.	3 50	
		8 25
Cost of one acre, in two years . .		20 75

	Dol. Cent.
Produce of an acre of Indian corn, 35 bushels, at 50 cents, the first year . .	17 50
Ditto, wheat, 25 bushels, at 75 cents, the second year	18 75
Value of the acre, in two years	36 25
Deduct cost	20 75
Profit	15 50

In the next two years, the two acres will cost
less by 8 dollars 75 cents, which, added to 15 dollars 50 cents, makes the net profit on two acres
24 dollars 25 cents, besides the increased value of
the land.

The proper expenses of a farmer, arriving with
a capital of 2,000 dollars, that is to say, his necessary expenses in establishing himself and family
the first year :

Dolls.

First year.—Entry of half section, or 320
    acres of land 160
House and stable, 80 dollars; smoke-house,
    pigstye, and hen-house, 40 dollars . . . 120
Two horses, good, 160 dollars; two ploughs
    and harness, 40 dollars 200
Four axes, four hoes, 16 dollars; waggon,
    100 dollars; harrows, 12 dollars . . . 128
Spades, shovels, six dollars; two cows, 36
    dollars; four sows in pig, 20 dollars . . 62
Corn crib and barn 60
Clearing 20 acres of land first year, foot and
    under, and fenced well 130
Ploughing, planting, hoeing, and turning . 130

                                  ————
                                  990
Twelve months' maintenance of family . . 250

                                  ————
                               1,240

So leaving him at harvest 800 dollars of his
2,000 dollars for the uses of the coming year; but
still, this money will not be wanted, as the farm
will now maintain itself and family; the money
then should be at use.

   " The foregoing statements," says Mr. Ingle,
" I will swear are correct, and they are in part reduced to practice this year." I think, however,
that the money should be at command for his own

use, as twenty acres more clearing, &c. unless he does most of it himself, (which he ought to do) wants 260 dollars the second year. All the labour, however, is to be done the first year by hired hands, if they can be found, and, if possible, to be done at a price per acre, not by the day.

Mr. Ingle insists on it that none of the old funds will be wanted the second year, but that the farm will maintain itself and family; as the pigs will supply plenty of bacon to eat and some to sell, besides the surplus of the first crop of corn, which will supply some money; but the second year, the work upon the farm must be principally done by himself and family.

He thinks that no more land should be under cultivation and fence, (say about forty or fifty, and thirty acres of grass) than the farmer can manage without hiring, which, at present, it is impossible to do with any thing like comfortable benefit and English regularity. He will not be so grasping as in England. A little will satisfy him; he is not so disposed to disquiet himself in vain. The habits and examples of the country will at length be imperceptibly followed.

New settlers in this state, men, women, and children, seem all exposed to an eruption, ten times worse than the itch, inasmuch as it itches more, runs all over the body, crusting and festering the hands and other parts, and is not to be

cured by the common treatment for the itch, which
has been tried without effect, and one instance has
been known, where the sulphur and grease killed
the patient by obstructing perspiration, and driving
in the eruption. The doctors know of no remedy,
and suffer it to take its tedious course. It comes
in the spring and fall, but not to the same person,
it is hoped, more than once. It is attributed to the
air, soil, and climate. Mr. Ingle's family are all
suffering severely under it. Although the climate
seems finer here than in the east, more humid and
temperate, yet the bite of every insect and reptile,
however insignificant, is highly poisonous; an evil
not to be remedied at present. New comers and
fresh flesh suffer most, and sometimes much inflammation is caused; but when the land becomes
more cleared, it is hoped this scourge will be less
afflictive.

Fine yeast: Take a small handful, or a good nip
of hops, and boil them ten minutes, in one quart of
water, then strain away the hops, and pour the
liquor into a quantity of flour, sufficient to give
the consistency of batter well beaten; a tea-cup
full, or something less than the usual quantity of
brewer's yeast, is sufficient for a half-stone loaf;
two spoonfuls of brewer's yeast to work the first
making; then, ever after, a little of the last made;
the yeast to be put to it while milk-warm, and kept
so until it ferments, which it generally does in
summer very soon, and in winter in a day, but it

must not be used until it does ferment. In winter it keeps one month, in summer (American) one week, two in England, and is a fine saving and a great convenience.

16th.—A poor emigrant farmer from Devonshire, called here in search of a home. His family, yet on the river, had been nine weeks in a stinking ark, coming from Pittsburgh, and ever since April last in getting from England, by way of Canada, hither. I asked him if he repented leaving England. " I do," said he, " a good deal, and so does my poor wife ;" and then he burst into tears. The tears of a man are hard-wrung drops. " You were getting, I suppose, a comfortable living in England?" " Oh no! taxes, tithes, rates, &c." " What money did you bring away?" " But a little, and besides my passage to Canada, where I could have had 100 acres for nothing, I have spent 50*l.* in getting to this western country. The captain told me that Canada was my best way, and I have now but little left." He thought of going to the Prairie. I told him he had better settle here. They of the Prairie were proud, and wanted only high-bred English. I encouraged this poor, desponding, ill-advised, weak man to hope for better times in this good land, where he said he was willing to labour.

Taverns are always charitable to moneyless travellers, if they are sure of their poverty, feeding them gratis as they pass along, as instanced in a moneyless female, and a sick man whom I met in the stage coming here. The Scots frequently plead poverty, and get fed gratis, while their pockets are full of dollars.

Mr. J. Ingle and maid started this morning, with a waggon, to Princeton, for boards, though living in a forest full of boards when sawn. He drove the waggon himself, and she was to get groceries and butter, if she could get it under twenty-five cents per lb. Thus, for two days, we were left without water, or an axe to hew firewood, or any person to milk and feed a kicking cow and pigs.

17th.—A stranger called and brushed out of the rain. He said he was short of money, and came ten miles to sell two pigs, fat, weighing 400lbs. the two, but was not able to sell them at more than four dollars a cwt. ; he could not afford to make pork at that price. No pigs fat this year at *mast*, only passable pork; but when quite fat they must have corn for two or three weeks to harden them, though they get no fatter, or else the bacon would drip all summer, and when boiled, the fat become oil and run out into the water. He has seventeen acres of corn ; a bad crop, not enough for his own use. Few farmers are ever able to hire labourers, though he thinks it would answer if they could; still it is best to do all the work by one's-self or family.

I went to turn the grindstone for J. Ingle's carpenter, at Mr. Maidlow's, one mile and a half

off. Went over his fine farm, that is to be. I
think it is the best I have seen in this settlement.
On it I saw a lick of singular size, extending over
nearly half an acre of land, all excavated three feet,
that is to say, licked away, and eaten, by buffaloes, deer, and other wild animals. It has the
appearance of a large pond dried. The earth is
soft, salt, and sulphurous, and they still resort to
it. Mr. Maidlow thinks that Cobbett is much
nearer the truth than Birkbeck, in his account of
the west. Had he now the chance of choosing,
he would purchase, in the east, improvements at
eighteen dollars an acre, like the farm of Mr.
Long, as he finds that making improvements in
the west costs much money. He believes Birkbeck is spending money fast. He does not think
that capital employed in farming here will answer,
or that cultivation will pay, if done by hired labour.
Out of 900 acres, (all he intends buying) he means
to cultivate and graze only about 100 acres; no
more than they can manage of themselves. He
does not expect to increase his capital, but by the
increase in value of land. He means to build a
mill, and plant a large orchard; is digging a well,
and finds some fine good burning coal in it, and a
vast mine of rich blue marl. The Missouri, says
he, is full of all the rich resources of nature; land,
very fine. Here is a large family of men, and
Mrs. Maidlow and daughter are drudges to the
house, cooking, scouring, and scrubbing, conti-

nually.   A young lady cleaning knives! How horrid!!

18th.—A few months since, J. Ingle agreed with a neighbouring Kentuckyan hunter, to build him a log-house, to be begun and finished in a given time. The fellow was procrastinating, and too idle to begin, yet for ever promising. At length Mr. Ingle told him, that unless he began on a certain day, at noon, at latest, the contract should be void, and others should begin it. He came on the day mentioned, but not until six in the evening, when others had begun the job. Greatly enraged, he said, he had come, and would begin in spite of any body. Mr. Ingle said he should never touch it. He said he would, or have Mr. Ingle's blood; "and to-morrow morn, I will come with men, and twenty rifles, and I will have your life, or you shall have mine." Mr. Ingle thought of having recourse to the civil power, which is very distant, insomuch that the people speak and seem as if they were without a government, and name it only as a bugbear.

J. Ingle returned this evening with his poplar boards, not worth carriage, and without being able to buy any tea, sugar, butter, cheese, or apples, for his use, at Princeton, though a county town, having a fine store out of stock, which it receives only once a-year.

19th.—A parson, with his wife, and sixty others, about eighteen months ago, came from the east, as settlers, to the big prairie of Illinois; in which, during the sickly season, last fall, an eighth of their number died in six weeks. Having lost his wife amongst the rest, he has cleared out, and lives by his itinerant ministrations.

It is useless to fence much more land than is cleared, because, until the country is cleared round about, the autumnal fires would destroy the fences. The cattle, therefore, must range in the woods, until some small inclosures, for pasture, can be made. Through the summer, both night and day, but mostly in the night, the mosquitoes, both in Indiana and Illinois, but chiefly in the latter, were, in their attacks, almost sufficient to drive English settlers out. If a man had been lashed naked to a post, he must have been stung to death, or unto madness. At Sandersville, says J. Ingle, they blinded several persons.

The Cherokee nation once wishing to war against the United States, sent their favourite chief, *old Double-head*, to Philadelphia, to sound parties, and return with his opinion either for or against it. "Oh," said he, on his return, " we must not war; I have seen more white men in one town, than would be sufficient to eat all the Indians, if made into a pie." They have never since thought of war, but what few remain, are friendly and civilized, and fight for *Uncle Sam*. Some cultivate their land, and possess negroes.

20th.—At nine this morning, after a fortnight's

stay at Sandersville, I mounted the neck of an ill mis-shapen, dull, stumbling beast, called a horse, the best that friendship and good-will could procure, for conveying me, in company with J. Ingle, to the state of Illinois, by way of the far-famed Harmony. I rode, in fear, all day, through woods and wilds; sometimes almost trackless. We were lost twice. The people seem to know nothing of time, and distance of places from each other; some telling us it was ten, when it was two, and three, when it was twelve o'clock; and as to distance, twenty when it was twenty-seven, and fifteen, when it was ten miles to Harmony. I expected to camp out all night, with no means of getting a fire. I saw nothing but good land, and (where any) fine corn; but no comfortable dwellings; all, miserable little log-holes, having neither springs nor mill-streams. We were very courteously shewn our way by a worshipful magistrate of Indiana, at work by the road side, hewing and splitting wood.

We rested, twenty minutes, at the log of one of Cobbett's Yankee farmers, with a fine family of boys, big enough for men, and handsome, sprightly, and free-looking, as ever walked the earth. I would have given something for a picture of them, being self-taught shoemakers, butchers, wheelwrights, carpenters, and what not, and having cleared, from 320 acres, 60 acres, and cropped them twice in two years. The mother sat, smoking her pipe, fat and easy. The father is ready to sell

out at 1,200 dollars ; a fair price, says Mr. Ingle.
They think well of this country, but were able to
grow more wheat per acre in Pennsylvania ; there,
thirty-four, here, twenty to twenty-four bushels an
acre ; they can have seventy-five cents at home, or
carrying it twenty miles or less, one dollar a
bushel, for wheat. The old fellow says that the
Harmonites do their business of all kinds better
than any body else.

I saw, on the Harmony lands and fields, of
great size, wheat, finer and thicker, planted with
two bushels, than in England with three and a
half bushels per acre. The fields, however, lie in
a vale of prodigious richness.

I reached Harmony at dusk, and found a large
and comfortable brick tavern, the best and cleanest
which I have seen in Indiana, and slept in a good,
clean bed-room, four beds in a room, one in each
corner ; but found bad beef, though good bread,
and high charges, one dollar, five cents, each.

A stranger present, asked our landlord of what
religion were the community of Harmony. In
broken English, and rather crossly, he replied,
" Dat's no matter ; they are all a satisfied people."
The spell, or secret, by which these people are
held in voluntary slavery, is not to be known or
fathomed by inquiry. We asked if strangers were
permitted to go to their church to-morrow. " No,"
was the answer. This is unprecedented in the
civilized world.

Sunday, 21*st.*—At Harmony till ten o'clock, when we were told, "we must then depart, or stay until after the morning service," which commences at ten o'clock. At the moment the bells began chiming, the people, one and all, from every quarter, hurry into their fine church like frighted doves to their windows; the street leading to the temple seems filled in a minute, and in less than ten minutes, all this large congregation, 1,000 men, women, and children, all who can walk or ride, are in the church, the males entering in at the side, the females at the tower, and separately seated. Then enters the old High Priest, Mr. Rapp, of about eighty, straight and active as his adopted son, Frederick, who walks behind him. The old man's wife and daughters enter with the crowd, from his fine house, which looks as if the people who built it for him, thought nothing too good for him. This people are never seen in idle groups; all is moving industry; no kind of idling; no time for it. Religious service takes place three times *every day.* They must be in the chains of superstition, though Rapp professes to govern them only by the Bible, and they certainly seem the perfection of obedience and morality. People who have left them say, that Rapp preaches, that if they quit the society, they will be damned, for his way is the only way to Heaven. He does much by signs, and by an impressive manner, stretching out his arm, which, he says, is the arm of God, and that they must obey it; and that when he dies, his spirit will descend unto his son Fred. The people appear saturnine, and neither very cleanly nor very dirty. They are dressed much alike, and look rather shabby, just as working folk in general look. None are genteel. The women are intentionally disfigured and made as ugly as it is possible for art to make them, having their hair combed straight up behind and before, so that the temples are bared, and a little skullcap, or black crape bandage, across the crown, and tied under the chin. This forms their only head-dress.

I rode round the town, which will soon be the best and first in the western country. At present, the dwellings, with the exception of Rapp's, and the stores and taverns, are all log-houses, with a cow-house and other conveniences. One is given to each family, and a fine cow, and nice garden; other necessaries are shared in common. Their horses, cattle, and sheep, are all in one stable; herds and flocks are folded every night, in comfortable sheds, particularly an immensely large flock of Merino sheep; and so secured from the wolves. They have a fine vineyard in the vale, and on the hills around, which are as beautiful as if formed by art to adorn the town. Not a spot but bears the most luxuriant vines, from which they make excellent wine. Their orchards, too, are of uncommon size and fertility; and in a large pleasure garden is a curious labyrinth, out of which none but those who formed it, or are well acquainted with it, can find their way.

Their granary is superb and large, and the barns and farm-yards are singularly capacious, as well as their cloth and other manufactories. It is the wise policy of this people to buy nothing which it is possible for them to make or raise, and their industry and ingenuity are irresistible. They have much to sell, at their own price, of almost every thing domestic and foreign. They cannot make shoes half so fast as they could sell them. It is not doubted but they are immensely rich, beginning in Pennsylvania with only 4,000*l.*, and being now worth 500,000*l.* They keep no accounts, and all business is done and every thing possessed in Frederick Rapp's name. They have been in this Harmony five years only ; they bought a huge territory of the richest land, which is all paid for, and keep an immense quantity in high cultivation, and continue to buy out bordering settlers, thus ever enlarging their boundaries. An American widower, with ten children, joined them some time ago, in distress for his children ; all are well off now.

They work very gently, but constantly. At eleven I left Harmony, wishing to see more of this singular community. Rapp came hither a poor, unlettered weaver from Germany.

I entered the woods again, on the banks of the fine river, the Big Wabash, wider than the Thames at London. There are no regular roads; but, over creeks and swamps, and the Black River, now dry, we took our way, and met six bastard Indian-like horsemen, drinking whiskey in the woods, looking wild and jovial, dressed in sky-blue and scarlet. Crossed the Big river into Illinois, after being lost one hour. Started a fine buck, and rode along rich bottom land, ten feet deep of water, in winter, and passed some smoke-dried women and children.

At four, p. m., I reached the English prairie, presenting a wide, rusty, black prospect, the fire having passed over it. I met Wood and Shepherd, the only two farmer-like men; saw no corn-fields; nothing done; rode into Albion at dusk, and called on Speculator Pugsley and Mr. E. P. Fordham, who never means to return to England, except rich or to be rich. If he fails here, he will turn hunter and live by his rifle on the frontiers. I supped and went to bed in a hog-stye of a room, containing four filthy beds and eight mean persons; the sheets stinking and dirty; scarcity of water is, I suppose, the cause. The beds lie on boards, not cords, and are so hard that I could not sleep. Three in one bed, all filth, no comfort, and yet this is an English tavern; no whiskey, no milk, and vile tea, in this land of prairies.

22nd.—At sun-rise I rose from our filthy nest. Mr. Simpkins, a dirty idle wife, with sons and daughters, late of Baldock, Herts, are the managers of this prairie tavern. A better one of brick is building by Mr. R. Flower, who owns the former, from which Simpkins is about removing to Evansville, because he and family, though all poor, are above being at the beck and call of every body, and pleasing nobody ; and besides (says Simpkins) the great folks are too aristocratical for me, and endeavour to oppress their countrymen. This, I believe, is not true. Simpkins, and better folks than he, need not come here, if they are unwilling to put their shoulders to the yoke. I walked round Albion. It contains one house only, and about ten or twelve log-cabins, full of degenerating English mechanics, too idle to work, and above every thing, but eating, drinking, brawling, and fighting. The streets and paths are almost impassable with roots and stumps, and in front of every door is a stinking puddle, formed by throwing out wash and dirty water. A good market-house, and a public library, is at the end, in which a kind of Unitarian worship is held on a Sunday, when a sermon and the church service purified is read by any one who pleases. The books are donations from the Flower family and their friends in England. By sending donations, people become honorary members, and Mrs. Flower has, by all legal means, secured perpetuity to this institution, which few expect to find in this distant wilderness.

Mr. and Mrs. Doctor Pugsley, late of London, live in the only house, which, if it had a servant,

would boast of English comforts, politeness, and
hospitality. She sighs to revisit England, where
she might see her friends, and rest her delicate
hands, now destined to all kind of drudgery. He
has purchased land largely, on speculation, without intending to cultivate any, and offers it at
three dollars an acre, or at a corn rent. Much of the
land has been thus purchased by capitalists here,
and is offered again on these terms, because the
Kentucky speculators, it is said, would otherwise
have bought all up and charged more for it, and
because the profit demanded, is thought to be
reasonable. But what is the effect? That of
driving away good little practical farmers to other
neighbourhoods. I was introduced to the young
Birkbecks, riding through Albion, and was struck
by their polished and prepossessing appearance.
I was introduced also to R. Flower, Esq., and
engaged to dine with him and his family, at their
house in the prairie. This gentleman much resembles the celebrated Benjamin Flower, though
of a finer person; but is fast fading away. The
shock which he received by the death of a favorite
son, a victim to the climate, has, together with
some disappointments, greatly impaired the vigorous mind and body of this noble man, and true
fearless friend of liberty all over the world. Mr.
G. Flower lives in the completest log-cabin I have
ever seen, near his father. It contains six or seven
rooms, with other needful buildings, and as a log-

establishment, I will venture to say, possesses more comfort and elegance than any ever seen in America. It is a model for all future log-builders. This gentleman is very polite, mild, gentle, and unassuming; trying scenes have made him rather silent and sombre. His lady seems the happiest and most elegant female I have seen, and perfectly suited to her present or any situation, being neither above the cottage nor below the palace. Well, indeed, might four gentlemen contend for the prize!

> " If some few failings to her portion fall,
>   Look in her face and you'll forget them all."

The gay, graceful, modest, hearty, anticipating kindness of this lady, makes every guest feel himself at home and loth to depart.

This family (the Flowers) own a large and beautiful domain of prairie, containing unnumbered acres of fine land, beautified by British park scenery. The visitor, coming here out of the forest, fancies himself in England, especially if he looks at the country through the windows of Messrs. Flower's and Birkbeck's houses, during the green and flowery season, when the scenery presents a wide waste of grass, flowers, and shrubs, of every hue; but the flowers have no fragrance, the birds no song. The sight of a flock of 500 Merino sheep, and a large herd of cattle, all their own, is indeed a novel and unexpected pleasure in these wild re-

gions; and, added to all these, the comfort of such
houses and harmonious families, escaped from the
embarrassments and anxieties of England, to quiet
rest and independence, makes it indeed a delightful spectacle. All say they have nothing to regret,
and are full of satisfaction, except the wish that
more friends would follow; whom, unless they
follow, they shall see no more. They acknowledge that they have much to do here, from want
of servants. One female, Biddy by name, recently
came and engaged to do only what she pleased,
and to sit at the same table. The terms were complied with, but a plan to cure Biddy was laid.
On a certain day many visitors were invited to
dinner, at which Biddy was not allowed to rise,
even to help herself to any thing, but all present
vied with each other in attending on Miss Biddy,
who, in great confusion, left the room, fully sensible of her folly, and next day determined to be
a servant for the future.

Mr. Flower and family recently visited Rapp,
the High Priest of Harmony. After dinner a band
of musicians entered. Mr. F. thinks highly of this
community, who, in religion and doctrine, are
Lutherans; in discipline, Presbyterians. He says,
that house-keeping here is nothing compared with
England. A fat buck, one dollar; beef, five cents;
mutton, six cents, per pound; and game, fine
prairie-hens, like grouse and turkeys, in sickening
abundance.

J. Ingle and family, eight in number, out of business, lived for four dollars a week at Princeton!

Mr. Flower would not live on woodland as a gift, if prairie land could be bought. The latter certainly seems most adapted for an English farmer; yet it costs as much to fence, and bring it into cultivation as woodland; for though less manual, yet more horse labour is necessary than in the woods. Six horses are necessary for the first ploughing, as the grass and shrub roots are deep down and uncommonly tough, having been growing for ages. It is, therefore, worth five dollars an acre to effect the first ploughing, and three or four dollars, the second. A summer's fallow is, besides, necessary for rotting the roots, and properly pulverizing the soil; and, unless so managed, it is badly managed. Both Flower and Birkbeck sowed nothing the first year, which came to any use. The latter planted corn, which the cattle destroyed, through want of a good fence, which must be hauled from the woodland, a considerable distance, to the prairie; the inclosing is, therefore, more expensive than on the woodland.

23rd.—Spending this day with Mr. G. Flower, I rode from ten till five o'clock round the prairie, in which is their fine park-like domain, and some smaller estates purchased for their friends in England, of which there is one with a house and some improvements belonging to Wed Nash, Esq., of Royston, Herts., and more rich and beautiful than

T

any he can see from the bleak, barren, chalky
hills of his native town. I called at an adjoining
farm, rented by a dirty, naked-legged French family, who, though born in this country, know
nothing of the English language. Then at Mr.
Hunt's, who is deaf and dumb, (the brother of
Henry Hunt, the Champion of Reform), who with
his nephew, a son of Henry, came here, about a
year since, to three quarter sections of land; of
which they have cultivated only six acres. They
live in a little one-room miserable log-cabin, doing
all the labour of the house and land themselves, and
without any female. We found them half-naked
and in rags, busily greasing a cart, or mending a
plough. They appeared only as labourers, but, on
being introduced to them by Mr. Flower, their best
friend, good sense and breeding shone through the
gloom of their forlorn situation. We entered their
cabin, and took some boiled beef on a board, and
sat on their bed and boxes, having no chairs,
stools, or tables, and only the mean clothes they
then wore; a fire having recently destroyed their
first cabin with all its contents. Being disappointed in English remittances, and unable to get
letters from thence, which they thought had been intercepted, they were out of funds, and their land was
uncultivated, unsown, and selling for the payment
of taxes. To prevent this, Mr. Flower called this
day. Mr. Hunt has a fine, animated, rather agi-
tated countenance. He converses in writing, with

great ease and rapidity, on any subject interesting
to him ; and his nephew, the orator's son, aged 20,
is a fine, tall, active, kind-hearted youth, pretty
well reconciled to his situation.   I offered to bear
any commands, or render them any services in my
power, on returning to England; an offer which they
gratefully embraced. I rode on towards the plantation of Mr. Lewis ; but losing our way, we returned without seeing him.   He spent much of his
capital idly in Philadelphia, and now, without
cultivating an acre of his land here, he has resold
it, intending to keep a boarding-house in Albion.
He, like the rest of his neighbours, knows nothing
of agriculture. The land here seems very tempting
to a British farmer, quite ready for the plough without any hewing or cleaving, or a blade of grass to
obstruct the plough. The fire has laid the surface black and bare as a stubble ground, burnt in
the fens of England.   But what is land with men
ignorant of, and too idle to work it? Without any
cultivation at all, it annually offers an infinite supply of hay and grass, for any who choose to mow
and gather it, or graze it ; yet few or none, saving
Birkbeck and Flower, have done so.   What is gathered, is green and fragrant, but not so sweet as
fine English hay.   It is hard, harsh, and dry.
Beef is well fattened on the grass, during the summer, the finest meat I ever saw ; and sheep, with
the assistance of corn, are fattened and now killing
from Mr. Flower's flock, which all day ranges over

the prairies with a shepherd, who pens them at night close to the farm-house, away from the wolves, which yesterday, in spite of the good shepherd, scattered them and devoured fifty. I tremble for the fate of this flock, which is now without grass or any substitute. The grass all dies in October; hard and dry food, which would starve an English flock, is now and must be their lot all winter. They drink constantly when water is near, like cattle, and water must be given them in troughs. And thus will they fare at lambing. What wasting, worrying, scattering, and death may not be expected? Would it not have been better to have waited for inclosures of cultivated grass for the herds and flocks?

Yesterday one of their fat bullocks was found dead near the Wabash, maliciously shot by a hunter; for the discovery of whom they offered 50 dollars reward.

It is the intention of these families to plough the land two years, and then turn it into English pasture, a portion every year. Mrs. G. Flower, while in Virginia, kissed a beautiful black babe before the owner, a lady, who felt great disgust and indignation at the act.—" Oh, take it away !"

Mr. Flower intends to form a society for freeing blacks, and employing free blacks. It is to be on the Harmony plan. He promises me the plan when matured. He thinks that 100*l.* in France is equal to 300*l.* in England for the support of a family, and in the former all is kindness, pleasure, and peace. He visited the Marquis de la Fayette, whose income is very small. By him he was furnished with a letter to the Hon. Thomas Jefferson, with whom he spent many happy days. This great philosopher and statesman, during the last 30 years, has been always up with the sun, noting down at sunrise the state of the mercury. He lives splendidly, in French style, on the top of the beautiful mountain Montecello, with his grandchildren and son-in-law, Mr. Randolph (not the orator). His last days are spent in writing incessantly a work for posterity. His patrimony is fast wasting, as it is in the slave states generally.

The hunters, or Illinois Rowdies, as they are called, are rather troublesome. They come rudely with their hats on into the parlour, and, when drunk, threaten Mr. Flower's life ; but they are great cowards ; firmness and a fearless resolution are necessary in dealing with them. One of a large offended party came drunk to Mr. Flower's house, and said, he would enter and shoot him. Mr. Flower got his rifle and pointed it at the fellow, on which he rushed up and put his mouth madly to the muzzle, and said, " Fire." Mr. F. then laid it down, seeing the effect was not good, and some less drunken members of the party dragged the fellow away. Law has no influence over these Rowdies. Violence must be opposed to violence.

The Flower family has bought out a good many

of these wretches. One, however, more violent
and lawless than any yet known, still remains, of
the name of Jack Ellis, the son of an old and industrious settler from Indiana, who says that he
expects this son will some time murder his mother;
and that if God does not take him, he, his father,
must kill him himself.

This rascal, with several others, in addition to
their hunting, go round stealing free negroes, on
pretence of being employed to find runaways.
The poor blacks are thus cruelly taken and sold
at New Orleans. I saw Jack with his rifle after
a negro, in the employ of Mr. G. Flower, who had
armed the poor fellow in defence of himself against
Jack, whom the settlement wish to be shot.

Mr. Flower, sen., one day found it necessary to
have his family carriage ferried over the river in a
flat, which had only one man to manage it, and
get the carriage on and off. Much delay being the
consequence, and the man unable to do alone,
Mr. Flower complained, and said, " If you do
not go and tell your master to send more help, I
will fine you for detaining me." The fellow very
rudely said, " *I have no master*, nor shall I go for
more help. I am not a servant." " How is that,"
said Mr. F., " the proprietor hires you; you serve
him, and he pays you. I am not above assisting
you; and being *your servant*, and you shall pay
me too." When landed on the other side, Mr.
Flower had two dollars demanded. " Very well,"

said he, " I have done half the work, and therefore I charge one dollar for my service !" The
fellow leered and looked humbled.

24th.—Left Mr. Flower and Albion for Wanborough, a village rising on the estate of Mr.
Birkbeck, and named after the village in Surrey,
where he last lived. Industry seems to have
done more for this village than for Albion;
every log-house has a cleared inclosure of a few
acres attached, and what is done, is done by the
occupants or owners, and not by Mr. Birkbeck;
whereas, in Albion, all has been done by the purse
of Mr. Flower. Both villages are the abode only
of the humble mechanic. The farmers live on their
quarter-sections, and both are but scantily supplied with water at a distance. Wells, however,
it is hoped, will soon be dug with an unfailing
supply. Wanborough has, I believe, and will have
the advantage over Albion, as it regards water;
but both Flower and Birkbeck have never-failing
water in wells close to their houses, to which people by permission come to draw it. Springs and
streams are found in other prairies. On stopping
at the tavern in the ville, we were met by the
young Birkbecks, who welcomed and conducted
us to the seat of their celebrated father, whom we
met near the house returning from shooting,
dressed in the common shooting jacket, &c., of
an English farmer, sporting over his own lands.
Knowing my friend, he received us both very gra-

ciously, and with a hearty welcome conducted us
in to the ladies. He approached us at first as
strangers, and, as is common with him, with a repelling sternness and earnestness of manner, seemed
to say, "Who are you?" But this manner, if he is
pleased with appearances, soon dies away into
smiling kindness and hospitality, which makes all
at home. "If I am not," said he, "pleased with
all who come, and I cannot, and will not, they go
away abusing me and the settlement." Gentler
and kinder manners, perhaps, to strangers indiscriminately coming from afar, would be no bad policy. Mr. Birkbeck is of a small, unformidable,
but erect stature, and swarthy Indian complexion.
The contour of his face, with the exception of a
fine nose, possesses little that is striking; and the
face, viewed as a whole, indicates little of the ex-
actness, ripeness, sweetness, and finished taste,
which are known to distinguish him. Notwithstanding the shock his feelings recently received,
he seems enviably happy in the bosom of his family, which consists of four sons and two daughters, mistresses of the lyre and lute, and of many
other accomplishments. Mr. B., and every branch
of this happy family, with the exception of his son
Richard, retire at ten every evening to their sleeping rooms, where a fire is kindled for them to read
and study by, half the night. "I am happy,"
said he, "in my family!" His favourite son Morris, a finished scholar, disliking a rustic life. is

about returning to England. Mr. Birkbeck had not the advantages of his children, but still is master of the dead and several of the modern languages. He, only a few days since, returned from a tour through Illinois, by way of Kascasky, where he was chosen President of the agricultural society of Illinois, one grand object of which will be, to rid the state of stagnant waters. He visited many settlements, but saw none so desirable as his own. On the Little Wabash, is one, of which he says Mr. Grant of Chatteris farms a part, very fine rich land, but rather sickly, and during the winter and spring inaccessible, by the overflowings of the Little Wabash, which then becomes five miles wide, imprisoning the settlement. Mr. Grant has been burnt out once, and lost cabin and all it contained. His daughter lives away from him at board. Not wishing to become prisoner to the Little Wabash, I declined, though I once intended, visiting this first-rate English farmer, late of Chatteris-ferry in the Isle of Ely. This gentleman died shortly afterwards, a victim to the climate.

Mr. Birkbeck says the Missouri territory partakes of an European character, in some respects, and is preferred by some English families on account of slavery, or rather the facility of getting labour and servants. Colonel Boon now lives thirty miles only from St. Louis, and in that flourishing town, Clark, the celebrated traveller up the Missouri river, lives, and has a museum.

Colonel Boon and his party, being without bread for six months, used wild turkey to their meat as a substitute.

After this conversation within doors, we agreed to walk out and view the house and estate. The first is very capacious and convenient, furnished with winter and summer apartments, piazzas, and balconies, and a fine library, to which you ascend by an outward gallery. Every comfort is found in this abode of the emperor of the prairies, as he is here called. It is situated out of the village, and on an elevation, having a fine view of his estate, and the prairies generally, in front. It is a pity that it is not built of brick or stone, instead of wood; once on fire, it will be inextinguishable, and the loss of comfort and property considerable, and, moreover, irrecoverable. There is no lime-stone here for mortar, but what is made, expensively, twelve miles off, of shells from the Wabash. Brick buildings are laid in muddy clay!

This estate, consisting of 16,000 acres, which he sells as customers offer, comprises some fine, and some wet land; and, at present, with the exception of a few acres of wheat just sown, too late, it is all uncultivated. Many acres are, however, enclosed by a ditch and rail fence, formed by stakes, bands, and split rails, which will oftener need repairing than the worm fence, without being so complete a protection. Less timber, however, is needed in this mode; and timber, drawn from a distance, is

now, and, in times to come, will, if no green
fences are raised, become a matter of great importance. I believe this fence will not be imitated by
any American. Land here is of no value without
fences, which will keep cattle in and pigs out. He
does not intend to farm much; " I had enough of
farming for thirty years in England. I came here
to rest. It ought not to be expected of me that I
should incumber myself with much business." He
means to plough two years, and then turn the land
into pasture, it being not desirable to have a large
surplus produce above what can be consumed by
the settlement; but of this there is little fear, as not
above six original farmers are yet here. Mr. B.
discovers that ditching and fencing removes the
cause of the fogs which hang over the low prairies.
About nine to twelve inches of surface, good soil,
rather light, is found. Underneath is white clay,
which an animal like a crab, but called a craw-
fish, throws up into numerous hills, bigger than
the large ant-hills in old English pastures. This
white clay, thus mixed, is, by Mr. B., deemed a
benefit. These curious creatures delve down into
the water under the soil. They are, like moles,
seldom seen but in their effects.

During our pleasant morning walk, John Ingle
said, " His father (the patriarch) wished to come,
but found it difficult, as his daughters were marry
ing, and giving in marriage, and therefore impeding
the father's wishes." " What," replied Mr. Birk-

beck, "What! stay and breed beggars in England! Well! with industry, we shall always have
an asylum for them here, but not soft independence."

Mr. B. said the Rowdies had threatened him
with assassination; but showing and convincing
them that he would shoot them if they attempted
to enter his house without permission, they had
abandoned their design. This circumstance, no
doubt, gave birth to a report of his death, which I
saw entered in the news-book at Wheeling, and at
Zainsville, Ohio.

25th.—After sleeping and breakfasting at Mr.
Birkbeck's, I called and dined with Joseph Hanks,
Esq. and his fine Irish family of sprightly sons, and
one little motherless daughter. They are Protest-
ants, and lived, as long as they could keep their
comforts, in Ireland. He was a banker, and a
correspondent of the Right Hon. N. Vansittart, and
George Canning, Esq. while the young sons were
the dandies of Dublin; but here, the father is a store-
keeper, and the sons are cooks, housemaids, carpenters, and drudges for all work. He brought
considerable property away. He has bought no
land, and professes to dislike the prairies and
America generally. He would have bought from
Mr. Birkbeck, but could get only a " cup," that is,
a swamp. He says his funds are yet entire, and he
means to leave the country, and live in England,
in a garret, in either London or Dublin, rather

than remain here, if he should be cast in a suit in
which he is the plaintiff, against the magistrates
of Illinois, who, he thinks, have unjustly taken
Birkbeck's part against him ; he and his family
having quarrelled with Mr. B. and family, about
water, &c. Mr. Hanks, is a wild, hot-headed,
sprightly Irishman, charging Mr. Birkbeck's writings with falsehood and deception, and him as a
deceiver, idly spending already 30,000 dollars ; no
farmer, and now out of funds, and embarrassed.
" I was caught," said he, " by his fascinating
writings ; it was impossible to resist them. Who
could ? Did ever man write like him ? I read his
letters to him ; he could not bear it. Persons were
employed to buy them up in the east. I admire
both him and his writings, and notwithstanding
all I say against him, I love him still. Whatever
may be his opinions, I hope and believe the
Almighty will never let such a man slip through
his fingers. He must, however, fail in his enterprize. Never come here, sir : here is no money,
no labourers. The English are the most dishonest." He says, Mr. Birkbeck maintained his
father during the last six years of his life. I returned to sup and sleep at Birkbeck's, who,
ou hearing where we spent the day, said, " You
have heard much falsehood. Hanks is a bad man,
having quarrelled with me, and nearly all around
him."

Cobbett now became the theme ; I said he had

sent the bones of Tom Paine to be enshrined at
Botley. " He cannot be such a fool?" " His
writings have been useful, and extensively read,"
said I. " Yes, that is true, but he sticks not to
truth; he is a caricaturist, and a dishonest man."
He then showed me his manuscript reply to Mr.
Cobbett's attack. In giving my opinion of it, I
pointed out what I conceived to be a grand omis-
sion, that of not noticing " no market for a surplus produce," and said, " he will fasten upon
that." " Yes, he probably will, but that is a
general question applicable to the whole western
country." " He will," said I, " have a rejoinder
for you." " Well, I must write again."

His opinion of Rapp and Harmony is unfriendly
to such a community. It is not firm as to temporals,
and as to spirituals, it is a priestly tyranny, interested in enslaving body and conscience, in order that
a few may some day divide the spoil. They keep no
accounts, and as the land is conveyed to Rapp and
his followers, those followers, by good management,
may become very few; then Harmony will be
divided. " No pleasurable feelings possess a man
who contemplates this community."

26th.—At breakfast, this morning, the young
Birkbecks said they had seen a general employed
in pig-killing, and a judge driving his own waggon. I asked the young ladies how they relished
the rattle-snake. They said, as it was of a prodigious size and tough and old, it was scarcely eat-

able, though it looked white and delicate, and tasted like a chicken.

The term elegant is no where so little understood as in this country. One of Mr. B.'s neighbours' sons falling sick, the father applied to Mr. B.'s chest for medicine, and received it. Mr. B. next morning said to the father, " Well, sir, how did the medicine operate?" " Oh, sir, elegantly," was the reply.

The hour was now come for quitting this distinguished man and harmonious family. He wished me to stay longer, and to hear of and from me after my return to England, and that his son, Morris, who is coming to a mercantile concern at Bristol, might accompany me.

I dined, on fine roast beef, with Dr. Pugsley, physician to the settlement. Here are English elegance and comfort, but no servant. What a change! And, as the settlement is said to be healthy, what a chance for a mere doctor! In the afternoon I called on Mr. Cowling, late of Spalding, Lincolnshire, who, with his brother, is settled on a corner of a quarter-section, living without any female, and fast barbarizing, in a most miserable log-cabin, not mudded, having only one room, no furniture of any kind, save a miserable, filthy, ragged bed for himself and his brother, who is lamed, and prostrated on the floor, by a plough-share, and who, though unable to move, yet refuses a doctor. Both were more filthy, stinking, ragged, and repelling, than any

English stroller or beggar ever seen; garments
rotting off, linen unwashed, face unshaven and unwashed, for, I should think, a month. Yet Mr.
Cowling is a sensible, shrewd man, quite a philosopher, though filthiness is against the law of nature. " Here (says he) a man learns philosophy
and its uses!" He expects his sisters and brothers
into this miserable abode. What a shock will such
a spectacle be to their feelings! He went, during
the summer, five miles for water, though a well
might have been dug on his farm. He grumbles
about having given 50*l.* per cent. profit to Birkbeck for his land, for by this policy the latter has
injured the settlement and himself; and as he does
not farm, as was expected, he must lose his capital as well as Mr. Flower. He says prairie
lands cost as much getting into cultivation as the
woodland. People coming here without fortune,
must have industry and work, if they would live.
He does not, however, regret emigrating, but people
should be taught the truth, and come with no in-
flated notions. Birkbeck has deceived himself
and the public. Cobbett's rubs against him are
good, but some are false.

I rested this night at the one-room log-cabin of
Mr. Woods and family, a real Nottinghamshire
farmer, on 400 acres of good land. Here we found
an excellent cleanly supper, good whiskey, segars, and a friendly welcome. The room contained four beds, for nine of us, standing on a

dirt floor, while the chimney poured nearly all its smoke upon us. With a scolding wife, instead of his pretty, cleanly English niece, things had been complete. But Mr. Woods lost his wife on the Ohio river, where many poor English, this summer, have either died or been drowned. He has brought with him four bushels of English hawthorn, for green fencing; without green fencing, woe be to the prairies! Mr. Woods seems a plain, judicious, industrious man, sensible of the wisdom of his choice. The Woods are men either for the prairie or the wood country. Not far from Mr. Woods live a Mr. Bentley and lady, late of London, who, here, with a little property, have turned farmers, doing all the labour in the field and loghouse themselves, and, it is said, seem very cheerful, happy, and healthy. In London he had the gout, and she the delicate blue devils, but here milking, fetching water, and all kinds of drudgery, in doors and out, have cured her, and ploughing, him. He never, he says, loved her or she him, half so much as in Illinois. At a distance of five miles from any dwelling live also two young gay gentlemen, late of London, of the name of Millor, now called children of the wood, who cultivate one quarter section, and shift for themselves in great comfort, cleanliness, and satisfaction, though they never saw a plough before. Here they do all. Mr. J. Cookson, of Bond-street, is now in Fordham's store.

U

27th.—By appointment, I revisited the Flower family. When it became known in England that they were about to emigrate, they were constantly assailed on the road and at home by inquiries, insomuch that it was necessary, for several days, to keep a servant posted at the anti-room door, to give a general answer to such inquiries, by saying that they neither wished nor wanted any body to go to America. At this time Mr. Birkbeck's notes appeared, after some difficulty in finding a respectable, independent bookseller, Mr. Ridgway. Mr. Flower read to me a manuscript letter, intended for publication, which he had recently written, addressed to Mr. Birkbeck, respecting the conduct of the latter gentleman; the object of which is to put him on his defence in all matters, public and private, relating to their mysterious and unfortunate quarrel. As I have heard both sides, from both parties, or at least as much of both sides as the parties, voluntarily and unquestioned, thought proper to give me, I shall endeavour to give a faithful account of what I heard. The Flowers charge Mr. B. with an intention of driving their family out of Illinois, and of deceiving the public generally, in the hope of monopolizing all the prairies to himself, so that he might sell, at what advanced price he pleased, to such of his countrymen as came hither, induced by his tempting publications. The second letter of that volume is to Mr. Flower, sen. Wishing to visit

America, to relieve himself from domestic unhappiness, Mr. G. Flower was the precursor of Mr. Birkbeck, who then was opposed to emigration, but who, soon after Flower's departure, suddenly changing his opinion, determined on his present measure, and wrote to G. Flower to that effect, who was so much pleased with the country, that he bought land in Virginia, intending to settle on it, if he could induce his family to follow. Mr. Birkbeck now met the Flower family, to persuade them to emigrate with him to their son George Flower, and make one property and share all things in common, a measure too Utopian for Mr. Flower, sen. to approve. Mr. Birkbeck then reproached Mr. Flower with *croaking;* and the emigration of the Flower family was deferred, while Mr. Birkbeck prepared for his departure. The Miss Birkbecks seeing a young lady at Mr. Flower's, Miss Andrews, wished her to accompany them to America, a measure to which the father objected, but soon afterwards consented, and away they sailed to Norfolk, in Virginia, where they were met by George Flower, who agreed to accompany them westward. Miss Andrews and George Flower, unknown to Birkbeck, were agreeing to marry; and on arriving at Vincennes, both parties made it known to Mr. Birkbeck, who, with considerable agitation and surprise, gave his consent and sanction to the marriage. This consent, however, was wildly given, and apparently with extreme reluctance, for he also was attached to this lovely female. Mr. Birkbeck having shewn strong feelings and emotions on this occasion, Mr. Flower and the Birkbeck family, in consequence, felt much alarm. Mr. Flower did not expect it, though he knew of the unfortunate attachment, for the fondness so little encouraged was but too evident; but as he had ingenuously told Mr. Birkbeck, and advised with him on the measure, and he had consented and acquiesced with apparent kindness, Mr. G. Flower had hoped that his strong emotions would subside. He offered to leave Mr. Birkbeck and his family for ever, to which Mr. B. would not consent, but, on leaving the happy pair at Vincennes, went on to Princeton, where all, in a few days, met in friendship, and proceeding into Illinois, subsequently settled in the prairies, as one family, until Birkbeck showed symptoms of violent attachment, which excited alarm as to consequences. It was then thought adviseable, as Mr. G. Flower was going to England, that Mrs. F. should not continue there, but go eastward, and remain there until her husband returned. She did so, and Mr. Birkbeck parted with them in friendship, promising to prepare houses and purchase land for them and the family before they returned. Mr. G. Flower was also the bearer of Mr. Birkbeck's celebrated letters for publication in England and Philadelphia. All seemed peace, and money was sent over express from

England to Mr. Birkbeck, for purchasing and
building; but, when the Flower family arrived, he
had done nothing, nor purchased any thing for them,
and on Mr. George Flower calling on Birkbeck,
the latter, shaking his head, turned his back, saying, " I am sorry to see you, I had rather not see
you—I cannot, will not see you." " But," said
Mr. Flower, " I must see you ; I have money for
you, and business with you."—"A third person will
do; I name your brother."   Mr. Flower then departed to his lady and brothers, now homeless
and exposed, in a little old, ruinous, dirt-floor
cabin, without doors or windows, or furniture, or
food, or water; and here, thus exposed to the damp
ground, camping out all night, in pestilential dews,
all fell sick but Mr. and Mrs. Flower, who had to
ride twenty miles for food, physic, and furniture,
denied them by Mr. Birkbeck.   At length Mr.
Flower fell sick, and thus was Mrs. Flower, the
only person in health, compelled to be servant of
all work to all, having water to draw and carry
herself from a distance, and wood to hew for the
fire, and no neighbours but the barbarian hunters,
who tendered that assistance which their dear
friend Birkbeck refused.   Mr. Flower's favorite
son, thus exposed and sick, never recovered. The
senior branches of the Flower family were now at
Lexington, ignorant of these evils, until a letter
from Mr. Birkbeck reached them, wishing they
should settle in the east, (where he supposed them

to be,) telling his reasons for so advising them,
namely, because he thought that they would all
make common cause with their son, George
Flower, and that he had not bought them any
land, but ordered the funds to be returned to
their banker in Philadelphia. Mr. Flower answered with great bitterness and asperity, accus-
ing Mr. Birkbeck of fraud, treachery, and cruelty,
threatening summary justice, and expressing a
determination to come and live there, to protect
his son and family against his malice. Mr. Birkbeck then offered peace, at least to Mr. Flower,
sen.; "but," said Mr. Flower, "I could not take
him by the hand now; it would be loss of character. I had done nothing to offend him, and why
was I thus made to suffer? I am bound up with
my family; their lives are precious in my sight."
This was a part of his letter to Birkbeck, which
he read to me, but when he came to that part, he
burst into tears, and rushed out, putting it into
my hands. I not being able to read it, Miss
Flower concluded it. Neither Mr. R. Flower,
nor Mr. G. Flower, have ever since met Mr. Birkbeck. "I avoid seeing him," says Mr. R.
Flower, "because, if I came near, I must lay
violent hands on him; I must knock him down.
I will never see him, or speak to him more; a re-
conciliation is impossible, to me it would be a
stain and loss of character." All the evil to both
families, and to the settlement, they impute to Birk-

beck. They wonder why he should have so changed, when he had sanctioned the conduct of George
Flower, and given him the lady in marriage. They
deem it hypocrisy, of the first order, as well as the
greatest impolicy; "but," say they, "he is now punished for it, being nearly in the situation of an
embarrassed man." Mrs. G. Flower, however,
more charitably, imputes nothing in Mr. Birkbeck's conduct to vile or corrupt motives, but all
to love, and to that kind of revenge, which such a
disappointment was likely to generate, when the
mind was lonely and abandoned to its own feelings. They deem the event a great evil to themselves and to the settlement, because it happened at
a time when the joint exertions of these two families were so necessary for its success. It de-
ranged every thing; and all connected with, or
who came nigh the prairies, wondered and felt the
evil, because the secret was unknown. Mr. G.
Flower professes not to defend his departure from
law and custom, in this second marriage, but very
ingenuously confesses, that having missed his
chance of happiness in his first, he was determined to try a second marriage, which promised
better things; and as Mr. Birkbeck knew his situation intimately, he would not have censured him,
had he not wished to marry the lady himself. As
this could not be, he and Mr. Birkbeck had, instead of consulting the good of the settlement, laid
by to give each other mortal stabs, or rather to

blast each other's good name. This ends one side of the case.

Mr. Birkbeck in reply, takes a disinterested, high, moral stand, suffering nothing to escape him relating to his own disappointments, though in a letter to Mr. Mellish, he admits " that scandal is busy with his name and affairs." He states, that soon after landing in this country, and being joined by Mr. G. Flower, he began to suspect a connection was forming between Miss Andrews and George Flower. At length it became unequivocal, and he consented to and sanctioned their marriage, as the least of two unavoidable evils; for the parties had determined either on marriage (if not impracticable), or at least on cohabitation; and, as he respected both as his children, he consented to the former as the least evil. The grand cause of a change of conduct to them (so much wondered at by the Flowers), and of not fulfilling his promises of purchasing and building for the reception of the families, will be seen in the following circumstances. He had been deceived; while G. Flower was gone to London, he became undeceived; he learnt, from the best authority, that Miss Andrews had been the cause of all the jealousy, unhappiness, and separation in G. Flower's former marriage; and that the senior branches had placed this young lady in his family for the express purpose of effecting their purposes, namely of marrying her to their son; a circumstance cal-

culated to injure the honour of himself and family
in the eyes of an uncharitable world.   Seeing himself, then, to have been made the innocent tool of
such iniquitous measures, it no longer remained a
matter of choice whether he should receive or
abandon them; it was impossible for him to act
otherwise than he had done, if he intended to preserve his reputation.   It was certainly not his wish
to quarrel with Mr. R. Flower, but as father and
son were one, it was impossible to avoid it; he
therefore declined purchasing the promised land
or using their money in any way.   He conceives
that Mr. Flower should not have taken part with
his son, but rather endeavoured, by all manner of
means, to make reparation for the indignity attempted to be put on his (Birkbeck's) family by
their illicit conduct.

Mr. Birkbeck rids himself of the charge of fraud
and breach of trust, by saying, in reply to Mr.
Flower's severe letter, that it was optional whether
he purchased lands with the money sent; it was
not binding upon him to do it.   And, moreover,
he thought it for the interest of both families, under
such circumstances, to be more distantly situated.

Thus have I given both sides of the question, as
completely as they could be gathered from verbal
statements.

The two villes of Albion and Wanborough, the
abodes of contention, party spirit, speculation, and
feuds, arose out of this greatly to be regretted

quarrel. If it had produced competition and extraordinary exertions in agriculture, and a desire to conciliate, accommodate, and invite settlers, it had been well; but the reverse was the consequence. It is true that no man, since Columbus, has done so much towards peopling America as Mr. Birkbeck, whose publications, and the authority of whose name, had effects truly prodigious; and if all could have settled in Illinois, whom he had tempted to cross the Atlantic and the mountains, it had now been the most populous state in the Union. America, and the western country generally, are benefitted by and indebted to him; but, not being a man of business, and therefore ill calculated to appreciate properly his advantages, the time to benefit himself is not yet come. He has land enough; but what is land without population and cultivation? Mr. Birkbeck declines the responsibility of advising people to emigrate; and Mr. Flower says, " Tell your countrymen to stay at home by all means, if they can keep their comforts."

The argument for and against speculation, so offensive and repelling to emigrants coming to the prairies, assumes the following shapes. First, It is necessary to keep out the Kentucky non-resident speculators, who are capricious and extravagant in their demands and profits, and remotely situated. Secondly, It is reasonable and just that speculators of capital, living on the spot, and who

have encountered the difficulties of first settlers,
and smoothed the way for followers, should derive
some remuneration from the latter, who now find
themselves surrounded with neighbours, facilities,
and conveniences of all kinds. Thirdly, That no
reasonable man can come, expecting to have the
land, under such circumstances, at the Old Congress price. Fourthly, That it is better worth four
dollars an acre now, than it was worth two dollars,
when they found it an inhospitable wild. Fifthly,
That as they have bought large quantities in the
mass, good and bad together, without knowing that
they should ever sell an acre, and that as they permit people to pick and choose, leaving much unsaleable land on their hands, they are entitled to get
all they can for what is good and saleable. Against
it, it is said. First, It is never right to do evil that
good may result; but, as evil is the consequence
of speculating, it is unjust, unreasonable, and unnecessary; and, besides, the public would rather
buy of native than of English speculators, if any
must speculate, and it is better that nuisances
should live at a distance. Secondly, That no beneficial improvements being made, the owners are
not entitled to any other remuneration than what naturally results from good neighbourhood. Thirdly,
That no reasonable honest man could desire it,
under such circumstances. Fourthly, That it is
foolish and impolitic to buy land in the mass, good
and bad together, when an infinite supply of the

good could be had separately in a better situation. Fifthly, That as property is created gradually by population only, then land, without followers, must sink rather than rise in value. Sixthly,
That as speculation had driven away settlers
calculated to improve and cultivate land, it had
become an evil, which should, if possible, be resisted and destroyed, and that no country affords
greater facilities than America for resisting the
prairie speculation. It was expected of Englishmen that they came to farm, not to speculate and
prey upon their more needy countrymen.

Sunday, 28*th.*—At breakfast this morning, Mr.
Flower, regretting the habit of duelling, said, that
a lady of Lexington, finding her nephew not inclined to fight a duel, encouraged him to go out;
and immediately on his departing for the fatal
spot, said to her black servant, " John, light up
and get the large drawing-room ready for the reception of a corpse." This order was given with
great *sang froid;* and in less than an hour, the
room was occupied by the corpse of her nephew !

So severely is the want of labourers felt here,
that Mr. Flower said he would pay to parishes in
England half the expense of getting their surplus
poor here.

We were now leaving this hospitable family and
the prairies, perhaps, for ever. We exchanged
blessings, and received parcels, letters, and kind
messages for friends in England; wild flower-

seeds, and a monstrous acorn from the ladies, and a racoon-skin from the young gentlemen, for a lady at Royston. " Enjoin," said Mr. G. Flower, " all those of our friends, who come, not to encumber themselves with merchandize and ventures; it is certain loss. When on the journey, they must endure with patience unto the end, or they will lose the reward of their toil. Tell them that I, whom they knew, and my father, have all our expectations answered; that we believe the country to be more healthy and suitable to Englishmen than any part; that we have soil, climate, and market. I am sure that were Archer, Greaves, J. Foster, and Elias Fordham here, they would enjoy themselves more than in any other place. You will, of course, tell what you have seen, which will do more to give my acquaintance a correct impression than a hundred letters. They must be confounded by the contradictory statements they hear."

We rode off on our way to Princeton, Indiana, through a cold, wet, marshy prairie, over which hang dense fogs, and on which lies water knee-deep in summer. When seen at a distance, it looks like a large lake of water, but on coming into it, the green grass, four feet high, conceals the stinking, stagnant, steaming water.

I crossed the Big Wabash, quarter of a mile wide, at La Valette's ferry, where is beautiful land, fine young orchards, and two lonely families of naked-legged French settlers, from whom I received two curious ears of poss corn. I thus quitted lonely Illinois, in which, this morning, I saw, for the first time, one running spring. The wild ducks on the river were very fat and fine, like our tame ones in England. One just shot floated dead to our flat. About eight miles from the river, we crossed a dismal swamp two miles wide, which, in winter, is ten feet deep of water from the river, and cuts off communication with Illinois, except by water. At the verge of this swamp, I stopped at a farmer's, sick and yellow with a bilious fever. My horse escaped from me, but was stopped by Judge Emberson. I rode all day without dinner, but reached Princeton to a good supper at Brown's tavern, which, but for Mr. Birkbeck, had been annihilated.

Mr. Birkbeck seems to have no theory on the formation of the ancient mounds and fortifications in the western country, but thinks them to be the work of the present race of Indians. Nor has he any hypothesis on the subject of the immense prairies. Though but partially planted with timber, he does not think the soil unfriendly to the growth of it, but deems the cause to be in the annual fires which run over the surface, checking the young plants, or destroying the seeds, or rather in a want of seed; and the decaying, dwarfish appearance of the trees, he attributes to the same fiery cause. That the prairies have been

lakes of water he much doubts. General Evans,
a gentleman with whom I, this day, held an interesting conversation on the subject, and who
has explored the prairie country generally, thinks
that as they are contiguous to the immense lakes
of Michigan, &c. without being intercepted by
any hills of magnitude, they must have been
formed by the receding of the lakes of which they
once constituted a part, and to this day, in the
sand, traces of surf and driving water are still
evident on and round about the gentle hills and
skirts of the prairies. This idea is opposed by
some, because, of the prairie rivers, some are found
running north into the lakes, and others south into
the Ohio and the Mississipi. The soil and sand,
however, of the prairies, are such as are found on
the lake shores, and shew, upon and below the
surface, the operations of water.

For the general purposes of agriculture, the
intelligent General considers the best prairie soil
to be deeper and more lasting than the woodland,
though at present more uncertain. It wants more
rain, and frequently fails in droughty seasons.
Cultivation, he conceives, will render it less porous
and more retentive of moisture: time is necessary
for rotting the tough, wiry grass-roots; its richness
and durability are proved by its having been constantly in cultivation at Vincennes, during the
last 200 years. The best prairies known in this
country, abounding with healthy situations, and

fine running never-failing springs, sufficient for
mill-streams, he saw from 70 to 100 miles above
Birkbeck's, on the banks of the Wabash, up to
its head waters, beyond Fort Harrison, and extending to the lake-streams. Between the Wabash, and a lake river, is only nine miles of land
carriage. Here is the richest land in the western
country, though at present more distantly situated
from market. The waters of the lakes, he thinks,
have recently experienced no diminution.

29th.—Two years ago, a young Yankee, of
the name of Williams, became the object of a
malicious prosecution here, on suspicion of robbing
a store. Circumstantial evidence of the worst
kind only could be adduced, and he was, as is
common in this country, acquitted. The people
of the place, however, prejudiced against him, as
a Yankee, deputed four persons to inform him,
that unless he quitted the town and state immediately, he should receive Lynch's law, that is, a
whipping in the woods. He departed, with his
wife and child, next day, on foot; but in the
woods, four miles from Princeton, they were overtaken by two men, armed with guns, dogs, and a
whip, who said they came to whip him, unless he
would confess and discover to them the stolen
money, so that they might have it. He vainly
expostulated with them; but, in consideration of
his wife's entreaties and cries, they remitted his
sentence to thirteen lashes. One man then bound

him to a tree and lashed him with a cow-hide
whip, while the other held and gagged him; the
alarmed wife, all the time, shrieking murder.
He was then untied, and told to depart from the
state immediately, or he should receive another
whipping on the morrow, as a warning and terror
to all future coming Yankees.

This poor fellow was of respectable parents at
Berlin, in the state of New York, and possessed
a well-informed mind. He quitted the state, and
returning, soon after, to prosecute his executioners,
died at Evansville, before he had effected so desirable an object. Here was liberty, with a ven-
geance! This poor fellow, a victim to popular
prejudice, had the liberty to travel 3,000 miles on
foot, twice, to this state, for a settlement; and no
sooner was he in it, than the inhabitants had the
liberty to whip him out again. He left behind
him an account of his journey, and of the treat
ment he here received. In walking through Kentucky, he found the people very inhospitable towards him, because he was a walking, working
Yankee man, on a journey, and, therefore, considered as nothing better than, or below, a *nigger*.

Thieving, it must be observed, at all times, and
in all places, thought to be most inexcusable, is
here deemed worse than murder, in consequence
of the very great facility of living.

30*th*.—Introduced last night to, and slept at
the farm log-house of the Rev. Mr. Devan, the

x

minister of a congregation, and one of the members
of a convention to form the government of this
state. He is a self-taught man of considerable
intelligence, originality, and amusing anecdote,
living on a quarter section of the richest land I
ever saw, bearing Indian corn, fifteen feet high,
yielding 80 bushels an acre. He has more land
than he occupies. His family is numerous; his hogs
almost innumerable, 400 in the wood, many wild,
and breeding faster in a wild, than in a tame state.
From these, the squatters supply themselves, in
defiance of a strict law against the act. Then the
wolves, wild cats, and bears, destroy, annually, a
great number. Until pigs are weaned, the wild
animals destroy them by cunningly quarrelling
with the sow, while a party of the wolves seize
the pigs in their nests. Mr. Devan, this morning,
shot a fat pig between the eyes; it fell dead instantly
the English mode, he says, is murder. He offered
me a fine pet deer, which follows him every where,
leaping over ten feet fences, and giving chace to
the fleetest dogs, which she instantly distances.
She holds communication with the wild bucks of
the wood, three or four of which follow her. I
regretted that I could not transport this beautiful
animal.

Mr. Devan manufactures and cultivates the tea
of China; I received from him some seed and tea for
use. The shrub resembles young quicking, or two
years old hawthorn. Its seed should be sown in

the autumn, and it will vegetate in May. He states that flax and currants are found wild in perfection, 1,500 miles up the Missouri territory, where also buffaloes are tamed for the yoke. He has a fine apple orchard, yielding plenty of fruit, the third year after being planted small from the nursery, and peach-trees from the seed, growing faster than osiers in England, being now from fifteen to twenty feet high, full of bearing branches. Fifteen years in England would not, I think, produce such an orchard. He has twelve children, and expects to leave them one quarter section each of improved rich land. The old gentleman tells many anecdotes respecting the uncommon cunning of the Indians. He believes that Birkbeck is sinking his capital by unskilful purchases and management, and by employing bad labourers, and omitting to cultivate. But the money goes, never to return. His land may rise to 15 or 20 dollars an acre, if he keeps it. He believes that skilful capitalists, even here in Indiana, after the second or third year, might enrich themselves from hired labour. Some have done it. Riches are relative things. Capitalists, however, not working themselves, would gain more money, in a good slave state, with good negroes. He thinks that J. Ingle's land is poor, but useful. An old settler upon it, says he, never got more than twenty bushels of wheat an acre, after corn; but, if fallowed, it would bring much more ; as it is, fifteen or sixteen is the average.

Mr. Devan, when preaching at Mr. Ingle's, stripped at it, taking off coat, waistcoat, and cravat, unbuttoning his shirt collar, and wildly throwing about his arms. He made the maddest gesticulations, for the space of two hours, ever seen in a man professing sanity. At parting with this eccentric, warm, true-hearted man, I said, "Tell me honestly whether or not we English should emigrate hither?" "In the language of the apostle," answered he, "Be ye content with such things as ye have. Remain where providence has placed you; but send me your travels." Be not offended, friend Devan!

December 1st. — Returned to Mr. Ingle's this evening. Till within the last five days, the last month has been warmer than an English summer, the mercury varying between 65 and 72, and with the exception of the all-pervading smoke, which vanished on the first coming rain, it has been the brightest and most delightful month I ever saw. How unlike an English November! I met, and shall meet daily, at the same table, J. Pedley, a native of Sutton, near Ely, once my father's ploughboy, who, with his wife and children, has begged his way to America, and all through it, 1,200 miles, to this place. The greatly needed hospitality and kindness which they met with, in passing down the river, in a pennyless condition, are highly honourable to this good poor-man's country. Our neighbour, Major Hooker, has killed fourteen

deer and one bear. The deer now killed, in such
abundance, fine and fat, are merely skinned, and
the hind quarters taken, while all the rest is left
rotting on the ground. Cook also met a fine bear,
which after he had fired thrice at it, in great rage
chased its destroyer, while the dogs were worrying its hind quarters; and, but for the dogs, Cook
had been worried by the bear. Two balls more
brought it to the ground, wondrous fat and fine,
a daily repast, three times a-day, in steaks, for
our table, and its skin for wigs for my host's aged
sire, the patriarch of Slyers. This morning Mr.
Ingle, in descending a ladder from his cock-loft
bed-room, into which sun, moon, and stars peep,
and all the winds and storms of heaven blow upon
us, was left suspended by his arms to the cham-
ber-floor, while the ladder fell from under him.
Such are the miserable shifts to which people
here submit without grumbling.

2nd.—Both our wooden chimneys caught fire,
which soon would have left us in the woods without a shelter. One building so fired, containing
3,000 dollars worth of store goods. What folly to
build wooden chimneys, as though a wooden house
were not hazardous enough! But a stone chimney
would cost a few dollars. Rather, too, than dig a
well at the door, Mr. Ingle and others yoke out a
horse and water-cart, bringing twelve gallons at a
time from a mile distance, having, he states, since
he came here, spent, in this work, 700 valuable

hours, much more than equal to digging the well.
I feel mad with people imposing inconveniences
upon themselves, which they would not have submitted to at home, though they might have gained
by it.

Saw twenty-two chattering parroquets on one
bough. Mr. Ingle, this day, offered ten dollars
an acre for cutting down all the timber, burning
some with the grubbing, and sawing others into
three lengths, but it was refused.

A young man came to the door and boldly asked if he could have a breakfast with us, and a job
of work after.

During the last month, three travellers in the
state of Illinois, on the lonely road from Vincennes to St. Louis, and one in Indiana, were
murdered; two being shot, and two having their
throats cut, one of whom recovered sufficiently
to tell his tale. The unfortunate man in Indiana
was sleeping at a lone tavern, in a room with another. In the morning, the landlord found that
both were gone, but following the traces of blood
on the floor, and along the road, into the wood,
they found the body covered with leaves. Law
and justice extend not thus far at present.

I met Mr. Maidlow, jun., who has abandoned
his wife in England. She would not come. I
saw also a poor man, of the name of Hall, just
come from Surrey, where he was a gardener, and
during his last year lost 50*l.* Finding it impos-

sible to live without spending all, he came away
with money enough to enter half a quarter section.
The gentry of Surrey, who respected him, endeavoured to prevent his coming.

9th.—Owing to want of pot-hooks, which are
dispensed with, because they cost money, we lost
our dinner. The pot, placed on the fire, became
dried, and pudding, meat, and sauce, all took fire,
and in the absence of all were burnt up. A black-
smith lives close by who could make pot-hooks,
but it is said a pair from Pittsburgh, 900 miles
off, will cost less money; they therefore wait,
suffering the pot to fire, or tumble off the logs.
There are several English families living without
bread, butter, milk, tea or coffee, for months, who,
if deprived of one of those articles in England,
would have cursed it and all in it, as the worst
country under Heaven. Some three families cook
and bake in one iron skillet, called the cook-all,
though plenty might be bought, or ovens made of
the stone near them. Some boast of having learnt
to do without sugar, because it is so dear in this
untaxed land, flowing with sugar, milk, and honey!
It is, perhaps, wise to reduce our wants, or rather
necessaries.

Met Mr. Stockwell, who is intimately acquainted with Messrs. Birkbeck and Flower. He
says that the former, though he refused purchasing
land for his friends in England, is now turning
over his own unsaleable land to them. He has

done no one thing which he promised to do. Corn
was carried in skiffs, from Harmony, down the
Wabash, at the enormous cost of two dollars a
bushel, yet the settlement has plenty of labourers,
land, and horses.   Mr. Birkbeck is very much
embarrassed, and G. Flower very short of cash.
The flock of sheep must perish, or subject him to
great loss.   When Mr. Stockwell called, in the
summer, on Mr. Birkbeck, the family was not up.
He rode to the house, through watery swamps
and wondrous fogs, insomuch that Mr. Birkbeck
found it necessary to apologize for the weather
and the fogs, saying, " it was the first fog seen, all
summer."   Mr. Stockwell is sure that all the
prairies, known to him, are naturally sickly, from
the lakes north, to the Gulf of Mexico south.
The cause is natural, and not to be completely removed in this climate. The numerous deaths, and
the yellow appearance of the native settlers, are
proofs not to be disputed. Mr. Birkbeck felt sure
of constructing a plough, (which he did) and
ploughing up the tough prairie turf, with a very
small horse power, but he broke his plough at the
beginning, and instead of 100 acres of corn, had
half an acre of potatoes!   The experienced native
farmers have found from six to eight oxen necessary for breaking up the land in the autumn; then
it lies till spring, and in summer is fallowed, and
lies a second winter till spring; then, being completely rotten, it is sown with corn.

I dined to-day with Mr. Wheeler, a mealman and baker, from Chelsea, who, having a wife and eight children, was determined on emigration, by soberly looking into his affairs, and finding that he had an increasing family and decreasing property, having lost, during his last year, amongst his tradesmen, 1,500*l.* He came here in expectation of finding America a land of labour, and had confidence in the prospect. He is not deceived, and expects many to follow him, but shall advise them all to come in their working jackets, and do as he and his family do, hew and split wood, and clear land themselves, without hiring. He finds that a house here, though he grows the wood, will cost nearly as much as a brick-house in England, finished both in the same style; the finishing determines the expense. He gave us for dinner a fine wild turkey, weighing 20lbs. The wild cat is a tiger cat; it kills the deer and pigs.

Mr. Kelhorn never expected to gain money by farming, but only by the increased rate of land. He is sorry that he settled not near flourishing Maddison, on land, at five dollars per acre. He abhors the prairies, which are all sickly, being either without water or drowned, with skiffs moving over swamps, covered with pestilent fogs and steamy heats. Birkbeck must fail, and Flower too!

16*th.*—Visited Scott's still-house, now building of rough logs, where corn and rye are to be turned into whiskey, half of which goes to the distiller; the grain to be brought, and the spirits to be carried away at the farmer's cost; so making the spirits as dear, if not dearer, than what can be bought of spirit-merchants. Besides, it is expected that Scott will take the best half for himself.

Farmer Montgomery came 10 miles this morning with one of his fat bullocks to kill for the English here. He killed and dressed it himself, or rather murdered it. The animal is either shot, or knocked down, in any part of the yard; then it is skinned and cut out immediately, not jointed, or cut into joints, but quartered, while hot, and drenched in blood, for it is not hung up to cool and dry. I begged for J. Pedley, the fine fat head and horns which the pigs had begun to devour. The farmer will not carry any out, but makes people come for it, and waits, if it is two days, or until all is sold. It was a fine treat to us, as we had not tasted tame meat for the last fortnight; nothing but lean, poor venison. I bought half a quarter, at four cents a pound, and fine beef it was.

Mr. Maidlow has bought several loads of corn, at thirty-three cents a bushel, 16d. English, and carted by the farmer, twelve miles, into the bargain. Forty bushels is a load for four horses, through the worst roads, taking two days, at four dollars a day for carriage, so leaving only 17s. sterling, for forty bushels, to the poor farmer! Or if bought at 25 cents, as it often is, only 9s. for the 40 bushels!!

But surely imperious necessity only can compel
the farmer so to sell, because if able to keep it
until summer, he gains from 100 to 200 per cent. ;
but he is sued and the corn goes. And in summer
he buys it at one dollar per bushel, for his own
eating!

Fifty cents is the usual price of carriage for
100lbs. for every 20 miles ; sometimes higher,
never lower. One bushel of corn weighs 50 to
56lbs., so that if it was hauled by weight, it would
not pay the carriage for 20 miles.

Western labourers, some of whom are quarter-
section farmers, very poor, dirty, and wretched,
because idle and semi-barbarians, work about
half the day and camp out all night, in all seasons and weathers. They surround a large fire,
and lie on leaves under a clap-board tent, or
wooden umbrella, wrapped in a blanket, with their
clothes on. Their houses and families (if any) are
perhaps, from 12 to 20 miles off, to whom they go
when the job is done, or their shirts are rotting off
their backs. They rarely shave, but clip off the
beard, and their flesh is never washed ; they look
pale, wan, yellow, and smoke-dried. They live on
the deer which they shoot. They are high-minded,
not suffering their children to go to service, because it is disgraceful, but not so to live at home,
in rags, idleness, and filth. The father is seldom
at home, because of being sued. If he has land,
he farms it not, because of bailiffs. He must then

work out, until judgment is had against him; when he either pays or makes arrangements, or the property, real and personal, is sold. These labourers, though complete workmen when they like, are pests to the English farmers for whom they work, generally, at meals, haunting the fire-side, where they stand in pairs with their backs towards the fire, to the exclusion of the family, at whom they gaze, expecting to be asked to dinner, breakfast, or supper. They come too, for work, and brush in at meal times with their hats on, expecting to be fed; but they never invite themselves, nor express thanks if invited; and if requested to reach this or that to the host, they do it ungraciously, saying, " Why, I can, I guess." If the female of the family is in bed, they stand and see her get out and dress. They will not be affronted with impunity, and it is necessary to shew or threaten them with a pistol. When the English first came to Evansville settlement, these Rowdey labourers had nearly scared them out. Time is not property to these men; they are eternal triflers.

Visited Evansville on the bluffs of Ohio. Behind it is an almost impassable road through a sickly swamp, none of which near the road is yet cultivated. It seems too wet. Here I met a few English mechanics regretting they had left England, where they think they could do better. J. Pedley, though he does well, says he would not have come could he have known what he must have suffered. Apples are here selling in boats from Cincinnati at eight dollars per barrel, and flour at eight dollars. A barrel of apples is two bushels and a half, and the barrel of flour contains five bushels of wheat which, to the consumer here, costs eight shillings sterling per bushel, though wheat is only 75 cents, or 3s. 6d. a bushel.

Cook, yesterday, shot another bear. He was camping out, and in the dead of the night saw Bruin, and with the first fire broke his neck. He weighed 400lbs. I bought the skin at four dollars ; worth four pounds in England.

The wolves last night howled horribly and prowled into town.

The case of first settlers here, particularly English, is hard, and their characteristic selfishness by no means tends to soften it. Nothing is to be had in the shape of necessaries but with great trouble, not even butter, cheese, or meat. They think that these are more trouble than they are worth, and that it is better to do without. The Americans make no trouble of it. If they can have money or credit, and can get good things, they have them. The English are too selfish to be provident ; their boast is that they can do without such a thing, and the habit of doing without is esteemed a fine thing, and causes those who express dissatisfaction to be despised. Thus my countrymen barbarize.

A skiff, last week before daylight, was seen floating on the Ohio, having in it one oar, a suit of shabby English clothes, two watches, and a small keg of whiskey half full. The owner, it was supposed, had tumbled out and was drowned, as have been many English before, on this excursion down the river.

The Rowdies of Kentucky, and in thinly settled parts of Tenessee where they are farmers, frequently decoy travellers, supposed to have money, out of the road, and then shoot them. A traveller, some two or three years since, had taken money near Red Banks, and was waylaid in the above manner by two farmer Rowdies, who shot him and were detected in the act, bearing away the traveller's horse and carriage. One was hanged, and the other nearly whipped to death, and ordered out of the state by the regulators, without time to sell his property. At another time the regulators overtook and shot a murderer, and stuck his head on a pole in Tenessee.

These regulators are self-appointed ministers of justice, to punish or destroy those whom the law cannot touch, such as suspected persons, persons acquitted through false witnesses, or lack of good evidence, but whom public opinion deems guilty. Such individuals rarely benefit by a legal acquittal. Whipping, death, or banishment, is inflicted by these regulators. The law, in itself inefficient, permits or winks at such matters.

Judge Waggoner, who is a notorious hog-stealer, was recently accused, while sitting on the bench, by Major Hooker, the hunter, gouger, whipper, and nose-biter, of stealing many hogs, and being, although a judge, the greatest rogue in the United States. This was the Major's answer to the question *Guilty, or Not Guilty*, on an indictment presented against him. The court laughed, and the Judge raved, and bade Hooker go out and he would fight him. The Major agreed, but said, " Judge, you shall go six miles into the woods, and the longest liver shall come back to tell his tale!" The Judge would not go. The Major was now, in his turn, much enraged by the Judge ordering him into court to pay a fine of ten dollars for some former offence, the present indictment being suffered to drop.

17th.—I was visited this day by General Johnson, a gentlemanly man, and Judge M'Creary, both of this state, the latter of whom is a preacher, and a shrewd, experienced, well-informed man, whom I promised to visit, but regret I did not. He said, " I will keep you well; come and stay a month or so, and I'll find you a good horse to carry you whithersoever you list." His son, a fine rustic youth of gentle manners, presented me segars of his own growth and making, better than the Spanish.

" For the appropriation of land," said the judge, " I prefer the western country ; but for information and education, the eastern states." He complains greatly of the choice of land made here by the British. He wonders they could not better inform themselves, because when they came, there was plenty of good land to be had, if not in bodies, yet in sections, or half-sections. " The soil," said he, " is as thin as a clapboard, or a deer-skin. I would not give one of my quarter-sections for all the neighbourhood of the barrens. They must have been deceived by speculators. But all the English must herd together." He deems Birkbeck's land much better; it is good land. " If the land, settled on by the deceived British, and thus near the Ohio, had been good, it would have been entered long ago. I gave my opinion, as above, to Hornbrook, the father of the settlement, whom it offended. I did not intend it; I was only giving him a friendly opinion, the result of my long experience in this state; but I smoothed him over a little, and said, " the soil would, though thin, deepen and improve."

20th.—This day four acres of woodland, (not thickly wooded) were put out to clear in the following manner, at ten dollars an acre, half in cash, half in store goods. All the wood to be cut down and burnt, save what is wanted for fencing the land with rails in the worm fashion, which rails they are to make and plant, and to root up the small roots, which is called grubbing, so as to render the land fit for the plough; and the grubbings are to be burnt. Thus land at twelve dollars an acre is bought and made fit for the plough.

I visited Mr. Canson and his agreeable wife, both young people, and one of the thirty-nine families, for whom Mr. Fearon was deputed to find an asylum. He brought a respectable sum, 1,500*l.* and now cares not about any business, except that of growing produce enough for his own consumption. He will receive Mr. Potts, a neighbour, as his partner in farming, not caring much about profits. This freedom from care is a fine thing. On his marriage in London, where he was a schoolmaster, he protested against all the absurdities of the marriage ceremony. When he removes from this settlement, it will be into the eastern states.

21*st.*—Met young Delaware Armstrong, the handsome simple son of a hunting Rowdey farmer, who grew only 80 bushels of corn off his whole farm last year.

This young man states his blood to be half Irish, half Scotch from his grandfather. He likes an English girl as well, or better than an American, if, as a wife, she could but make his clothes. But at any rate she must milk; he could not neglect his business to milk. Milking is disgraceful; or, if he agrees to do the milking, she must do all the washing herself, though it is common for him, and his father, and other farmers to assist in the washing. "Many a day," said he, "have I and father washed." I said, if he agreed to milk for his English wife, who certainly would not, he must always do it, or she would comb his hair,

Y

pull his ears, scratch his eyes, or take the hot
poker to him. " 1 can't always milk, and she
would thus act only once; but if we could not
agree, I would go to Squire Russel's and be parted. I would leave her, and marry again in another state. But if she did scratch and poker me,
I would knock her down, and the devil's a hog, if
I would not kill her." Before this, he said his
mode of courtship would be, on the first time of
meeting, to put the question whether she would
have him ; he should see at first sight if she liked
him ; he would not try again if she refused him.
I told him our ladies always refused at first,
though they meant otherwise, and wished him to
come again, and look silly, and say little things.
" That," said he, "cannot be right; she cannot
be an honest woman who so acts." "But," said I,
" you must get your quarter-sections, horse, cows,
pigs, orchard, &c., before you take an English
wife ; she likes all these things." " Aye, but I
would not let her know that I had any thing but
what's on my back ; she should not have me at all;
for all I should want her to bring from her father
would be decent clothes, and a bed and bedding.
You English despise a man, and leave him to
starve in England, if he is poor. We are a hospitable people. If a fellow, sick or poor, comes to us,
we feed, and keep, and treat him as one of the family
as long as he likes; and if he can work a little, give
him half a dollar a day besides, and grumble not

if he makes not above an hour or two a day.
When I court, I shall go at noon and sit up all
night with her, and go once a week."

23rd.—Met a party of Rowdey hunters, who
state that the bear in the month of June is fierce
and chases the hunters, and all who molest it. They
say that it climbs the tallest tree and falls from
the top without injury, rolled up in the form of a
ball.

The mode of tempering clay (which is used as
mortar) is to confine and feed hogs upon it. Corn
is strewed on it daily, and they tread and turn it
all over with great industry.

Cock and hen, or common poultry feathers, are
made to furnish down for beds in the following
manner, fill a barrel with these feathers, and place
it under a shed, bottom upwards, on the earth;
when, in a few months, the common earth-worms
eat up all the stalk or stem of the feather, and leave
the remainder a well manufactured mass of down,
fit for use.

Mr. Maidlow states that Judge Waggoner, at
the celebration of the 4th of June last at Evansville, was chairman, when by some gentlemen present it was proposed that due provision should
be made for the coming day in the form of a sub-
scription. This, without passing to a vote, was
amended by another rising to say, " I motion, that
as some cannot command money they should bring
vegetables, such as beef, mutton, venison, and

pork!" which amendment was put by the judge, and carried in the above form.

A traveller through Illinois to Missouri was, while in bed, twice disturbed in one night by a fellow entering with an axe on his shoulder. The traveller pointed his pistol and told him that if he did not start, he would shoot him; he retired, but in two hours after returned, and was repulsed again by the wakeful traveller. A line of houses on the lonely road to Missouri is, (says Mr. Birkbeck to Mr. Wheeler) in existence, and kept up by these Rowdey robbers and murderers for the reception of travellers, and villains to rob them. These houses are known by extravagant, unprecedented charges, such as 20 dollars a night for man and horse, which must be paid, or the traveller is exposed to robbery, and, perhaps, murder.

24th.—I was indebted to Mr. Phillips for the company of Mr. Wheeler, a pleasant young Englishman from Bristol, with his wife, seeking a refuge here.

At midnight a severe hail-storm preceded a heavy fall of snow. The hail fell thick through the roof and floor on my pillow, and into my mouth, and I licked in the hail-stones as a luxury.

25th.—Partridges, or quails, are here so tame, that, at noon-day, a man may kill them by throwing a stick into the covey; or, by staking a large net, coveys are drawn into it with great ease.

Met a Mr. Gordon, from the Isle of Ely, who

states that the English at, and near Cincinnati,
are much dissatisfied, and wish themselves back
again.   Many have purchased land at thirty to
sixty dollars an acre.

John Pedley bargained to-day with Mr. Ingle for
one year, to receive thirteen dollars a month, and
to have a house, and four acres of cleared land,
for his use, while he continues in his service.

Sunday, 26th. — At noon, this day, Colonel
M'Greary called at Mr. Canson's with Major
Hooker, and others, and demanded whiskey, either
to be given or sold to them.   They were quite
drunk, and armed with rifles from their camp, in
which they had lain all night.   Mr. C. refused them;
when they attempted to force the door, threatening to kick Mrs. C. out, and whip and shoot
Mr. C. who had treated them rather coarsely, and
with great impolicy.   Hooker wished to shake
hands and forget it.   Mr. C. refused.   They then
became more furious.   These Rowdies do not
always mean violence.   They only want whiskey;
and there is little to fear from them, if properly
treated.   Mr. Canson applied to Squire Russel
for a warrant against the Rowdies for the outrage.

Visited the Chatteris Pecks.   Twelve of us sat
down to tea and coffee without milk, sugar, or
butter.   The females and the son think of Chatteris with regret, and would not have come, if
they could have known what they now know.
The father is an exception to this, but he regrets

that so much untruth, in favour of America, should have been said.

27th.—I went one mile and a half, to borrow, from Mrs. Delight Williams, six tumblers, for the use of our coming Christmas party. This step was necessary, or our friends, the Dons of the settlement, must drink out of tin cups or pots. Mrs. Williams is the widow of the whipped Yankee, whose story I have related; she lives in a house without a chimney, having only a hole in the roof to let out the smoke, the fire being made in any part. She was rather unwilling to lend these tumblers, because they came from England, and money could not replace them if broken. She should expect five dollars, though, in England, one dollar bought six.

Mr. Hornbrook observed, this evening, that he did not intend to cultivate much; he did not care much about business.

28th.—A young man, from the state of New York, near White's town, reports that the farmers are nearly all farming their own land, which is, however, deeply mortgaged. They keep no house-servants, and would think it ruin to do so; all work, and the women milk. They give no money in marriage with daughters, but sometimes a little land, or stock, or a bed. They hire but little, and only in harvest. People are comfortable, but have no money to employ him and other mechanics. Gentlemen, one or two, here and there,

have a negro or two in the house. Wheat is one
dollar a bushel.

Mr. Ingle spent 200*l.*, out of 550*l.*, in getting
here. He bought a house at Princeton for 300
dollars, to let. He has seventeen acres the first
year, and will have forty acres the second year,
in cultivation; his stock consists of three horses,
one cow, eight buds, and many hogs, or small pigs.
He bought four hogs, half fat, 600lbs. weight, for
twenty dollars. If he had money, he could buy
bacon at four dollars, and sell it at sixteen dollars;
and sugar, from New Orleans, would pay fifty per
cent.; costing ten cents, and selling at twenty-five
cents: two and a half cents being deducted per lb.
for carriage. The store goods, bought at Washington, which he is selling cheaper than his neighbours, pay twenty-five per cent. profit. He has
640 acres of land entered, for which the first in-
stalment is paid, and the next is to be paid in
twelve months hence. He has entered, for G.
Sutton, 328 acres.

After a sound dressing of aqua-fortis and grease,
and scrubbing and washing in strong hot lie, I
prepared for quitting Indiana, to-morrow, and
wrote the following epistle to T. Drakard, Esq.
in Old England.

*" Once for all, from an inquiring Englishman in
the United States.*

To the Editor of the Stamford News.

*Ingle's Refuge, Banks of Ohio, State
of Indiana, 25th December,* 1819.

Sir,

To my esteemed friends and countrymen,
living within the wide circuit of your paper, and
expecting many long promised epistles, say that
the task is impracticable, and therefore justly abandoned. What they need, *truth,* is always difficult
to attain; and a correct impression of things, made
by weight of unwilling, or long concealed evidence,
examined and cross-examined, will, perhaps, be
found in my journal, calculated to undeceive, dis-
appoint, and, as usual, offend, nearly all those of
whom, and for whom I have written.

It is, I regret to say, too true, that the writings
of emigrants, however respectable, present a partial or unfaithful portraiture; *" shewing things as
they should be, not as they are."* Such authority,
then, is questionable and deceptive. Each individual destined never to return, wants, and tempts,
his friends to follow; the motive, perhaps, is innocent, or venial, but the consequences are evil
and disastrous.

My peregrinations, visits, and visitations, to
many points and intersections of the compass, and

to all ranks of native and adopted citizens, on this continent, are little short of eight thousand miles. Of those visited, and added to the number of my acquaintance, exclusive of excellencies, honourables, generals, majors, captains, judges, and squires, are our two distinguished expatriates, Birkbeck and Flower, with whom I have spent days more interesting than fall to the lot of travellers in common. Of their success or failure, satisfaction or disappointment, I, at present, say nothing. By me, they were met with feelings of respect, and quitted with regret.

My inquiries have been, as promised, directed to one grand object; that of ascertaining, by firstrate means, the past and present condition, and future probable prospects, of British emigrants, and the consequent good or evil of emigration, in the hope of clearly defining and exposing its character, so that it may no longer remain a doubtful or desperate enterprize, a journey in the dark, alternately praised or blamed, but a cause, attaching to it *certain* consequences, which, for some persons to embrace, or shun, is become a visible, tangible, matter of duty.

To my countrymen disposed to emigrate, but who can, by encreased exertion, keep their unequalled comforts and honour unimpaired, I would say, in a voice which should be heard from shore to shore, " *Stay where you are;* for neither America, nor the world, have any thing to offer you in exchange!" But to those of *decreas-ing* means, and *increasing* families, uprooted, wi-thering, and seeking a transplantation *somewhere*, full of hard, dirty-handed industry, and with means sufficient for location here, I would say, "*Haste away;* you have no other refuge from poverty, which, in England, is crime, punishable with neg-lect, and contempt everlasting! But, if you come, come one and all of you, male and female, in your working jackets, with axes, ploughshares, and pruning-hooks in your hands, prepared long to suffer many privations, expecting to be your own servants,—no man's masters; to find liberty and independence, any thing but soft indulgence; and America, a land only of everlasting, well-reward-ed labour. Thus, morally and physically qua-lified, the dark, lonely wilds and interminable forests, which now surround me, shall bow before you, yielding to your cultivation every common good thing, but not satisfaction, which is not of earthly growth! For you, even *you,* escaped from prisons and pauperism, will, sometimes, ' hang your harps on the willow, and weep,' when you remember distant England. Very few emigrants, whatsoever may have been their disgusts and evils in the old country, or their successes in the new, can forget their ' dear native land.' The recollec-tion is, indeed, an impediment to their prosperity; distance only enhances her value, and, as a much-loved, ungrateful mistress, her charms only are remembered and cherished. This seems an indestructible feeling; the incurable mania of the British exile.

I am now living on wild bucks and bears, mixed up, and barbarizing with men almost as wild as they: men, systematically unprincipled, and in whom the moral sense seems to have no existence: this is the lot of all coming here. The climate is not good in any season, and though better here than east of the mountains, is yet unfriendly to industry every where. Summer, amidst breezy shades, champaigne and brandy; and winter, with two down beds, one over and one under you, and a hickory fire continually, are just tolerable! The autumn is pleasant enough, but too generally pestilential.

Having to commence in the morning, a journey of one thousand miles, on horseback, on my way to England, through the Cities of Washington and Charleston, and the worst roads and weather in the universe, the mercury being now three degrees below zero; riding, and not writing, presses on the attention of, Sir,

Your obedient servant,

W. Faux.

30th.—I bade a long, final farewell, to this kind family, and the best woman in Indiana, whom I left in tears. In company with Mr. Ingle, I mounted a young colt, three years old, bough. for me at 100 dollars. My saddle was covered with a bear-skin; myself dressed in three shirts, two waist-coats, three coats, three pair of breeches, three pair of hose, and a seal-cap. I called to warm at Squire Russell's, who makes his own shoes, in a one-room log-hole, where hung a wild turkey on the chimney-piece, for dinner. He could not find a man to serve the warrant, at the suit of Mr. Canson, on Hooker, and means to impanel a Rowdey jury, and try the matter before himself. The cold this day is two below zero.

We reached Princeton at four o'clock; and here I met Mr. R. Birkbeck, a partner with Mr. Peel in the store at Wanborough.

31st.—Intense cold, three below zero, the wind blowing from the North Lakes; the water on my head and face freezes, while I am washing, and much cuts my lips and face. Three suns rose this morning, say the astronomers of Princeton. I spent the evening with Judge Hart. Fifty pounds per cent. profit is made on store goods in the west.

January 1st, 1820.—I left Princeton at ten o'clock, with Mr. Phillips and Mr. Wheeler; and here parted with my good and kind friend Ingle.

I met and spoke, ten miles off, with two hog-jobbing judges, Judge Prince and Judge Daniel, driving home twenty fat hogs, which they had just bought.

I reached, and rested at Petersburgh, consisting of fifteen houses. I passed good farms. Our landlord of this infant town, though having an ostler, was compelled to groom, saddle, unsaddle, and to do all himself. Having fifty dollars owing to him, from a gentleman of Evansville, he arrested him, when he went into the bounds; then he sued one of the bondsmen, who also entered the bounds. The squire is next to be sued, who, it is expected, will do likewise.

Sunday, 2nd.—I rode thirty-one miles this day, and rested at Edmonstone, in a little cold log-hole, out of which I turned an officer's black cat, which jumped from the roof into our faces, while in bed; but she soon found her way in again, through a hole in the roof. The cat liked our fire. We got no coffee nor tea, but cold milk and pork, and corn cake.

3rd.—Travelled all day, through the mud-holes formed by springs running from countless hills, covered with fine timber, to breakfast, at three o'clock, p. m. I supped and slept at Judge Chambers's, a comfortable house, and saw again the judge's mother, of eighty, whose activity and superior horsemanship, I have before mentioned. I smoked a segar with Mrs. Judge, while she smoked her pipe, (the first pipe I have seen here.) She, as well as the old lady, is a quaker. The judge was gone to the metropolitan town of Coridon, being a senator, on duty. The land which I passed over all this day, seemed poor, but full of wild turkeys and bears.

4th.—I reached Miller's to supper, but found no

coffee; cold milk only, as a substitute. The ride hither is interesting, through a fine rolling country. The wolves howled around us all night.

5th.—Passed the Silver Hills, from the summit of which is a fine, extensive prospect of Kentucky, the Ohio, and of Louisville, where we breakfasted. I called with Mr. Flower's letter to Archer, who was out. I received the present of a cow-hide whip, from a lady, and promised to treat the beast kindly, for her sake. Judge Waggoner recently shook hands at a whiskey-shop, with a man coming before him that day, to be tried for murder. He drank his health, and wished him well through.

I rode seven miles with an intelligent old Kentucky planter, having four children, who cultivate his farm, without negroes. He says, "Kentucky is morally and physically ruined. We have been brought up to live without labour: all are demoralized. No man's word or judgment is to be taken for the guidance and government of another. Deception is a trade, and all are rogues. The west has the scum of all the earth. Long ago it was said, when a man left other States, he is gone to hell, or Kentucky. The people are none the better for a free, good government. The oldest first settlers are all gone or ruined. Your colt, sir, of one hundred dollars, is worth only fifteen dollars. At Louisville, as good a horse can be bought at ten dollars, or fifteen dollars. You are therefore cheated."

The Missouri territory boasts the best land in

the country, but is not watered by springs. Wells are, however, dug, abounding in good water, says our hearty landlord, just returned from viewing that country.

The bottom land is the finest in the world. Corn, from sixty to eighty bushels, and wheat, from forty to sixty bushels an acre. The best prairies are full of fine grass, flowers, and weeds, not coarse, benty, sticky grass, which denotes the worst of prairie land. Grass, of a short fine quality, fit for pasture or hay, every where abounds. The country is full of wild honey, some houses having made seven and eight barrels this season, taken out of the trees, which are cut down without killing the bees. These industrious insects do not sting, but are easily hived and made tame. Our landlord likes the Missouri, but not so well as Old Kentucky.

Two grim, gaunt-looking men burst into our room, at two, this morning; and by six, the landlord disturbed us by cow-hiding his negro, threatening to squeeze the life out of him.

6th.—I rode all day through a country of fine plantations, and reached Frankfort to supper, with the legislative body, where I again met my gay fellow-traveller, Mr. Cowen. It was interesting to look down our table, and contemplate the many bright, intelligent faces around me: men who might honour any nation. As strangers, we were

invited by the landlord, (the best I have seen) to
the first rush for a chance at the table's head.

7th.—I travelled this day through a fine country
of rich pasture and tillage, to Lexington City, to
Keen's excellent tavern. I drank wine with Mr.
Lidiard, who is removing eastward, having spent
1,100*l.* in living, and travelling to and fro. Fine
beef at three cents per lb. Fat fowls, one dollar
per dozen. Who would not live in old Kentucky's
first city?

8th.—Being a wet day, I rested all day and this
night. Prairie flies bleed horses nearly to death.
Smoke and fire is a refuge to these distressed animals. The Indian summer smoke reaches to the
Isle of Madeira.

Visited the Athenæum. Viewed some fine horses,
at two hundred dollars each.

Sunday, 9th.—I quitted Lexington, and one of
the best taverns in America, for Paris, Kentucky,
and a good, genteel farm-house, the General Washington, twenty-three miles from the city, belonging
to Mr. Hit, who, though owning between four hundred and five hundred acres of the finest land in
Kentucky, does not think it beneath him to enter-
tain travellers and their horses, on the best fare
and beds in the country. He has been offered
sixty dollars, and could now have forty dollars an
acre, for his land, which averages thirty bushels of
wheat, and sixty bushels of corn per acre, and, in

natural or artificial grass, is the first in the world. Sheep, (fine stores) one dollar per head; beef, fine, three cents per lb., and fowls, one dollar per dozen.

10*th.*—Rode all day in the rain and mud, and through the worst roads in the universe, frequently crossing creeks, belly deep of our horses. Passed the creek at Blue-lick, belly deep, with sulphurous water running from a sulphur spring, once a salt spring. The water stinks like the putrid stagnant water of an English horse-pond, full of animal dung. This is resorted to for health.

Five or six dirkings and stabbings took place, this fall, in Kentucky.

11*th.*—Breakfasted at Washington, (Kentucky) where we parted with Mr. Phillips, and met the Squire, and another gentleman, debating about law. Rested at Maysville, a good house, having chambers, and good beds, with curtains. The steam-boats pass this handsome river town, at the rate of fifteen to twenty miles an hour. To the passenger, the effect is beautiful, every minute presenting new objects of attraction.

12*th.*—Crossed the Ohio in a flat, submitting to Kentuckyan imposition of seventy-five cents a horse, instead of twenty-five, because we were supposed to be Yankees. "We will not," said the boat-man, "take you over, for less than a dollar each. We heard of you, yesterday. The gentleman in the cap (meaning me) looks as though he

z

could afford to pay, and besides, he is so slick
with his tongue. The Yankees are the smartest
of fellows, except the Kentuckyans." Sauciness
and impudence are characteristic of these boat-
men, who wished I would commence a bridge
over the river.

Reached Union town, Ohio, and rested for the
night.

13th.—Breakfasted at Colonel Wood's. A fine
breakfast on beef, pork-steaks, eggs, and coffee,
and plenty for our horses, all for fifty cents each.
Slept at Colonel Peril's, an old Virginian revolutionary soldier, living on 400 acres of fine land,
in a good house, on an eminence, which he has
held two years only. He now wishes to sell all at
ten dollars an acre, less than it cost him, because
he has a family who will all want as much land
each, in the Missouri, at two dollars. He never
had a negro. He knows us to be English from
our dialect. We passed, this day, through two
or three young villages.

14th.—Breakfasted at Bainbridge, where is
good bottom land, at twenty to thirty dollars an
acre, with improvements. The old Virginian complains of want of labourers. A farmer must do
all himself. Received of our landlady a lump of
Ohio wild sugar, of which some families make
from six to ten barrels a-year, sweet and good
enough.

Reached Chilicothé, on the Sciota river, to

sup and rest at the tavern of Mr. Madera, a sensible young man. Here I met Mr. Randolph, a gentleman of Philadelphia, from Missouri and Illinois, who thinks both sickly, and not to be preferred to the east, or other parts of the west. I saw three or four good houses, in the best street, abandoned, and the windows and doors rotting out for want of occupants.

15th.—I rode all day through a fine interesting country, abounding with every good thing, and full of springs and streams. Near Lancaster, I passed a large high ridge of rocks, which nature has clothed in everlasting green, being beautified with the spruce, waving like feathers, on their bleak, barren tops. I reached Lancaster to rest; a handsome county seat, near which land is selling occasionally from sixteen dollars to twenty dollars. A fine farm of 170 acres, 100 being cleared, with all improvements, was sold lately by the sheriff, at sixteen dollars one cent an acre, much less than it cost. Labour is to be had at fifty cents and board, but as the produce is so low, it is thought farming, by hired hands, does not pay. Wheat, fifty cents; corn, $33\frac{1}{2}$ cents; potatoes, 33 cents a bushel; beef, four dollars per cwt.; pork, three dollars; mutton none; sheep being kept only for the wool, and bought in common at 2*s.* 8*d.* per head.

Met Judge and General ——, who states that four millions of acres of land will this year be offered to sale, bordering on the lakes. Why then should people go to the Missouri? It is not healthy near the lakes, on account of stagnant waters, made by sand bars, at the mouth of lake rivers. The regular periodical rising and falling of the lakes is not yet accounted for. There is no sensible diminution, or increase of the lake-waters. A grand canal is to be completed in five years, when boats will travel.

Sunday, 16th.—I left Lancaster at peep of day, travelling through intense cold and icy roads to Somerset, eighteen miles, in five hours, to break-fast. Warmed at an old quarter-section man, a Dutch American, from Pennsylvania. He came here eleven years since, cleared seventy acres, has eight children, likes his land, but says, produce is too low to make it worth raising. People com-fortably settled in the east, on good farms, should stay, unless their children can come and work on the land. He and his young family do all the work. Has a fine stove below, warming the first, and all other floors, by a pipe passing through them.

I slept at a good tavern, the keeper of which is a farmer. All are farmers, and all the best far-mers are tavern-keepers. Farms, therefore, on the road, sell from 50 to 100 per cent more than land lying back, though it is no better in quality, and for mere farming, worth no more. But on the road, a farm and frequented tavern is found to be a very beneficial mode of using land; the produce selling for double and treble what it will bring at market, and also fetching ready money. Labour is not to be commanded, says our landlord.

17th.—Started at peep of day in a snow-storm, which had covered the ground six inches deep. Breakfasted at beautiful Zainsville, a town most delightfully situated amongst the hills. Twelve miles from this town, one Chandler, in boring for salt, hit upon silver; a mine, seven feet thick, 150 feet below the surface. It is very pure ore, and the proprietor has given up two acres of the land to persons who have applied to the legislature to be incorporated. He is to receive one-fifth of the net profits.

18th.—I rode all day through a fine hilly country, full of springs and fountains. The land is more adapted for good pasture than for cultivation. Our landlord, Mr. Gill, states that wheat at fifty cents is too low; but, even at that price, there is no market, nor at any other. In some former years, Orleans was a market, but now it gets supplied from countries more conveniently situated than Ohio, from which it costs one dollar, or one dollar and a quarter per barrel, to send it. Boats carrying from 100 to 500 barrels, sell for only 16 dollars.

From a conversation, with an intelligent High Sheriff of this county, I learn that no common debtor has ever lain in prison longer than five

days.   None need be longer in giving security for
the surrender of all property.

19th.—Reached Wheeling late at night, passing
through a romantic, broken, mountainous country,
with many fine springs and creeks.   Thus I left
Ohio, which, thirty years ago, was a frontier state,
full of Indians, without a white man's house, between Wheeling, Kaskasky, and St. Louis.

20th.—Reached Washington, Pennsylvania, to
sleep, and found our tavern full of thirsty classics,
from the seminary in this town.

21st.—Reached Pittsburgh, through a beautiful
country of hills, fit only for pasture.   I viewed
the fine covered bridges over the two rivers Monongahela and Allegany, which cost 10,000 dollars each.   The hills around the city shut it in,
and make the descent into it frightfully precipitous.   It is most eligibly situated amidst rocks,
or rather hills, of coal, stone, and iron, the coals
lying up to the surface, ready for use.   One of
these hills, or coal banks, has been long on fire,
and resembles a volcano.   Bountiful nature has
done every thing for this rising Birmingham of
America.

We slept at Wheeling, at the good hotel of Major Spriggs, one of General Washington's revolutionary officers, now near 80, a chronicle of years
departed.

22nd.—Bought a fine buffalo robe for five dollars. The buffaloes, when Kentucky was first settled, were shot, by the settlers, merely for their tongues; the carcase and skin being thought worth nothing, were left where the animal fell.

Left Pittsburgh for Greensburgh, travelling through a fine, cultivated, thickly settled country, full of neat, flourishing, and good farms, the occupants of which are said to be rich. Land, *on* the road, is worth from fifteen to thirty dollars; *from* it, five to fifteen dollars per acre. The hills and mountains seem full of coal-mines and stone-quarries, or rather banks of coal and stone ever open gratuitously to all. The people about here are economical and intelligent; qualities characteristic of Pennsylvania.

Sunday, 23d.—We agreed to rest here until the morrow; finding one of our best horses sick; and went to Pittsburgh church.

24th.—My fellow traveller finding his horse getting worse, gave him away for our tavern bill of two days, thus paying 175 dollars for two days board. While this fine animal remained ours, no doctor could be found, but as soon as he became our landlord's, one was discovered, who engaged to cure him in a week. Mr. Wheeler took my horse, and left me to come on in the stage, to meet again at Chambersburgh.

The country round about here is fine, but there is no market, except at Baltimore, at five dollars a barrel for flour. The carriage costs two and half dollars. I saw two young ladies, Dutch farmers' daughters, smoking segars in our tavern, very freely, and made one of their party. Paid twelve dollars for fare to Chambersburgh.

Invited to a sleying party of ten gentlemen, one of whom was the venerable speaker (Brady) of the senate of this state. They were nearly all drunk with apple-toddy, a large bowl of which was handed to every drinker. One gentleman returned with a cracked skull.

25th.—Left this town, at three o'clock in the morning, in the stage, and met again at Bedford, and parted, perhaps, for ever, with my agreeable fellow-traveller, Mr. Wheeler, who passed on to New York. Passed the Laurel-hill, a huge mountain, covered with everlasting green, and a refuge for bears, one of which was recently killed with a pig of 150lbs weight in his mouth.

26th.—Again mounted my horse, passing the lonely Allegany mountains, all day, in a blinding snow-storm, rendering the air as dense as a November fog in London. Previous to its coming on, I found my naked nose in danger. The noses of others were wrapped up in flannel bags, or cots, and masks for the eyes, which are liable to freeze into balls of ice.

Passed several flourishing villages. The people here seem more economical and simple, than in other states. Rested at M'Connell's town, 100 miles from Washington city.

27th.—Crossed the last of the huge Allegany mountains, called the North Mount, nine miles over, and very high. My horse was belly deep in snow.

Breakfasted at Mercersburgh, at the foot of the above mountain, and at the commencement of that fine and richest valley in the eastern states, in which Hagar's town stands, and which extends through Pennsylvania, Maryland, and Virginia, from 100 to 200 miles long, and from 30 to 40 broad. Land here, three years ago, sold at 100 to 120 dollars, although now at a forced sale, 160 acres sold for only 1,600 dollars, with improvements, in Pennsylvania. And if, says my informant, the state makes no law to prevent it, much must come into the market, without money to buy, except at a ruinous depreciation.

Passed Hagar's town, to Boonsburgh, to rest all night, after 37 miles travel.

The old Pennsylvanian farmer, in answer to " How do you do without negroes?" said, " Better than with them. I occupy of my father 80 acres in this valley, and hire all my hands, and sell five loads of flour, while some of the Marylanders and Virginians cannot raise enough to maintain their negroes, who do but little work."

28th.—Breakfasted on the road; passed Middletown, with two fine spires, a good town; and also Frederick town, a noble inland town, and next to Lancaster, in Pennsylvania, and the first

in the United States. It has three beautiful spires.
It is much like a second rate English town, but
not so cleanly; something is dirty, or in ruins. It
stands at the foot of the Blue Ridge, in the finest,
largest vale in the world, running from the eastern
sea to the Gulf of Mexico.

Rested at Windmiller's, a stage-house, thirty
miles from Washington, distinguished only by
infamous, ungenerous, extortion from travellers.
Here I paid 75 cents for tea; 25 cents for a pint
of beer, 9*s.* sterling for a bushel of oats and corn,
and 50 cents for hay for the night. The horse
cost 6*s.* 9*d.* in one night.

29*th.*—Rode from seven till eleven o'clock,
sixteen miles to breakfast, at Montgomery-court-
house, all drenched in rain. I reached Washington
city, at six this evening. Here, for the first time,
I met friend Joseph Lancaster, full of vision-
ary schemes, which are unlikely to produce him
bread.

Sunday, 30*th.*—Went to Congress-hall, and
heard grave senators wrangling about slavery.
Governor Barbour spoke with eloquence.

Friend Lancaster's daily and familiar calls on
the great, and on his Excellency, the President,
about schooling the Indians, and his praises of
the members, are likely to wear out all his former
fame, already much in ruins. I was this day introduced by him to —— Parr, Esq., an English
gentleman of fortune, from Boston, Lincolnshire,

who has just returned from a pedestrian pilgrimage
to Birkbeck and the western country.

February 1st.—I again went to Congress, where
I heard Mr. Randolph's good speech on the Missouri question. This sensible orator continually
refers to English authors and orators, insomuch
that all seemed English. These American statesmen
cannot open their mouths without acknowledging
their British origin and obligations.—I shall here
insert some observations on the constitution and
laws of this country, and on several of the most
distinguished members of Congress, for which I am
indebted to the pen of G. Waterstone, Esq., Con-
gressional Librarian at Washington.

*Observations on the Constitution and Laws of the
United States, with Sketches of some of the most
prominent public Characters.*

Like the Minerva of the ancients, the American
people have sprung, at once, into full and vigorous maturity, without the imbecility of infancy,
or the tedious process of gradual progression.
They possess none of the thoughtless liberality and
inconsiderate confidence of youth; but are, already, distinguished by the cold and cautious
policy of declining life, rendered suspicious by a
long acquaintance with the deceptions and the
vices of the world.

Practitioners of jurisprudence have become almost innumerable, and the great end of all laws, the security and protection of the citizen, is in some degree defeated. It is to the multiplicity and ambiguity of the laws of his age, that Tacitus has ascribed most of the miseries which were then experienced; and this evil will always be felt where they are ambiguous and too numerous. In vain do the Americans urge that their laws have been founded on those of England, the wisdom and excellence of which have been so highly and extravagantly eulogized. The difference, as Mably correctly observes, between the situation of this country and that is prodigious;* the government of one having been formed in an age of refinement and civilization, and that of the other, amidst the darkness and barbarism of feudal ignorance. In most of the states the civil and criminal code is defective; and the latter, like that of Draco, is often written in blood. Why should not each state form a code of laws for itself, and cast off this slavish dependence on Great Britain, whom they pretend so much to dislike?

With a view of explaining more perfectly the nature of this constitution, I will briefly exhibit the points in which the British and American governments differ.

* Observations sur le Gouvernement et les Lois des U. S. p. 20.

In England.	*In America.*
1. The king possesses imperial dignity.	There is no king; the president acts as the chief magistrate of the nation only.
II. This imperial dignity is hereditary and perpetual.	The presidency lasts only four years.
III. The king has the sole power of making war and peace, and of forming treaties with foreign powers.	The president can do neither, without the consent of Congress.
IV. The king alone can levy troops, build fortresses, and equip fleets.	The president has no such power: this is vested in Congress.
V. He is the source of all judicial power, and the head of all the tribunals of the nation.	The executive has only the appointment of judges, with the consent of the senate, and is not connected with the judiciary.
VI. He is the fountain of all honour, office, and privilege; can create peers, and distribute titles and dignities.	The president has no such power. There are no titles, and he can only appoint to office, by and with the consent of the senate.
VII. He is at the head of the national church, and has supreme control over it.	There is no established church.
VIII. He is the superintendent of commerce; regulates the weights and measures, and can alone coin money and give currency to foreign coin.	The president has no such power.
IX. He is the universal proprietor of the kingdom.	The president has nothing to do with the property of the United States.

X. The king's person is sacred and inviolate; he is accountable to no human power, and can do no wrong.

The president is nothing more than an individual, is amenable like all civil officers, and considered as capable of doing wrong as any other citizen.

XI. The British legislature contains a house of lords, 300 nobles, whose seats, honours, and privileges are hereditary.

There are no nobles, and both houses of Congress are elected.

It may, perhaps, be unnecessary to adduce more points of difference to illustrate the nature of the American government. These are amply sufficient to demonstrate the entire democratic tendency of the constitution of the United States, and the error under which those persons labour, who believe that but few differences, and those immaterial and unimportant, exist between these two governments. They have, indeed, in common the Habeas Corpus and the Trial by Jury, the great bulwarks of civil liberty, but in almost every other particular they disagree.

The second branch of this government is the legislature. This consists of a Senate and House of Representatives; the members of the latter are chosen every two years by the people; and those of the former, every six years by the legislatures of the different states. It is in this branch that the American government differs from the republics of ancient and modern times; it is this which

makes it not a pure, but a representative demo-
cracy; and it is this which gives it such a decided
superiority over all the governments in the world.
Experience has demonstrated the impracticability
of assembling a numerous collection of people to
frame laws, and their incompetency, when assembled, for judicious deliberation and prompt and un-
biassed decision. The passions of illiterate and
unthinking men are easily roused into action and
inflamed to madness. Artful and designing dema-
gogues are too apt to take advantage of those im-
becilities of our nature, and to convert them to
the basest purposes

The qualifications of representatives are very
simple. It is only required that they should be
citizens of the United States, and have attained
the age of twenty-five. The moment their period of
service expires, they are again, unless re-elected,
reduced to the rank and condition of citizens. If
they should have acted in opposition to the wishes
and interests of their constituents, while performing
the functions of legislation, the people possess the
remedy and can exercise it without endangering the
peace and harmony of society ; the offending member is dropped, and his place supplied by another,
more worthy of confidence. This consciousness
of responsibility, on the part of the representatives,
operates as a perpetual guarantee to the people,
and protects and secures them in the enjoyment of
their political and civil liberties.

It must be admitted that the Americans have attained the *Ultima Thulé* in representative legislation, and that they enjoy this inestimable blessing to a much greater extent than the people of Great Britain. Of the three distinct and independent branches of that government, one only owes its existence to the free suffrages of the people, and this, from the inequality of representation, the long intervals between the periods of election, and the liability of members, from this circumstance, to be corrupted, is not so important and useful a branch as might otherwise be expected. Imperfect, however, as it is, the people, without it, would indeed be slaves, and the government nothing more than a pure monarchy.

The American walks abroad in the majesty of freedom ; if he be innocent, he shrinks not from the gaze of upstart and insignificant wealth, nor sinks beneath the oppression of his fellow-man. Conscious of his rights and of the security he enjoys, by the liberal institutions of his country, independence beams in his eye, and humanity glows in his heart. Has he done wrong? He knows the limits of his punishment, and the character of his judges. Is he innocent? He feels that no power on earth can crush him. What a condition is this, compared with that of the subjects of almost all the European nations !

As long as it is preserved, the security of the citizen and the union of the states, will be guaran-

teed, and the country thus governed, will become
the home of the free, the retreat of misery, and the
asylum of persecuted humanity. As a written com-
pact, it is a phenomenon in politics, an unprecedented and perfect example of representative de-
mocracy, to which the attention of mankind is now
enthusiastically directed. Most happily and ex-
quisitely organized, the American constitution is,
in truth, at once " a monument of genius, and an
edifice of strength and majesty." The union of its
parts forms its solidity, and the harmony of its
proportions constitutes its beauty. May it always
be preserved inviolate by the gallant and high-
minded people of America, and may they never
forget that its destruction will be the inevitable
death-blow of liberty, and the probable passport
to universal despotism !

The speaker of the House of Representatives is
Mr. Clay, a delegate from Kentucky, and who, not
long ago, acted a conspicuous part, as one of the
American commissioners at Ghent. He is a tall,
thin, and not very muscular man; his gait is stately,
but swinging; and his countenance, while it indicates genius, denotes dissipation. As an orator,
Mr. Clay stands high in the estimation of his
countrymen, but he does not possess much grace-
fulness or elegance of manner ; his eloquence is
impetuous and vehement ; it rolls like a torrent,
but like a torrent which is sometimes irregular,
and occasionally obstructed. Though there is a

want of rapidity and fluency in his elocution, yet he has a great deal of fire and vigour in his expression. When he speaks he is full of animation and earnestness; his face brightens, his eye beams with additional lustre, and his whole figure indicates that he is entirely occupied with the subject on which his eloquence is employed. In action, on which Demosthenes laid such peculiar emphasis, and which was so highly esteemed among the ancients, Mr. Clay is neither very graceful nor very imposing. He does not, in the language of Shakespear, " so suit the word to the action, and the action to the word, as not to o'erstep the modesty of nature." In his gesticulation and attitudes, there is sometimes an uniformity and awkwardness that lessen his merits as an orator, and in some measure destroy the impression and effect his eloquence would otherwise produce. Mr. Clay does not seem to have studied rhetoric as a science, or to have paid much attention to those artificial divisions and rhetorical graces and ornaments on which the orators of antiquity so strongly insist. Indeed, oratory as an art is but little studied in this country. Public speakers here trust almost entirely to the efficacy of their own native powers for success in the different fields of eloquence, and search not for the extrinsic embellishments and facilities of art. It is but rarely they unite the Attic and Rhodian manner, and still more rarely do they devote their attention to the ac-

quisition of those accomplishments which were, in
the refined ages of Greece and Rome, considered
so essential to the completion of an orator.   Mr.
Clay, however, is an eloquent speaker; and notwithstanding the defects I have mentioned, very
seldom fails to please and convince.   His mind
is so organized that he overcomes the difficulties
of abstruse and complicated subjects, apparently
without the toil of investigation or the labour of
profound research. It is rich, and active, and
rapid, grasping at one glance, connections the
most distant, and consequences the most remote,
and breaking down the trammels of error and the
cobwebs of sophistry. When he rises to speak he
always commands attention, and almost always
satisfies the mind on which his eloquence is intended to operate. The warmth and fervor of his
feelings, and the natural impetuosity of his character, which seem to be common to the Ken-
tuckians, often indeed lead him to the adoption
of opinions, which are not, at all times, consis-
tent with the dictates of sound policy. Though
ambitious and persevering, his intentions are good
and his heart is pure; he is propelled by a love
of country, but yet is solicitous of distinction; he
wishes to attain the pinnacle of greatness without
infringing the liberties, or marring the prosperity
of that land of which it seems to be his glory to
be a native.

The prominent traits of Mr. Clay's mind are quickness, penetration, and acuteness; a fertile invention, discriminating judgment, and good memory. His attention does not seem to have been much devoted to literary or scientific pursuits, unconnected with his profession; but fertile in resources, and abounding in expedients, he is seldom at a loss, and if he is not at all times able to amplify and embellish, he but rarely fails to do justice to the subject which has called forth his eloquence. On the most complicated questions, his observations made immediately and on the spur of the occasion, are generally such as would be suggested by long and deep reflection. In short, Mr. Clay has been gifted by nature with great intellectual superiority, which will always give him a decided influence in whatever sphere it may be his destiny to revolve.

Mr. Clay's manners are plain and easy. He has nothing in him of that reserve which checks confidence, and which some politicians assume; his views of mankind are enlarged and liberal; and his conduct as a politician and a statesman has been marked with the same enlarged and liberal policy. As Speaker of the House of Representatives, he presides generally with great dignity, and decides on questions of order, sometimes, indeed, with too much precipitation, but almost always correctly. It is but seldom his decisions are dis-

puted, and when they are, they are not often re-
versed.*

" A Statesman," says Mirabeau, " presents to
the mind the idea of a vast genius improved by experience, capable of embracing the mass of social
interests, and of perceiving how to maintain true
harmony among the individuals of which society
is composed, and an extent of information which
may give substance and union to the different
operations of government."

Mr. Pinkney is between fifty and sixty years of
age; his form is sufficiently elevated and com-
pact to be graceful, and his countenance, though
marked by the lines of dissipation, and rather too
heavy, is not unprepossessing or repulsive. His
eye is rapid in its motion, and beams with the animation of genius; but his lips are too thick, and
his cheeks too fleshy and loose for beauty; there
is too a degree of foppery, and sometimes of
splendor, manifested in the decoration of his person, which is not perfectly reconcileable to our

---

* The House of Representatives, like the House of Commons, is
sometimes very disorderly. Heat and cold have the same effect
upon the feelings of the members; for both make them quit their
seats, and the authority of the speaker often fails to bring them
back. It is in vain to call to order; cold has benumbed their
fingers, or heat has dissolved their solids, and they can neither
think nor act.

ideas of mental superiority, and an appearance of
voluptuousness about him which cannot surely be
a source of pride or of gratification to one whose
mind is so capacious and elegant. It is not improbable, however, that this character is assumed
merely for the purpose of exciting a higher admiration of his powers, by inducing a belief that, without the labour of study or the toil of investigation,
he can attain the object of his wishes and become
eminent, without deigning to resort to that painful
drudgery by which meaner minds and inferior in-
tellects are enabled to arrive at excellence and distinction. At the first glance, you would imagine
Mr. Pinkney was one of those butterflies of fashion,
a dandy, known by their extravagant eccentri-
cities of dress, and peculiarities of manners ; and
no one could believe, from his external appearance, that he was, in the least degree, intellec-
tually superior to his fellow men. But Mr. Pinkney is indeed a wonderful man, and one of those
beings whom the lover of human nature feels a delight in contemplating. His mind is of the very
first order ; quick, expanded, fervid, and powerful. The hearer is at a loss which most to admire, the vigour of his judgment, the fertility of
his invention, the strength of his memory, or the
power of his imagination. Each of these faculties
he possesses in an equal degree of perfection, and
each is displayed in its full maturity, when the

magnitude of the subject on which he descants
renders its operation necessary. This singular
union of the rare and precious gifts of nature, has
received all the strength which education could
afford, and all the polish and splendour which
art could bestow. Under the cloak of dissipation
and voluptuousness his application has been indefatigable, and his studies unintermitted: the oil of
the midnight lamp has been exhausted, and the
labyrinths of knowledge have been explored.

Mr. Pinkney is never unprepared, and never off
his guard. He encounters his subject with a mind
rich in all the gifts of nature, and fraught with all
the resources of art and study. He enters the list
with his antagonist, armed, like the ancient cava-
lier, cap-a-pee; and is alike prepared to wield the
lance, or to handle the sword, as occasion may require. In cases which embrace all the complica-
tions and intricacies of law, where reason seems
to be lost in the chaos of technical perplexity, and
obscurity and darkness assume the dignified character of science, he displays an extent of research,
a range of investigation, a lucidness of reasoning,
and a fervor and brilliancy of thought, that excite our wonder, and elicit our admiration. On
the driest, most abstract, and uninteresting questions of law, when no mind can anticipate such an
occurrence, he occasionally blazes forth in all the
enchanting exuberance of a chastened, but rich

and vivid imagination, and paints in a manner as
classical as it is splendid, and as polished as it
is brilliant. In the higher grades of eloquence,
where the passions and feelings of our nature are
roused to action, or lulled to tranquillity, Mr.
Pinkney is still the great magician, whose power
is resistless, and whose touch is fascination. His
eloquence becomes sublime and impassioned, majestic and overwhelming. In calmer moments,
when these passions are hushed, and more tem-
pered feelings have assumed the place of agitation
and disorder, he weaves around you the fairy
circles of fancy, and calls up the golden palaces
and magnificent scenes of enchantment. You
listen with rapture as he rolls along: his defects
vanish, and you are not conscious of any thing but
what he pleases to infuse. From his tongue, like
that of Nestor, "language more sweet than honey
flows;" and the attention is constantly rivetted by
the successive operation of the different faculties of
the mind. There are no awkward pauses, no he-
sitation for want of words or of arguments: he
moves forward with a pace sometimes majestic,
sometimes graceful, but always captivating and
elegant. His order is lucid, his reasoning logical,
his diction select, magnificent, and appropriate,
and his style, flowing, oratorical, and beautiful.
The most laboured and finished composition could
not be better than that which he seems to utter

spontaneously and without effort. His judgment, invention, memory, and imagination, all conspire to furnish him at once with whatever he may require to enforce, embellish, or illustrate his subject. On the dullest topic he is never dry: and no one leaves him without feeling an admiration of his powers, that borders on enthusiasm. His satire is keen, but delicate, and his wit is scintillating and brilliant. His treasure is exhaustless, possessing the most extensive and varied information. He never feels at a loss; and he ornaments and illustrates every subject he touches. *Nihil quod tetigit, non ornavit.* He is never the same; he uses no common place artifice to excite a momentary thrill of admiration. He is not obliged to patch up and embellish a few ordinary thoughts, or set off a few meagre and uninteresting facts. His resources seem to be as unlimited as those of nature; and fresh powers, and new beauties are exhibited, whenever his eloquence is employed. A singular copiousness and felicity of thought and expression, united to a magnificence of amplification, and a purity and chastity of ornament, give to his eloquence a sort of enchantment which it is difficult to describe.

Mr. Pinkney's mind is in a high degree poetical; it sometimes wantons in the luxuriance of its own creations; but these creations never violate the purity of classical taste and elegance. He

loves to paint when there is no occasion to reason;
and addresses the imagination and passions, when
the judgment has been satisfied and enlightened.
I speak of Mr. Pinkney at present as a forensic
orator. His career was too short to afford an
opportunity of judging of his parliamentary eloquence; and, perhaps, like Curran, he might have
failed in a field in which it was anticipated he
would excel, or, at least, retain his usual pre-eminence. Mr. Pinkney, I think, bears a stronger
resemblance to Burke than to Pitt; but, in some
particulars, he unites the excellences of both. He
has the fancy and erudition of the former, and the
point, rapidity, and elocution of the latter. Compared with his countrymen, he wants the vigour
and striking majesty of Clay, the originality and
ingenuity of Calhoun; but, as a rhetorician, he
surpasses both. In his action, Mr. Pinkney has,
unfortunately, acquired a manner, borrowed, no
doubt, from some illustrious model, which is emi-
nently uncouth and inelegant. It consists in raising one leg on a bench or chair before him, and
in thrusting his right arm in a horizontal line from
his side to its full length in front. This action is
uniform, and never varies or changes in the most
tranquil flow of sentiment, or the grandest burst
of impassioned eloquence. His voice, though not
naturally good, has been disciplined to modula-
tion by art; and, if it is not always musical, it is

never very harsh or offensive. Such is Mr. Pinkney as an orator; as a diplomatist but little can
be said that will add to his reputation. In his
official notes there is too much flippancy, and
too great diffuseness, for beauty or elegance of
composition. It is but seldom that the orator possesses the requisites of the writer; and the fame
which is acquired by the tongue sometimes eva-
porates through the pen. As a writer he is inferior to the present Attorney-General, who unites
the powers of both in a high degree, and thus in
his own person illustrates the position which he
has laid down, as to the universality of genius.

Mr. R. King is a senator from the State of New
York, and was formerly the resident minister at the
court of St. James's. He is now about sixty years
of age, above the middle size, and somewhat inclined to corpulency. His countenance, when serious and thoughtful, possesses a great deal of
austerity and rigour; but at other moments it is
marked with placidity and benevolence. Among
his friends he is facetious and easy; but when
with strangers, reserved and distant; apparently
indisposed to conversation, and inclined to taci-
turnity; but when called out, his colloquial powers
are of no ordinary character, and his conversation
becomes peculiarly instructive, fascinating, and
humourous. Mr. King has read and reflected
much; and though long in public life, his atten-

tion has not been exclusively devoted to the political sciences; for his information on other subjects is equally matured and extensive. His resources are numerous and multiplied, and can easily be called into operation. In his parliamentary addresses he always displays a deep and intimate knowledge of the subject under discussion, and never fails to edify and instruct if he ceases to delight. He has read history to become a statesman, and not for the mere gratification it affords. He applies the experience of ages, which the historical muse exhibits, to the general purposes of government, and thus reduces to practice the mass of knowledge with which his mind is fraught and embellished. As a legislator he is, perhaps, inferior to no man in this country. The faculty of close and accurate observation by which he is distinguished has enabled him to remark and treasure up every fact of political importance, that has occurred since the organization of the American government; and the citizen, as well as the stranger, is often surprised at the minuteness of his historical details, and the facility with which they are applied. With the various subjects immediately connected with politics, he has made himself well acquainted; and such is the strength of his memory, and the extent of his information, that the accuracy of his statements is never disputed. Mr. King, however, is somewhat of an

enthusiast, and his feelings sometimes propel him
to do that which his judgment cannot sanction.
When parties existed in this country, he belonged
to, and was considered to be the leader of what was
denominated the federal phalanx; and he has often,
perhaps, been induced, from the influence of party
feeling, and the violence of party animosity, to
countenance measures that must have wounded
his moral sensibilities; and that now, when reason
is suffered to dictate, cannot but be deeply regretted.   From a rapid survey of his political and parliamentary career, it would appear that the fury of
party has betrayed him into the expression of sentiments, and the support of measures, that were,
in their character, revolting to his feelings; but
whatever he may have been charged with, his intentions, at least, were pure, and his exertions, as
he conceived, calculated for the public good.   He
was indeed *cried down* by a class of emigrants
from the mother country, who have far too great
a sway in the political transactions of the United
States; and though, unquestionably, an ornament
to the nation which has given him birth, his countrymen, averse to him from party considerations,
joined in the cry, and he became a victim, perhaps,
to the duty he owed, and the love he bore to his
country.   Prejudice, however, does not always
continue, and the American people, with that good
sense which forms so prominent a feature of their
character, are beginning justly to appreciate those

virtues and talents, they once so much decried.
Mr. King has a sound and discriminating mind,
a memory uncommonly tenacious, and a judgment, vigorous, prompt, and decisive. He either
wants imagination, or is unwilling to employ a faculty that he conceives only calculated to flatter
and delight. His object is more to convince and
persuade, by the force of reason, than to amuse
the mind by the fantastic embroidery and gaudy
festoonings of fancy. His style of eloquence is
plain, but bold and manly; replete with argument,
and full of intelligence; neither impetuous nor vehement, but flowing and persuasive. His mind,
like that of Fox, is historical; it embraces consequences the most distant with rapidity and ease.
Facts form the basis of his reasoning. Without
these his analysis is defective, and his combinations
and deductions are often incorrect. His logic is
not artificial, but natural: he abandons its formal
divisions, non-essentials, moods, and figures, to
weaker minds, and adheres to the substantials of
natural reason. Of Mr. King's moral character I
can say nothing from my own personal knowledge,
as my acquaintance with him has not been long
and intimate enough to enable me to judge correctly. I have not, however, heard any thing alleged against it calculated to lessen his reputation as an honourable statesman, or a virtuous
member of society. He is wealthy, and has, no
doubt, something of pride and hauteur in his man-

ner, offensive to the spirit of republicanism, and inconsistent with the nature of equality; but, as a father, husband, and friend, I have not yet heard him charged with any dereliction of duty, or any violation of those principles which tend to harmonize society, and to unite man to man by the bonds of affection and virtue. I must now beg permission to despatch the portrait of Mr. King, in order to submit to your inspection an imperfect likeness of another member of the same body. This is not the country to look for the blazonry and trappings of ancestry; merit alone claims and receives distinction; and none but the fool or the simpleton, ever pretends to boast of his ancestry and noble blood, or to offer it as a claim to respect or preferment. The people alone form the tribunal to which every aspirant for fame or honour must submit; and they are too enlightened and too independent to favour insignificance, though surrounded by the splendour of wealth, or to countenance stupidity, though descended from those who were once illustrious and great.

James Barbour is a senator from Virginia, his native state. He was in his youth a deputy sheriff of the county in which he was born, and received an education which was merely intended to fit him for an ordinary station in life. He felt, however, superior to his condition, and stimulated by that love of fame which often characterizes genius, he devoted himself to study, and became a practitioner of the law. He rose rapidly in his profession, and soon acquired both wealth and reputation. Like most of the barristers of this country, he conceived that to be a lawyer was necessarily to be a politician, and he rushed forward into public life to extend his fame and enlarge his sphere of action. From a member of the house of delegates he was elevated to the gubernatorial chair of Virginia, and received the highest honour his native state could confer. Gratified thus far in the wishes he had formed, he became desirous to enter on a more enlarged theatre, where his talents would have a greater field of action, and his eloquence a wider range and better effect, and he accepted the situation of senator of the United States.

Mr. Barbour commenced his career with a speech against the establishment of the national bank, which was then in agitation. He had come fraught with prejudices against this mammoth institution, and in the fervor of the moment gave vent to those prejudices in a manner certainly very eloquent, but not very judicious. When he had soberly weighed the good and evil with which it might be attended, the peculiar condition of his country, and the necessity of adopting some scheme by which the difficulties of government should be obviated, and its financial embarrassment relieved, he very candidly confessed the error into which his feelings had betrayed him, and in a speech, conceived and uttered in the very spirit of true eloquence, supported the measure.

Mr. Barbour is, in person, muscular and vigorous, and rather inclined to corpulency. His eyebrows are thick and bushy, which gives to his countenance a little too much the appearance of ferocity, but this is counterbalanced by a peculiar expression in his visage, that conveys a sentiment of mildness and humanity. He seems to be above forty years of age, and is about five feet ten inches high. Of his mind, the prominent characters are brilliancy and fervor. He has more imagination than judgment, and more splendor than solidity. His memory is not very retentive, because it has never been much employed, except to treasure up poetical images, and to preserve the spangles and tinsel of oratory. As an orator, Mr. Barbour has some great defects. His style is too artificial and verbose, and he seems always more solicitous to shine and dazzle than convince or persuade. He labours after splendid images, and strives to fill the ear more with sound than sense. His sentences are sometimes involved and complicated, replete with *sesquipedalia verba*, and too much charged with " guns, trumpets, blunderbuss, and thunder." He has unfortunately laid down to himself a model, which, with reverence be it spoken, is not the best that could have been adopted. Curran has gone a great way to corrupt the taste of the present age. His powers

2 B

were certainly very extraordinary, but his taste was bad, and by yielding too much to the impulse of a highly poetical imagination, he filled the mind of his hearer with fine paintings indeed, and left it at last glowing, but vacant, delighted, but unconvinced. Too many of the youths of this country seem to be smitten with the model which he has thus given, and which is certainly calculated to fire an ardent mind, and lead it astray from the principles of correct taste and genuine oratory. Mr. Barbour, however, is frequently not only very fluent but very persuasive, and he often employs his full flowing oratorical style to great advantage in setting off his argument, and in decorating and enforcing his reasoning. From the want of opportunities, his reading, like that of most of the politicians of this country, has been confined, and his range of thought, from the absence of that knowledge which books afford, is necessarily limited. He has, indeed, derived advantages from an association with men of literary and scientific attainments, but he has still much to acquire to render him eminent as a statesman. The contributions, which, from this circumstance, he is compelled to levy on his own unaided native resources, have, however, tended to sharpen his intellectual powers, and to give them vivacity and quickness. Mr. Barbour seldom thinks deeply, but he is always rapid; and though his observations are sometimes trite and ordinary, there is almost always something new and gratifying in the manner in which they are uttered. His mind does not appear organized for long continued investigation, and nature has formed him more for a poet than a mathematician. He is rather too anxious to be thought a great orator, and this over-ruling propensity is manifested even in common conversation; when, instead of ease, simplicity, and conciseness, he discovers the formal elocution of the public speaker, on the most unimportant and incidental subjects. In private circles, Mr. Barbour is always very pleasant, and exhibits a politeness, which, flowing from the heart rather than the head, delights all who have the pleasure of his acquaintance, and renders him an acceptable guest, and an agreeable companion.

There is a native openness and benevolence in his character, which excite the love of all who know him, and which powerfully attract the stranger as well as the friend. He seems superior to the grovelling intrigues of party, and always expresses his feelings, in the bold and lofty language of conscious independence and freedom. There is a marked difference between this gentleman and his brother, Mr. Philip P. Barbour, a member of the House of Representatives, in the respective faculties of their mind; the latter is more logical, and also more laborious and indefatigable. He seems to have a peculiar tact for those constitutional and legal questions which

are involved and obscure, and possesses that clear-
ness and vigor of mind necessary to unfold what
is complicated, and illuminate what is dark. He
casts on such subjects so powerful a light, that
we wonder we should ever have doubted, and behold at once the truth, stripped of all its obscurity. The former seldom attempts an analysis of
such questions. He reasons, but his reasoning
is not so much that of a mathematician, as of
an advocate who labours to surprise by his novelty, and to fascinate by the ingenuity of his
deductions, and the ease and beauty of his elocution. He has more genius than his brother, but
less judgment ; more refinement and elegance, but
less vigor and energy. It appears to me that there
is a vast deal of what may be denominated *law mind*
in this country, which will ultimately reach a point
of excellence that must astonish the world. The
fondness for the profession of the law, at present,
is wonderful ; almost every man, whatever be his
means of support, or grade in society, if he have
children, endeavours to make one of them, at least,
a disciple of Coke, or a " fomentor of village vexation," and you cannot enter a court-house, without being astonished at the number of young men,
who are either studying or practising the law.
This, however, is not a matter of surprise, when
we consider the facility with which this profession
leads to preferment and distinction, and the ease
with which it seems to be acquired. Amidst such

a mass of *law mind*, therefore, as exists here, excellence must hereafter be attained, if it has not
now reached its climax; and the Cokes, the Mans-
fields, and Ellenboroughs of England are, or will
soon be, equalled in this country. The future destinies of this republic cannot be fully anticipated;
the march of mind is progressive and resistless,
and intellectual pre-eminence must be attained
where so many inducements are offered to effect,
and so few impediments exist to prevent it. Mind
is often regulated by the circumstance in which it
is placed, and fashioned by the objects by which
it is surrounded. This country is, therefore, peculiarly favorable for the expansion and develop-
ment of the intellectual powers. Physical, as well
as moral causes, operate to this end. The eye of
an American is perpetually presented with an
outline of wonderful magnificence and grandeur;
every work of nature is here on a vast and expansive scale; the mountains, and lakes, and rivers,
and forests, appear in a wild sublimity of grandeur,
which renders the mountains, lakes, and rivers of
Europe, mere pigmies in comparison. The political
and religious freedom, too, which is here experienced, removes all shackles, and gives an elasti-
city, a loftiness, and an impetus to the mind that
cannot but propel it to greatness. Thus operated
upon by moral and physical causes, what must be
the ultimate destiny of the people of this country,
and the range and expansion of intellect which they

will possess? Devoted as they are for the most
part to studies and professions, which have a tendency to enlarge and liberalize the mind, and influenced by the causes I have mentioned, it would
be worse than stupidity to suppose they could
long remain an inferior people, or possibly avoid
reaching that point of elevation of which mankind
are capable. The *law mind* of this country has
now attained a high degree of splendor, and is in
rapid progress to still greater excellence. There
are many men, in this country, though so much
calumniated by British writers, who would shed
a lustre on the bench of that nation, and not suffer
by a comparison with some of the brightest lumi-
naries of English jurisprudence.

Before I quit this body of American worthies,
I must introduce to your acquaintance, as suc-
cinctly as possible, another member of the senate,
who, though not so conspicuous as the two former,
in the walks of public life, is not inferior to any
in this country, in all that constitutes and dignifies
the patriot and the statesman. Mr. Roberts is
from Pennsylvania. He is a plain farmer, and
was, once, I understand, a mechanic. Though
he cannot boast of a liberal education, yet nature
has given him a mind, which, with early improvement, would have made him prominent in any
sphere in life. It is vigorous and powerful in no
ordinary degree, and the sophistry of art, and the
dexterity of learning, are often foiled and defeated

by the unaided and spontaneous efforts of his native good sense. But he has that which is of more sterling advantage, both to himself and his country,—immoveable political and moral integrity. It is gratifying, in this age of corruption and voluptuousness, to contemplate men like Aristides, Fabricius, and Cato. They exhibit to us the true dignity of man, and hold out examples that we must feel delighted to imitate. They show us to what pitch of excellence man is capable of attaining, and rescue the exalted condition of human nature from that odium and disgrace which profligacy and corruption have heaped upon it. No spectacle can be more sublime or more elevating than he, who, in the hour of public danger and trial, and amidst the allurements and fascinations of vice, stands like a rock in the ocean, placid and immoveable, and endures the dangers that surround, and braves the storms and tempests that beat upon him, with undeviating firmness, for the safety of his country and the glory of his God! The mind rests upon such a character as the eye upon a spot of fertility, amidst deserts of sand, and we rise from the blood-stained page of history, and the corruptions of the living world, with a heart filled with love, admiration, and reverence, by the contemplation of the few who have shed an imperishable lustre on the exalted character of man. This description is not exaggerated; it is drawn from nature and truth, and fancy has nothing to do with the picture. But I must now hasten to finish my portraits of American characters.

Mr. Bagot,* the English minister to this government, appears to be about thirty-five years of age. He is tall, elegant, and rather graceful in his person, with a countenance open and ingenuous, an English complexion, and eyes mild though dark. He has ingratiated himself with the Americans, by the real or affected simplicity of his manners, and by assimilating himself to their usages and customs. He has thrown aside the reserve and hauteur of the English character, as not at all suited to the meridian of this country, and attends to all with equal courtesy and politeness. I can say nothing of the powers of his mind, but they do not appear to be more than ordinary. It has always seemed to me very strange policy on the part of the British cabinet, to appoint ministers to this country of inferior capacity and inconsiderable reputation, while the Americans send to our court only their most prominent and leading men, who have distinguished themselves by their ability and their eloquence.

The French minister, M. Hyde de Neuville, is a " fat, portly gentleman," with a broad chest, big head, and short neck, which he seems almost incapable of turning *ad libitum.* He is full of

---

* Now Sir Charles Bagot.

Bourbon importance and French vivacity; has
petits soupers every Saturday evening during the
winter, and spends his summer at the springs, or
his country residence, in extolling the virtues of his
beloved Louis *le desiré*.   I do not think that M.
Neuville, though an amiable, and, I understand,
a benevolent man, has that kind of talent which
would qualify him for the station he holds, or that,
in the event of any difficulty arising between this
country and France, he could counteract the intrigues of diplomatic ingenuity, or benefit his
nation, by inducing the American cabinet, though
I believe he is highly esteemed, to adopt any
measure not manifestly advantageous to the United
States.   He has been many years a resident of
this country, and was driven from France by the
persecutions of Buonaparte.   He is said to have
evinced for his exiled countrymen much feeling
and interest, and to have given them, while strangers and unknown in a foreign land, all the aid
he could afford.   His acts of benevolence certainly redound to the credit of his heart, and I
should be sorry to say any thing that would dis-
parage the qualities of his head.   He is too much
occupied with his own, or other people's concerns,
to attend to the little or the complicated intrigues
of courts, and though he resides here as a representative, yet he now represents a cypher.

4th.—To tea with J. C. Wright, Esq., to meet a young man, Mr. Dawson, who is giving up a school here to go as " Teacher to the Cherokee nation of Indians." Much enthusiasm takes him there; little will be needed to bring him back again. Since my return, Washington has been visited by some very distant and interesting tribes of Indians, with the following account of whom I have been favoured by a friend residing there.

Some account of the Indians who visited all the Chief Cities in the Eastern States, and made a long stay in Washington in the winter of 1821.

These Indians were the chiefs and half-chiefs of tribes from the most western part of this continent with which we are at all acquainted, and came under the guidance of Major O'Fallan from the Counsel Bluffs. All of them are men of large stature, very muscular, having fine open countenances, with the real noble Roman nose, dignified in their manners, and peaceful and quiet in their habits. There was no instance of drunkenness among them during their stay here. The circumstances which led to their visit were singular. A missionary, who had been amongst them a few years back, on renewing his visit recently, found an old chief, with whom he was acquainted, degraded from his rank, and another appointed in his place. This led to inquiries after the cause, which proved to be that this chief having, during a considerable

absence from his tribe, visited some of the cities of
the whites, carried back such a report of their
houses, ships, numbers, wealth, and power, that
they disbelieved his account, and degraded him as
a man unworthy of being longer their chief. They
inquired of their missionaries, who confirmed the
statement, and they met in council with other
tribes, and resolved that a deputation should, in
company with the representative of the great father, " see if things were so," and if they were, the
chief should be reinstated. They have returned,
saying the " half was not told them." Red Jacket
(of whom you have heard) used to say, that " the
great spirit was too great a being to overlook red
men; that he listened to the talk of red men as well
as to the talk of white men ;" but these natives of
the forest thought the great spirit favoured white
men more than red. An anecdote is related of
one of the chiefs (a Pawnee) which is a well au-
thenticated fact, and recorded by Dr. Morse in his
account of visits to the western regions. The
tribe of the Pawnees had taken a woman prisoner
from a neighbouring tribe with whom they were
at war, and, as was their custom, they made every
preparation to offer her a sacrifice to the great
spirit. Every thing was prepared, the wood, the
green withes, and the fire, and the victim, when
this chief suddenly flew and seized her, carried
her under his arm to a neighbouring thicket, where

he had prepared horses for her and himself, and riding away at speed, he, after three days' travelling through the woods, returned her in safety to her tribe and friends. This event was considered by the Pawnee tribe as an interference of the great spirit in her favour, and on the return of the chief no questions were asked him on that subject, nor has a woman been offered a sacrifice by that tribe since. As a compliment justly due to his gallant exploit, a number of ladies in this city had a medal made, and presented to him in due form, in the presence of all the Indians; on one side of which was represented the preparation for the sacrifice, and on the reverse the chief running off with a woman under his arm, and two horses stationed at a short distance, surmounted by this inscription, " To the bravest of the Braves," (the Pawnees are also called the Braves). These Indians excited so much interest from their dignified personal appearance, and from their peaceful manner, that they received a great number of rich presents, sufficient to fill six large boxes in New York, Philadelphia, Baltimore, and Washington; these were forwarded before they left us. Their portraits, which are gone with them, were taken in oil by Mr. King in their native costume, buffalo skins, with the hair inside, turned back at the neck and breast, which looked very handsome, like fur collars. Eight, however, the chiefs and

the squaw, Mr. King copied and keeps himself.
He received 400 dollars from *Uncle Sam* for it.
There was a notice in the papers that the Indians
would dance and display their feats in front of
the President's house on a certain day, which
they did to at least 6,000 persons. They shewed
their manner of sitting in council, their dances,
their war whoop, with the noises, gesticulations, &c.
of the centinels on the sight of an approaching
enemy. They were in a state of perfect nudity,
except a piece of red flannel round the waist and
passing between the legs. They afterwards performed at the house of his Excellency M. Hyde
de Neuville. They were painted horribly, and
exhibited the operation of scalping and tomahawk-
ing in fine style.

The Otta half-chief and his squaw have taken
tea with and frequently visited us. She was a
very good natured, mild woman, and he shewed
great readiness in acquiring our language, being
inquisitive, retaining any thing that he was once
informed, and imitating admirably the tones of
every word. He spent the evening with us before
they finally left the city. I took himself and squaw
into Dr. Barber's room, and opened gently the
skeleton case. He looked slyly in, and the wife
wanted to look, but he put himself in an attitude
to represent a dead person, and said, " *no good,
no good.*" She still wanted to see, but he would

not let her. Three others came afterwards wanting to see it, who, when I opened it, raised themselves up in a dignified manner and said, " *very good*," one of them taking hold of the hand said, " how you do."* The Otta half-chief and squaw afterwards saw it together and were very well pleased. Our children were all full of play with them, and the squaw nursed the younger ones. Margaret wanted to go with them. The calumet of peace (the tomahawk pipe and their own sumach tobacco) frequently went round, and they expressed a wish to see us again.

I have recorded much of the vocabulary of these Indians, and would transcribe it, but have not room. They count by tens as we do, for instance, *noah*, two; *taurny*, three; *crabraugh*, ten; *crabraugh no ah*, twenty; *crabraugh taurny*, thirty, &c. They hold polygamy as honourable; one wife, *no good*, three, *good*; four, *very good*. In their talks with the residents they shew no wish to adopt our habits.

5th.—To dine with Dr. Dawes at his poor, worn out farm, of which he is already tired. The Doctor seems one of the best Englishmen I have met in America.

Sunday, 6th.—Dr. Rice preaching this day in Congress-hall before the senate, and representa-

---

* I made them understand the man was hung for murder, which seemed to please them.

tives, called the assembly, polite, just, respected, respectable, and deemed it unnecessary to mention sin and human depravity.

American husbands abound in outward politeness and respect to their wives; and gentlemen, in general, are excessively attentive to the fair sex, rising and leaving their seats, even at church, to accommodate the late coming ladies. I gave much offence, on a recent occasion, by my want of gallantry in this particular. The meanest white woman is here addressed by the title of *Madam*.

It may also be mentioned, as a proof of superior civilization and refinement in manners, that a stranger cannot, in this country, enter and join a party or social circle, without being publicly presented by name, and exchanging names and hearty shakes of the hand with all present. Should he, however, happen to enter and take his seat without submitting to this indispensable ceremony, he must remain dumb and unnoticed, as an intruder, or as a person whose character renders him unfit for introduction, and for the acquaintance of any. But, on the other hand, when properly presented, he is instantly at home; and ever after, at any distance of time and place, acknowledged as entitled to the goodwill and friendship of all who thus met him. Friendships are thus formed and propagated, and the boundaries of society in the new world extended. It would hence be impracticable for me to be half an hour, as has happened to me in England, unknowingly present with a person of distinction; and many unpleasant mistakes and misunderstandings are thus obviated.

8th.—I heard Mr. Speaker Clay deliver a splendid speech of four hours long on the Missouri slave-question. His voice fills the house; his action is good and generally graceful.

I met this evening Mr. Smith, a young gentleman from Lincolnshire, the fellow-traveller of Mr. Parr, who walked through the west, and admired all! He is not determined on continuing here; he has a good farm in England. He and Mr. Parr have been introduced by a member of Congress to the President, who sat half an hour familiarly talking with them, in a plain, domestic, business-like manner.

Sunday, 13*th.*—From the Speaker's chair in Congress-hall, I heard the young, learned, and reverend professor Everett, of Cambridge University, (aged 29) preach most eloquently to the President and legislature of this great empire. His voice, bewitchingly melodious, yet manly, filled the house, and made every word tell, and every ear hear. " *Time is short,*" was the subject. His discourse was full of high praise of this land, it being, he said, (in my own language) " the only resting place for liberty, who, when driven hence, must ascend in her pure, white robes to heaven. No more new continents will be discovered for her reception, and therefore let this nation wisely keep her asylum here." He then spoke very warmly against kings, lords, and priests, and what he called the toleration of man and his rights. "In England they tolerate liberty; and what is liberty there? A shadow! But here, a substance! There her existence is only nominal. She is mocked by her very name." Independent of its moral instruction, this sermon was a fine specimen of oratory, and greatly interested the members of both houses, who very cordially shook the preacher by the hand. Though not forgetting slavery in his discourse, the professor seemed too partial to it.

This gentleman had just returned from his tour through Europe, where he visited Sir Walter Scott, and other distinguished literati, and preached in London.

I met Mr. Lowndes, the Howard of America, at Mr. Elliott's. He says, that "Harmony presents much moral philosophy in practice. Flesh and blood had hard work at first, but now they have but few desires to gratify. Nature seems under the hatches, and they have little to wish, want, or fear. But theirs is a stagnant life."

14th.—Read Mr. John Wright's pamphlet on Slavery, in which he uses my name in reference to my negro letter, and shows very clearly the evil effects of slavery on the character of this country, and proves the unalterable nature of the black man's right to liberty, and its benefits.

2 c

Mr. Rufus King, a member for New York, a gentlemanly English-like speaker, confines himself to business, and to the grand fundamental principles of every political question, and the consequences likely to result from extending slavery over the continent. " In time," says he, " you will enable the blacks to enslave the whites. Why, therefore, should we of the free, be compelled to suffer with you of the slave states ?"

18*th*.—I supped with Dr. Alison, Chaplain to Congress, a gentleman possessing every variety of knowledge. He is the friend and correspondent of the Ex-presidents Jefferson and Adams, and of the present President, and is known all over the country by his virtues. This gentleman was visited by the black Baron de Vasey, and his friend, from St. Domingo, who supped with him. On their quitting the room, the doctor's black servant set up a laugh, which might be heard by the baron, and all, far and near. " What's the matter, Sam?" said the doctor. " Why, two niggers sat and took tea with my massa, at the same table! !" In Virginia, the doctor complained of his fears of being murdered by the negroes, one hundred of whom were owned by his hostess. She cried and said, " she hoped the Lord would protect her." " Oh, no! you must not look to the Lord for it; it is not there." She said she would free them, if she could find any body to support them. Freed slaves must quit the states, or be sold by it for slaves again!

Colonel Taylor has a black uncle, a slave, for his body guard, and most owners are related to their black cattle. A gentleman of Washington, too kind-hearted to whip his house-negroes himself, leaves it to his wife, a fashionable, beautiful female, holding, and going to levees, yet able to cow-hide her negroes, whose screams, under the lash, scare Mrs. Little and family. A cow-hide is no uncommon appendage of ladies here !

Squire Simpson, an old emigrant from England, whom I have before mentioned as living near this city, once acted as a magistrate. Two parties came before him for justice, but neither of them seemed disposed to submit to his worship's decision. At last, the most choleric of the two thus addressed Mr. Simpson: " Well! I don't see, I guess, that we can settle it fairly. So here's at you. I'll fight you, Squire!" Both then went out, magistrate and man, and decided the affair by battle. Simpson was victor.

24th.—Revisited Dr. Dawes, who is full of improving his farm by a summer fallow, and turning it into grass without a crop. He has paid only half the cash for his farm of 500 acres, because the title cannot be completed. Any one, says ex-squire Simpson, would take it off his hands. The doctor deems, as does Sir H. Davy, that plaster of Paris is the natural food of plants ; and it is found, more or less, in almost all soils, particularly in England,

where manuring with plaster is found to have but
little effect, but in this country vice versâ.

Visited Mr. Plant, who holds 400 acres, all
cleared and enclosed long ago, and exhausted too,
at 100 dollars a year rent, offered for sale at fifteen dollars an acre, poor but useful, light, sandy
loam, shining bright with silvery mica. He ma-
nages this estate without a capital, by the labour
of himself, one slave and a boy; he hires none.
He has sold Bradford's Rest, a large estate, costing
seven dollars, for 20 dollars per acre; well sold!

26th.—I rode this day to the bench of his worship, Squire Arden, with Doctor Dawes, who was
served with a warrant for a small debt for goods.
I carried the Doctor's diploma, to prove him a
physician, authorized to write prescriptions. The
plaintiff is a neighbour of the Doctor's, who had
prescribed for his family, and therefore pleaded a
set off. The plaintiff then swore he would prove
that the Doctor never was sent for nor came! The
Doctor considers almost all here as unprincipled
and conspiring against his cash. Quitting the diploma for the plough, he gave up a practice of 400
or 500 pounds a year, at Wisbeach, in England,
where he was highly esteemed. His humanity
here to poor exiles, distinguishes him as a patriot
and a philanthropist, and entitles him to the applause and goodwill of all mankind. In September last, poor John Steed, the English Quaker,

was fed, housed, physicked, and restored to health, by this benevolent man. Steed was returning to England; but how to return without money? There was money for him! My warm-hearted friend, *the watchman*, a dear friend of the Rev. I. Leathes, brother-in-law of the late Bishop of Bristol, put into Steed's empty hands a purse, amply sufficient for his land and sea expenses. This was noble! It is well to praise man for his humanity to a suffering brother, but better to ascribe all the glory to his Maker, who gives all, and blesses him with a generous heart, and who has promised that " He who deviseth liberal things, by liberal things shall he stand."

March 11th. — I revisited the astronomical, mathematical, and philosophical Mr. W. Elliott, dining on vegetables only. He states that it is impossible for a sensible, honest Englishman to prefer this country to his own; and in knowing that he has quitted England for ever, he experiences a feeling indescribably painful. To return no more is a word next to death. Although he would not, at present, desire to live in England, yet he would not advise any to quit who can live in it. The soil here is unfit for man, and for an Englishman particularly. Both mind and body barbarize and degenerate. He feels, at first, sanguine, but soon after he begins to judge and compare, and finds that though the government allured him here, yet that all is not gold that glitters. He becomes weak and emaciated, and drinks into the habits of the country, where he is no longer the man he thought himself at first. The labouring poor here are far behind, and more miserable than the poor, bold peasantry of England. No man needs labour here long, if he would work and not drink excessively ; but he drinks and is undone.

Sunday, 12*th*.—Met J. C. Wright, Esq. who has consumed, in segars, for his own use, since he began smoking, twenty years since, 700 barrels of flour, at the present price. One hundred and fifty dollars annually is the cost of his smoking.

14*th*.—The Hon. T. Law brought, it is said, half a million sterling with him to this country, but has lost two-thirds of it. He married the niece of General Washington, the most beautiful lady in Virginia; and, at her uncle's request, Mr. Law settled on her, in case they parted, 15,000 dollars a year. The event, which seemed thus to be anticipated, soon after occurred; for Mr. Law visiting England soon after his marriage and leaving his wife in America, she, during his absence, eloped with a young dashing officer in the army. Mr. Law returned only to part with one of the most accomplished ladies in the land. She still lives in high style, and her house is the resort of the most fashionable parties.

By Mr. Sutton, an English gentleman from Cheshire, I was this day introduced to an hour's conversation with Mr. John Law, a lawyer of this

city, son of Mr. Thomas Law, above mentioned.
This gentleman occupies a mean office, but seems
very sprightly and acute, and though a plain republican, has much of the blood of the Laws in
him. He states that he is in expectation of receiving 80,000*l.* from Sir Wm. T———, for purchasing land in the wilds of the west, which is to
increase in value greatly in twenty years. For
the same purpose, he also wishes to get 150,000*l.*
from English capitalists, who never mean to emigrate, but who only wish to invest money in western lands. There are several millions of acres,
some of which, military lands in Illinois, are selling at 37 and 50 cents an acre. Mr. Law pro-
poses to be the agent, and live on the spot, to
settle poor emigrants from England on it, by finding them implements and money for commencing,
which is to be repaid in produce. They are to
live seven years rent free. He would make it his
business to interest emigrant societies in favor of
this speculation, by which the posterity of such
cap talists are to benefit greatly. Mr. Law is to
receive only one quarter of the cash for his own
trouble, that is, *only* about 37,000*l.* or 40,000*l.*
out of the 150,000*l.*

Birkbeck (he says) must be rich in ten years;
which ten years of life he admits a man must sacrifice before he can arrive at *comforts.* Ohio, he
states, has proved what time can do for a wilderness; and I say, that time has proved that those

enriching improvements made by hands, and not by time, can be bought any where for less than they cost in that State, or almost in any other, Kentucky perhaps excepted.

A reflection or two on litigation!—The Judges here have not legal knowledge enough for their station; and of course not weight of character or dignity sufficient to fill it well. Counsellor Jones and Key, of "*star-spangled banner*" fame, influence, and carry their honours almost as they please. The bar is greater than the bench!

Litigation frequently arises here from the imaginary independence which one man has, or fancies he has of others, to show which, on the least slip, a suit is the certain result. It is bad for the people that law is cheap, as it keeps them constantly in strife with their neighbours, and annihilates that sociability of feeling which so strongly characterizes the English. From the constant litigation amongst the people of this country arise that antisocial apathy, and want of those kindly feelings of the heart, which shew themselves on all occasions, in the conduct and character of the people of the old country. There were more suits for debt in Washington county court, in a late term, (seventeen hundred), than, perhaps, in all England! Further comments are left to the reader.

Judge Parsons, while only an advocate, completely upset the evidence against a prisoner who employed him, and that in the following manner.

The witnesses against the prisoner were all sailors.
The advocate disguised himself as a sailor, and offered to bet them twenty dollars that the accused
would not be hanged. They readily accepted the
bet, and when they came, over anxious to give evidence and convict the prisoner at the bar, the
learned counsel confounded them with their bet,
the court spurned their evidence, and the prisoner,
though guilty, escaped by this learned stratagem.
At another time, in an important case of law,
where several parties were interested, he was requested to plead, he said, " No! I cannot see my
way clear." They then offered him 1,000 dollars
for his neutrality, which he took. The other side
then came. " No," said he, as before. " Well then,"
said they, " if you will not plead for us, we will
give you 1,000 dollars not to be against us;" which
sum he took, and left other advocates to talk.

Edward C———, late in the service of Joseph
Vipan, Esq. of Sutton, is here elevated from the
smock frock and stable, to the dress and society
of a merchant in this city. So great is the change
and so mighty the tyranny of custom, that what
were his duties last year, would now be a disgrace to him. Another would-be gentleman, in
the same store, was requested to assist his em-
ployer, a polished Englishman, in rolling a barrel
of dried fish out of the cellar into a cart only.
" Oh! no, that is *nigger*'s work," said he; and
then left a good situation within two hours after

he came to it. Such are the blessed effects of slavery!

15th.—Met Mr. Cooper, an English gentleman, at Washington, who has grown comfortably rich, and has recently bought about 300 acres of land, near this city, so exhausted, that no produce can be had from it for years to come. The system pursued here, if carried into the old country, would soon lay it waste, more effectually than either fire or sword. It is more difficult to raise a hundred dollars here than a hundred pounds in England. Individuals, who are rich in land, are generally without cash, and have their personalty seized, and sold for small debts, of a few dollars only.

16th.—All kinds of fruit and vegetables (potatoes excepted) are now remarkably scarce, and enormously dear, insomuch that they are not seen, during the winter and spring, except on the tables of the rich. In summer they cost as much or more than butcher's meat; yet thousands of acres, all round the city, close to water and manure, are to be had by any body free of rent! In summer the potatoes were one dollar fifty cents per bushel; now, eastern potatoes sell for 50 to 75 cents, and nothing but potatoes come on the tables of the bulk of the people. What is the cause? " Why," says one, " the gardeners get rich and ride in their single horse chaise, because the business is so profitable. They have no competition.

Whatever they send to market is sold only at their own price. It is their will to have 150 per cent. above the value of an article. Rather than under-sell, they would carry home their vegetables for the cattle and pigs!" So that the will of the gar-dener governs the price, although the means of op-position are open to all! The poor farmer comes to market with his flour, but *his* will is to take just what is offered him. He is not in the gar-dener's secret of insisting and willing to have ten dollars a barrel for flour, when worth only four dollars and a half. But what is the real cause of the high price of vegetables in this soil and climate of Washington? Why, no body gardens; not even the rich; because they can buy cheaper than they can raise them; and it is found that none but the poor, humble man, who has no capital, will at-tempt it, because others can employ capital more profitably than in gardening. It is therefore an undoubted fact, that the soil and climate do not admit of vegetables being raised, at a much lower price than that at which they are actually sold. In summer, continual watering and shading are absolutely necessary, and the soil is poor into the bargain; insomuch that the seed rises so weak, that the sun would burn up the plants instantly, without great attention to shade and watering, and if this were not so, myriads of grasshoppers would eat all in spite of any measures for their preservation.

Winter Prices of Garden-stuff.

Winter greens, lightly put in, one quarter dollar per peck.

Spinach, the same.

Cabbages, of about four oz. weight, yellow and bad, having been buried from the frost, four cents each.

Potatoes, seventy-five cents a bushel.

Carrots, bad and scabby, 9*d.* sterling, to one quarter dollar per peck.

23rd.—Commodore Stephen Decatur fell this day in a duel, having killed five men in the same way himself. He swore shamefully at the doctors while dying, because they could not extract the fatal ball from his bowels. He is called by the National Intelligencer, " One of the bright stars of Columbia, set for ever!" And the country is summoned to mourn for him. The president and the heads of departments, with military and naval officers and citizens, walked in procession at his funeral. The laws of heaven and earth, on this subject, are here quite insulted, by common consent. A lady of this district, hearing that her husband was gone to fight a duel, fifty miles off, sent an express, charging that he should be brought home a corpse rather than disgraced. It is a rule here always to take skilful aim, and if one party chooses to reserve his fire, he may go up and shoot the other, if he does not beg for his life.

A gentleman once would not beg it, but the other said, " If your life is not worth asking for, it is not worth taking!"   And so fired in the air.

A sinecure, or something in the nature of one, is held by Joseph Paulding, Esq. of Washington. The holder of this situation is enjoined to write in defence of the American character and government, and at the same time to vilify the British. Mr. Colvin, late editor of the National Register, in a critique on Lancaster's lectures, says, " that we (meaning America) are more virtuous than the people of other nations, I cannot believe. It is sufficient that we are equal, not worse." That there is no great superiority of moral worth on the part of America, the following anecdote will prove.   A gentleman seduced the sister of his own wife, and then, to hide her disgrace, disguised his wife in the uniform of a lieutenant of the United States' navy, and married the young woman to her.   The lieutenant of course went to sea immediately, and, poor man! was never heard of more.   The nuptials were celebrated by candlelight, and all the gay company, except the priest, were parties to this ingenious trick!

24*th*.—Flour now is only four dollars and a half a barrel, five bushels to a barrel.   After hauling, grinding, and the cost of the empty barrel, are deducted, it is seen that the farmer only receives two dollars fifty cents, for five bushels of fine wheat. Under such circumstances, where is profit?

Sunday, 26th.—I left this city and old friends, to return, perhaps, no more. At Baltimore, on my way to Philadelphia, I met Joseph Lancaster, teaching a few small children.

28th.—Again at Philadelphia, where British and French goods are selling at 200 per cent. under cost. So great is the distress for money, that the regular merchants are sending their stock to auction. I visited Mr. Potter, an English merchant, who has been established here ever since the peace of 1786. He is now rich, but loves England still. He was intimately known to the Duke of Kent. He says that corruption is rising into an English sense, even here; and adding the state and general taxes together, they make a sum little short of English taxation.

29th.—Six hundred prisoners are this day in a state of mutiny, endeavouring to escape by violence from the Philadelphia state prison. One is shot, and three or four are wounded. The mail robbers now in custody killed the driver of the mail, but they have restored all the money, and pray that they may not be hanged.

31st.—I parted with my old friend C., who promised to meet me again at Baltimore, in June. I reached Newcastle, Delaware State, and visited its old Golgotha, on a bluff, near the river Delaware, which washes the feet of the dead, exposes a great part of the coffin, and bleaches the skulls and bones of men. Numbers of horses tread on the graves and break in the coffins, for here is nothing to protect these bones from insult.

I saw the effect of the late freezing rain on the trees, which, over an extent of country six times as large as England, has despoiled trees as completely as if chain shot had passed through them all. The trees and shrubs are laden with ice, a weight ten times that of their own boughs. Many farmers lost nearly all their timber and orchards: a ship also was upset by the great weight of the ice adhering to her rigging.

April 7th.—I met with a black gentleman who has bought a beautiful farm, with a good house and improvements, six miles only from Philadelphia, at twenty dollars an acre, at a sheriff's sale. A law has just passed to prevent any more selling under two thirds of a fair valuation. A quaker whom I met, states that Joseph Lancaster injured himself by going to Baltimore. He did not succeed at Philadelphia, the only place where he could have succeeded, because he expected more attention from the inhabitants of that city, than they ever pay to any body.

Visited Peale's museum, a fine collection of native and foreign curiosities, amongst the former of which are the skeleton of a mammoth, 15 feet high, and horns, nine feet long, under the belly of which, as under an arch, a horse might run full gallop. I crept down the throat of an alligator.

Several bodies of Indian chiefs are here to be seen dried, standing in their usual dresses and attitudes, as well as some Otaheiteans. There is also the skin from the thighs and legs of an Indian, tanned by Indians into fine leather, for thus they use their prisoners taken in battle. I saw the manuscript of a poem of Major André, penned about two months before his execution. Here is also a fine collection of national portraits.

8th.—I this day set sail from Philadelphia for Charleston, in the *General Wade Hampton*, and anchored at Newcastle in the evening.

Sunday, 9th.—I rode with the captain, in his chariot, to the beautiful seat and extensive powder mills of E. S. Dupont, Esq. on the Brandywine creek, a fine stream full of natural falls and working many mills. We went for 500 barrels of gunpowder. Mr. Dupont, who pressingly invited us to dine, seems a liberal, intelligent Frenchman, of large capital, which sometimes vanishes by explosion, together with the doors and windows of his elegant mansion.

During this twenty miles ride, I observed that thorn-quicks are here generally used as an outward fence, but they are badly managed. I saw, on poor wet lands, large heaps of lime, formed by oyster shells and stone, gathered and burnt for manure; in this way cheaply turning stone into bread.

We received this evening three or four physicians and other passengers, to the number of ten or twelve, on board the *Wade Hampton*.

10th.—At three, this morning, we got under weigh, sailing into the bay of Delaware, and by noon arrived opposite to the light-house.

A family (says the Captain) from England, of the name of Clementson, recently bought an estate from a scoundrel old countryman, of the name of Watson, living at Philadelphia, at a price 200 or 300 per cent. above its value. They paid in part about 6,000 dollars, but being unable to pay the remainder, and having no written contract, he induced them to quit and go to the wilds of Ohio, where, he said, he had much land at a low price, which they should have for the money in his hand. He also kindly gave them a letter of credit to his agent there; but on arriving, they found that he was unknown, and had no land, nor agent; and they were in consequence forced to sell their horses, waggon, and every necessary, to enable them, in unspeakable distress, to return to prosecute this scoundrel; but they had no evidence against him, and therefore found it advisable to lose their money without going to law. Having about 2,000 dollars left, they purchased and stocked a farm bigger and better than the one for which they were to have paid 8,000, or 10,000 dollars. Old countrymen, it is said, make the most complete rascals.

11th.—Now at sea, exposed to head-winds and sea-sickness. An Irish gentleman from Missouri, states that last week, on board the steam-boat, he met a black archbishop and several of his inferior clergy. This most reverend father in God was endeavouring to prove that Adam, Noah, and all the prophets, and patriarchs, down to Jesus Christ, were blacks, and that a small portion of mankind, and that the worst, are whites, of whom Cain is the progenitor.

The Missouri Irishman has invested 50,000 dollars in land, the advantages of which he deems to be yet dubious and prospective. He says that society is bad, and that the people are unprincipled.

12th.—Two old German gentlemen, heroes of the revolution, now on board, state, that they knew the accomplished and unfortunate Major André. When taken by three militiamen, in the capacity of a British spy, endeavouring to seduce West Point, he was dressed as a citizen, instead of appearing in the regimentals of his country, which greatly aggravated his crime. He offered his gold watch and purse, and large pecuniary compensation to be released, but the three men were firm. Both sides regretted, and were unwilling to witness, his death; and the American government would have saved him, if the British would have given up the traitor Arnold. He was fairly tried, and no precipitation evinced towards him. He thanked the court martial for their gentlemanly treatment, submitted to his fate as a matter of course, and with great firmness prepared himself for it. Three months elapsed between his apprehension and execution. But when he was led out to execution, and saw the gallows instead of the rifle, his firmness, in some measure, forsook him. He was elegantly dressed in his martial suit, and on giving his cravat to his waiting man, only said, "I die for the honour of my king and country;" at which General Green, the American commander, who presided in the midst of the surrounding army on this sad occasion, shook his head, and observed, "No! you die for your cowardice, and like a coward!"

General Washington signed the order for his death with great reluctance; but the army were dissatisfied and demanded the sacrifice. The example was necessary and salutary, and in its general consequence calculated to deter men of honour and respectability from such military meanness. Major André hoped to the last to escape. The tories, of whom he was one, had previously murdered some of the citizens and officers, in consequence of which, General Washington determined on retaliation by executing one of the British tory officers then prisoners, and ordered them to draw lots to decide who of their number must die. The lot fell on Sir Charles Asgill, who, but for the French influence of Count Vergennes, and a most pathetic letter from the baronet's mother, would have been executed.

The quakers, about New Jersey, were very loyal, and locked up the wells, and withheld all aid from the rebels!

Sunday, 16*th*.—Fine breeze; sailing by Cape Hatteras, to pass which occupied two days. A strong current of air is here found, rushing to the land, accompanied generally with tempestuous gales. A gap in the Allegany mountains, towards which this current rushes, is said to be the cause.

18*th*.—At three o'clock this afternoon I landed at Charleston, and found all nature in its most beautiful attire. Peas and all kinds of summer vegetables are in great abundance, and the peach-trees full of fruit. I found that my much respected friend, N. Russell, Esq. had died only a fortnight since; he kindly inquired after me in his extremity.

19*th*.—I met my old shipmate, Mr. Moses Wood. I bought twilled nankeen trowsers for two dollars and a half. London clothes of good and best kinds sell at lower prices than in London.

Rattlesnakes.—A gentleman informed me that he once shot a rattlesnake as thick as his thigh, and 26 years old. Its age is known by its tail. It was near biting him. A neighbour of his left his house in search of his swine, and being long away, his wife went after him and found him dead, killed by a snake, to the bite of which the poor deceased had applied a quid of tobacco, then found sticking on the wound. Another neighbour, who was also bitten, managed to walk home before he fell, but died very soon after his arrival. I was told, also, of a planter, out with his dogs and rifle after a deer, which he shot; but on bringing it to lay on the horse, a rattlesnake struck the man, who was found dead, with the buck and horse, which being tied to a tree was starved to death. Thus they were all found dead in one heap together.

20th.—By conversation with Judge King, to whom I presented J. Wright's pamphlet on slavery, I learn that my negro case was much noticed, and its exposure much and indignantly regretted. Mr. King says that it was indiscreet in me to report facts, except from the evidence of my own senses! If no testimony is to be received, but that of our own eyes, half the evidence in the world is worthless. The Carolinians love slavery, and hate all who hate it. Both Mr. King and Mr. Duncan state, that in consequence of that affair, and of my being a foreigner, a stranger in a strange land, if Gregory should prosecute me for an advertisement, which I found it necessary, in pursuing the claims on the Rugeley property, to publish against him, I should meet with but little mercy from the jury!

21st.—Called on Patrick Duncan, Esq., and took a final leave of him and his beautiful gardens, in which are oranges, figs, sugar-canes, pomegranates, and the prairie grass of South America, soft as silk in hand.

Received, from my warm-hearted Irish friend, Mr. Wood, 50 dollars, an unsolicited loan, although he knows me not. Here is faith, greater than almost any I have yet found in America.

The slave-owners, in this state, must maintain all their helpless and infirm slaves, or kill them privately. They cannot become chargeable to the parish, or state. O humanity, where art thou!!! As a punishment for the lassitude of age, or the idleness of youth, a *nigger* is stripped naked, well flogged, then dressed all over with treacle (or molasses) and hung up by his heels on a tree, in a swamp full of flies and mosquitoes, which lick up the sweets, and sting and bleed him dreadfully into the bargain. He is then a living lump of inflammation. What ingenious torture this! how refined! how honourable to the taste and ingenuity of a nation, the freest of the free, and who boast of superabundant polish and civilization!

When with my cousin, Major Rugely, in May last, I was presented with a beautiful black female qaby, that could just creep, and which was given and intended to be sent as a keepsake to my lady in England; but I, not being qualified for a nurse at sea, nor indeed by land, declined this well-intended gift. The Major then possessed a poor negro, who wishing to die, was constantly detected in the act of eating dirt or lumps of earth, a habit which procured for him a cow-hiding daily! I might have had him, and branded him with my own brand, **F.** As cattle it is necessary so to distinguish one herd from another, and if they stray, or are stolen, to advertise their persons, correctly describing the mark, or brand, which is deeply burnt in, and never obliterated, unless it is cut out!

Sunday, 23rd.—I bade, this morning, a willing and final farewell to Charleston city, and to all its bugs, mosquitoes, negroes, and alligators, and a race of people, many of whom seem not much better than they. I left behind me some copies of J. Wright's pamphlet on slavery, for his Excellency, Governor Geddiss, the Attorney-General Haines, the editor of the Courier, Mr. Thomas Mitchel, and Mr. Judge King, the latter of whom promised to keep his a profound secret. The press seems here to be more enslaved than under the most despotic government. At night I found myself at sea, 60 miles from Charleston, in the *President* for New York. Fare, 25 dollars.

25th.—I saw two young alligators emigrating to the north. Mr. Morse (the son of the geographer, Dr. Morse) states, that at Newhaven University, Connecticut, an education of four years costs only 1,000 dollars, board included. The same gentleman states, that in Connecticut, republicanism and equality exist in greater purity than in any other part of the union. The farmers and people generally live economically and comfortably, surrounded with a cheap abundance of all the

necessaries of life, but they keep no domestic servants, male or female. They are their own servants. As to negroes, scarcely one is to be seen
in a day's travel. The people generally are so
well educated in this state, that almost any man is
qualified for a schoolmaster in any of the sister
states. Dr. Paley's moral philosophy is a text
book in their college.

26th.—A young gentleman on board, from the
state of Albania, says that Mobile, out of 600, lost
530 inhabitants, by the yellow fever last summer.
In winter the population is from 2 to 3,000.

A dashing English gentleman travelling through
this state with a white servant behind him, rode
up to a one-room log-tavern, and begged the landlord to let him have a room to himself, which
was agreed to. In a few minutes up came two
native travellers, *equals*, who entered without ceremony, when the Englishman began to curse the
landlord for permitting the intrusion. He replied,
that he meant that the gentleman should have the
room to himself until other travellers came up.

29th.—At ten this morning we made Sandyhook
light-house. The scenery here, all the way up to
the city of New York, is delightful. Perhaps the
views presented by this city and neighbourhood
are unequalled, both as it respects the beauties of
nature and the works of art. I landed at six
o'clock, and was introduced by Messrs. Morse

and Co. to the boarding-house of Mrs. Mudge,
where I met Mr. Dwight, a brother of the late
eminent Dr. Dwight, now editor of the New York
Advertiser. In person this gentleman is said to
be much like the Doctor.

Sunday, 30*th.*—I accompanied Mr. Morse to
the splendid Presbyterian church of the eloquent
Dr. Romaine, whose prayers are the most appropriate in manner and matter, and whose sermons
are, with the exception of Dr. Storton's, superior
to any I have heard in America. On this day,
the appearance of this large city is most orderly
and christian-like. This laudable change is attributed to Sunday-schools. All places of worship are thronged. How unlike Washington city!
Mr. Morse states that not only in New York, but
in all the east, a religious feeling generally pervades the people.

May 1*st.*—Passed over to Brooklyn, a beautiful
gay-looking village of great extent in Long Island,
in quest of my old friend, and western fellow-traveller, Mr. Wheeler, whom I found three miles
from the city, living on a hired farm of about
30 acres of arable land, and six in wood, or rather
cedar, on which is a beautiful house, to which I
was warmly welcomed. It consists of six small
rooms and piazzas on each side, standing in an
orchard fronting the public road, which, for four
miles, is like one continued suburban village all
the way from New York. The farm cost, two

years ago, without a house or well, 3,500 dollars, and the house and well have since cost 1,500 dollars. Mr. Wheeler has hired this situation for one year only, at the rent of 300 dollars, ten dollars an acre, all poor and long-exhausted land, insomuch that nothing can be raised without manure, which is bought at one dollar per load, and hauled three miles.

Land, thus situated, is expected to be devoted to raising garden-stuff, or to be occupied only as a suburban retreat. The mere farmer can scarcely live out of it, even if it is his own, unless he cultivates vegetables, and carries his milk to New York market, in small quantities, daily. Those who have lived here eighteen or twenty years, on their own estates, have only just lived, saved nothing, and been always their own servants. Mr. Wheeler has three servants, one black man, and a white man and woman. The white man has 100 dollars a-year; the black man ten dollars a month; and the woman five dollars and board, working from sun-rise to dark.

2nd.—After dinner, Mr. Wheeler ordered out of the plough into the carriage, his pair of handsome greys, when, with the ladies, we drove to the beautiful neighbouring villages of New-town, Flushing, and Jamaica, at the latter of which is the residence of Rufus King, Esq. a house by no means equal to those of the village squires of England, yet very inviting. Perhaps no where, except in the vicinity of London and Bath, can a more attractive ride of twenty miles be found; the whole distance of road, from the city, seeming one continued village of new and handsome farm-houses, with either a pleasure-garden, or green pasture, or orchard, or all of them, in front of almost every house, any of which may be bought, boards being up, *For sale, this farm.* But the land, in every direction, is poor, except where superior and expensive management exists. Every thing is sold from the land, which might make manure and enrich it. The leaves of the forest trees now begin to appear. The spring is late, yet the orchards are in full bloom. The frost was severe last night.

Though he has three servants, Mr. Wheeler cleans his own boots. They would not absolutely refuse, but would do it reluctantly, and feel disgraced by the act; yet two of them are good servants. A black servant lately broke into the cellar and dairy of Mr. Wheeler, and stole all the bread and meat he could find; he is now in gaol. About two years ago, in great rage with his sister, he caught hold of her head, and endeavoured, with an axe, to chop it off; but not being able to get it into a fit place, he chopped off two of her fingers, and nailed them on the door-post!

4th.—I made, on horseback, the tour of York island, about ten miles in length and two in breadth. On one side is the noble Hudson, or great North River, and on the other, the East River and Hell-gate, and the beautiful villages of Manhattan, Haarlem, and Greenwich. All the road from the city, to the extremity of, and beyond the isle, is adorned, on both sides, with the country-seats and pleasure-grounds of rich citizens, who, like those of London, every morning and evening drive to and fro in great numbers. Perhaps no city in the world is so happily situated as that of New York, standing on this island, with the sea to the south, and these majestic rivers, from one to two miles wide, on the north and east, the banks of which are very high, and for twelve miles crowned with mansions. The houses on the roads, thus leading through the isle to the city, have each from five to ten acres of green pasture, park, or pleasure-gardens, which renders them more rural, though less splendid than those on the roads leading to London. I saw from fifty to 100 convicts, heavily ironed, forming a new road for the state; receiving no pay nor shirts, but only food.

I visited the supreme court, and inquired for Messrs. Emmett and Sampson, but saw not these celebrated refugees.

Mr. Wheeler agreed to purchase a quantity of seed corn from a neighbour, which was to be picked, but much of it came in rotten. Mr. W. returned the rotten part, and begged other corn to be sent in its place. "No, send it all back! that is not the way we deal here;" in great rage, said the farmer, " you may do so in your country, but not here."

5th.—Bade farewell to Long Island, and my much esteemed friends, the Wheelers, who pressingly invited me to stay longer. I renewed my invitation to them to come and make Whitehall their home, when, if ever, they came to England.

I quitted New York, for Philadelphia, at ten this morning. Left a history of Somersham for Mr. F. Morse of Newhaven.

Visited one of the packet-ships, the *James Monroe*, the most complete I ever saw; every birth is a state room. For forty guineas, it transports passengers to Liverpool in high style. All are fed luxuriously.

6th.—At six this morning, I left Borden town, on the Delaware, where are the ruins of Joseph Bonaparte's house, about to be rebuilt. Sixty men are employed already. The estate, consisting of 300 acres, all poor land, is now laying out into pleasure-grounds, and park, enclosed with a fine fence; it cost five dollars an acre. Joseph came hither, it is said, with ten millions of dollars from the Spanish treasury.

I reached the City of Philadelphia at ten this morning, just twenty-eight days after I left it, since which time I have travelled about 2,000 miles, and rested eleven days.

Sunday, 7th.—I was present when Dr. Storton,

administered the rites of baptism to a large, re-spectable auditory. He is rather pompous in his expressions, and theatrical in his action and man-ner, but certainly an accomplished man. He has said that there is no preaching talent in America but what is imported; but this is not strictly true.

11*th.*—I wrote the following epistle to Mr. Day, of St. Ives in England, by the ship Electra, bound for London.

May 11, 1820.

Dear Sir,

At this distance of time and place, the recollec-tion of you is replete with all that is good and pleasant to me; while the esteem and regard al-ways professed and felt for you demand, at least, one epistle, as a thing not to be withheld. I should have had great pleasure in your correspondence, but it is now too late, as my duties here are nearly at an end, and by the time this reaches you, I hope, under the guidance of gracious Providence, that the compass, in unison with my heart, will be pointing me towards my own home and country.

The inducements to emigrate, and the facilities of living here, are neither so great nor so many as I wished and expected to find them. The majority of those who come are without capital and above useful labour. Of this kind seem our friends —— and ——, and others known to you, whose

prospects are, I assure you, very shadowy.   I
speak impartially.   Even capital, I believe, can
any where be better employed than here.   And
as to labourers, there are more than can be paid.
By the late report of this city, it appeared that
11,000 within these walls were in a state of unemployed pauperism; while in one prison only, are
600 thieves and incendiaries, the natural fruits of
increasing poverty.

Land, generally, is not property in this country,
because there is infinitely more than enough; the
surplus, therefore, is worth nothing.   What is already in cultivation by hired hands lessens, rather
than augments capital.   Even potatoes, you know,
cannot be produced from one without the agency
of the other.   The markets are all glutted, and
without foreign demand, a surplus produce is not
desirable, because unsaleable and perishable.

All travel is restless labour, and " vanity and
vexation of spirit."   Its idea was once so supremely
fascinating to my ambition, that I thought I never
could have enough of it, and therefore wished myself doomed to perpetual travel.   I have my wish,
or something like it, and it disappoints me.   During the last two years I have indeed found " no
continuing city;" it is well if I seek and find one
to come.   I fly from city to city, town to town,
state to state, climate to climate, with the velocity
of an eagle.   I have frigid and tropical latitudes,
polar cold and equinoxial heat, wintry desolation,

and the summery foliage of oranges and myrtles,
all in the short space of one week, or less. For
although this beautiful city of William Penn lies in
an Egyptian latitude, winter has not long been
over; whereas, it never enters the city of Charleston, which I have just quitted, where

> " Blossoms and fruits and flowers together rise,
> " And all the year in rich confusion lies."

The male youth generally of this, and other cities,
are remarkably polished, sprightly and prepossessing in their exterior; being of tall and slender
figures, and looking free and easy, without any thing
like levity, for each puts on all the airs, manners,
actions, and opinions of men, with his *first* pair of
breeches, and expects to be treated as a man. But
ringlets decorate the faces of both sexes, and in
other respects all are *dandies*, male and female! The
young ladies generally are not so handsome as the
males; though beauty is not rare amongst them.
A woman's duties and province are, I think, yet
undiscovered. She is here, that is, in all sections
south of the Delaware, a little divinity, to whom all
must bend, give place, and pay idle homage; her
tyranny is great, her influence unbounded. Her
lover, or husband, is outwardly her slave; but as
a wife, mother, mistress, she must yield to my unequalled countrywomen. Youth here, is of very
short duration; all soon look old; and " all the
days of the years of this vain life," soon come to
an end. Religion and duty seem but little under-

stood, and less regarded, except it be to ascertain how little of either may suffice. Paley's Moral Philosophy has been, perhaps, the text book of the educated, who are very numerous; yet but few live and die practical philosophers. Death is little dreaded, and often, as in duelling, voluntarily embraced. Two selfish gods, Pleasure and Gain, enslave the Americans. The scum of all the earth is drifted here.

As this is sent off about a month after my other, and will be my last letter from this country, I wish you to inform my good father, if living, and Mr. Ingle, of my present refuge and intended return, and assure them of my best regards. My beloved child, who, by-the-bye, would become in part your ward if I returned no more, is very precious in my sight; if you knew her, I should beg you to pronounce a father's blessing on her; but it comes to her on every western breeze. When I can, I will teach her to esteem you, and perpetuate, what is of little value, the disinterested and most sincere friendship of,

Dear Sir,

Your very obedient servant,

W. FAUX.

11*th.*—Mistrust and suspicion are general in Philadelphia. The cause is a general disregard or violation of duty. Two respectable quakers would not suffer Mr. ——— to owe them eight

2 E

dollars for a day or two, though guaranteed by
a second person, who, for any thing they knew,
might be respectable; so they took out two pieces
of muslin to reduce the bill down to the funds in
hand. "Notwithstanding this guarantee," said the
quaker, "I will, and must have the thing squared."
The representative of my friend then paid the complete balance. I was present at this transaction,
and feeling both pained and amused, began to speculate upon it, and to consider what could have
generated this general suspicion and mistrust. It
is the common effect of some cause. What cause?
A general violation or neglect of some prominent
duties, not directly guarded by the laws, but the
observance of which is indispensable to the good
of mankind every where. Culpability of this kind,
in not doing to others as we would be done by,
does more injury to the world than all the thieves
and incendiaries put together; because the consequence in one case is particular, in the other illi-
mitable. If I act justly towards my neighbour,
I confer both temporal and moral good on him and
on myself. But it stops not here: he learns thereby its value, and acts in like manner towards
others. On the other hand, if I violate my duty to
him, he retaliates not only on me, but on others
indiscriminately. He thinks he has been honest
and unsuspicious long enough, and bids adieu to
rectitude perhaps for ever.

Last month at Dover, Delaware, Squire Loper

received sentence of the court for passing forged
notes, knowing them to be so. He had been in
the commission of the peace for 20 years, and received the forged notes from a gang convicted before him of forgery. The notes had remained in
his hands ever since. A month ago, he desired a
gentleman, a neighbour of his, going to Philadelphia, to buy him some iron, and meeting the gentleman privately, gave him fifty dollars, saying,
" Take notice it is a fifty dollar note," and gave
it him carefully wrapped in paper. When the
bearer offered it for the iron, it was discovered to
be one of the forged notes, well known to have
been offered by the gang before. The gentleman
had some difficulty in keeping out of the Peniten-
tiary. On proving himself not to be a party con-
cerned, and promising to bring the Squire forward,
he was released. The Squire admitted the note
to be forged, and said, he gave it to his friend only
in joke. On being arrested, he was treated with
great liberality, but he acted haughtily and foolishly. On his trial he would not employ counsel
nor set up any defence; but in a cool, sneering manner said, that the note was given in joke, and the
court might do as they would. He was sentenced
to six months' solitary confinement, thirty-nine
lashes, and never after to pass out of his own house
in Dover without the letter F, a foot long in scarlet,
on his back, on pain of another six months' confinement and thirty-nine stripes. But so great was the

public pity for him, in court and out, both with judge and jury, that the prison door was left open for him in hope that he would escape and quit the neighbourhood for ever. He did escape into the town only, and came back to prison voluntarily, where no such chance is again to be afforded him.

At night, I went to the black church, where the black minister shewed much uncultivated talent. After sermon they began singing merrily, and continued, without stopping, one hour, till they became exhausted and breathless. "Oh! come to Zion, come!" "Hallelujah, &c." And then, "O won't you have my lovely bleeding *Jasus,*" a thousand times repeated in full thundering chorus to the tune of "Fol de rol." While all the time they were clapping hands, shouting, and jumping, and exclaiming, "Ah Lord! Good Lord! Give me *Jasus!* Amen." At half-past ten this meeting broke up. For an hour it seemed like Bedlam let loose. At the close, one female said, striking the breasts of two male friends, "We had a happy time of it."

16*th.*—Last week, in the state of Delaware, the High Sheriff had to perform the duty of Jack Ketch, and hang his own nephew, for the murder of his *own* mother, the Sheriff's sister. The youth killed her by striking her with a club on the temple. In the same neighbourhood and the same week another youth was sent to gaol for poisoning his uncle, a rich old gentleman, who being childless, had taken this nephew into the house and made him heir to all; but the youth being impatient, went to a druggist for arsenic, which he said was to kill the rats, that every night kept his uncle from sleeping. He mixed a portion of it in a glass of apple-toddy and gave it to his uncle, but in so large a portion that it began to operate immediately, on which the old man said, " You have given me something to do me harm." The youth denied it, but the old man grew rapidly sick, and feeling conscious that he was poisoned and should die before the distant doctor could arrive, got out the will in favor of the ungrateful youth, and having burnt it, died soon after.

A short time ago, the friends of a murderer, under sentence of death in Pennsylvania, conspired together to procure a pardon from the governor, by threats and intimidation. Their plan was to get the governor into a room to themselves, and offer him his own life for the pardon of Lieut. Smith, the convict, who had cohabited with Mrs. Carson, and taken possession of her house and property, during the absence of her husband, Captain Carson. When the latter returned and demanded his wife and property, he was shot dead in his own house by Smith. The governor had intelligence of the plot, and seized the conspirators before they could carry their design into effect.

Sunday, 21*st.*—Quitted Philadelphia on board the steam-boat. A gentleman, Lieut. Skinner, of the United States' navy, from the Franklin, just arrived from Gibraltar, states, that the sailors, on settling accounts, will go on shore and spend the balance, several hundred dollars, in two or three days, lavishing from 100 to 200 dollars a-day, until all is gone, when they re-enter. So indifferent are they to the use and value of money, that they give it away, and suffer any person to plunder them with impunity. The cause, says he, of this indifference and insane extravagance, is to be found in the strictness and severity of the discipline on board, where money is of no use to them.

Duelling.—So frequent were these meetings between the officers of the United States' navy and the British garrison, that the governor felt compelled to interfere, in order to save life, as one or two duels occurred daily, originating in the most foolish disputes.

The parties met always on neutral ground. For any expression uttered by one officer of the 64th regiment, a general challenge was sent by the officers of the United States' navy to the regiment; wishing to include *all*, from the colonel down to the lowest in rank.

Two young Americans, of New York, at Gibraltar, met in consequence of a trifling dispute. The offending party fired three times without hitting, while his opponent fired every time into the air, begging the other to apologize, saying, " If I take aim I shall kill you, but I can stand all your fires." This concession was, however, obstinately refused; on which the seconds stepped forward, and said to the party who had acted so generously, "Sir, you must fire in your own defence!" Both again charged, and Sands, the aggressor, fell dead. The survivor was arrested, but acquitted with honour; being told by his commander, that if he had not acted thus, he would not have received him again into the service. The young reprobate who fell, was a classical scholar, of fine person and great mental accomplishments, but ripe for perdition.

22nd.—I reached Washington city, now emptied of the wise men, and which, after quitting Philadelphia, seems mean, indeed, both morally and physically. All the bogs and swamps, in and round the city, are now full of melody, from the big, bellowing bull frog, down to the little singing mosquito, while rotting carcases and other nuisances perfume the warm southern breezes.

A lady, in a letter to Mr. Thomas Coote, from New Orleans, states that eighteen American pirates under sentence of death, in the jail of that city, have many friends, much intent upon effecting a rescue, by forcing the prison, which is strongly guarded by the military. Every night almost, for this purpose, mobs collect around it and set fire to distant parts of the city, in order to divert the attention of the guards from the prison. Great alarm exists on the subject, and it is feared, that on the day of execution, much blood will be spilt.

One hundred sail of slave-ships, full of slaves, appeared in sight, one day, during this spring, off the coast of Africa. Several of them were fast-sailing vessels, built, owned, and manned by the free citizens of free America. Some were chased and taken by the British and American navy. This trade is now considered to be more extensive than ever.

30th.—Visited Mr. Dunn, who states that the small red squirrel, of this state, is seen to seize and castrate, in a moment, the large grey squirrel, which greatly fears and always flies at the sight of the former.

Are those English people who are now in America happier than they were in England? I will take upon me to pronounce, that in the aggregate, they are not. Happiness and misery are not mere localities, for as God is the father of all, the earth is his and the fulness thereof; his frowns or smiles are not bounded by geographical lines and latitudes; the whole human family are under his wise economy. God's management is always right. He can blast prosperity and bless disappointment, so as to keep it from disappointing; thus bringing good out of evil, light out of darkness, blessings out of curses, and curses out of blessings. Blessings unblessed are curses in disguise, and adversity blessed is a blessing. We need his blessing upon every thing, even on his blessings. I am sometimes disposed to think that the blessings of American liberty are unblessed.

Mr. Elliott deems universal suffrage, as it exists in America, an universal evil, because the worst and meanest of mankind, who are the most numerous every where, are enabled to exert an overwhelming influence over the good and the honourable. Every man here is a segment of the government. Mean and evil men seek to represent their like. A good man cannot descend to the mean mode of popularity; he cannot bribe with whiskey; he cannot promise what is evil to perform; and therefore but few good men are in the government. Antipathy to Englishmen, and whatever they suggest, is general and nearly national.

For the following very interesting, original, and last letter of a distinguished, yet unfortunate artist, I am indebted to an old philosophical friend, whose well-judged opinions of and extensive acquaintance with men and things, make his sentiments precious and almost oracular. Let him here receive my thanks for the many pleasant hours which I spent in his company, and for the rich materials of thinking gathered from him.

Washington, September 5th, 1820.

Dear Sir,
I embrace the opportunity of writing to you by the favour of Mrs. Orris. I enclose a letter received

from the celebrated *Francis Guy*, landscape painter, who lately died at New York. He was at the
head of his profession in this country, and perhaps in the world. He was born near Keswick,
in Cumberland, England. I knew him well, and
esteemed him highly, as well for his virtues as his
talents. In this letter, (which I believe was the
last he wrote, it being dated only a few days before his death) you will know the opinion of many
artists, who have left their country to seek for
food and fame in this, and see how they are re-
warded for the exercise of their talents in this
great republic of North America. *He (Guy) told
me that he had not received 50 cents per day for his
labours!* You are welcome to any use of this
letter.

Buildings seem to rise very fast, notwithstanding the badness of the times, as they are termed.

Please to favour me with a letter as soon as convenient. I am in daily expectation of the nuts,
&c. The ground has been ploughed some weeks
for their reception. I am in good health, but my
mother, my wife, my brother, his wife, and oldest
child are all very sick.

Please accept my best wishes for your welfare.
The club also wish to be remembered to you.

Your Old Friend.

To Mr. Faux.

Brooklyn, Long Island,
June 29th, 1820.

My Dear Friend,

I received yours, with its inclosures, in due time, and it would be a difficult thing for me to describe the pleasure I feel at seeing such a proof of your continued friendship. There is, indeed, a something in a real upright and downright honest John Bull, that cannot be found in the sly, say-nothing, smiling, deep speculating, money-hunting Jonathans of this all-men-are-born-equally-free-and-independent, negro-driving, cow-skin republic.

It is surely wrong to be content with nothing, because not blessed with all. We see bad effects, we hate them, and we grumble, but ten to one it is because we are unacquainted with the cause from whence they spring; but there is one self-evident, hell-born cause of endless ills in this land, which, for want of a better name, we will call avarice. From Maine to Georgia, on all occasions, the general question is, How much shall I get by it? What will it fetch me? Pray what benefit will that be to me? &c. &c. From this, man-stealing, mail robberies, piracy, murders, thefts, swindling, forgeries, lying, cheating, slavery, whips, gags, chains, and all the black catalogue of monstrous ills proceed. Indeed, that angel who is described by Milton as being more fond of admiring Heaven's golden pavement, than any thing glorious aloft, is the ruling god of this nation; and in imitation

of him, they are for ever chasing dollars, walking
half bent under the accursed dominion of selfish
views. But death, the mighty hunter, will catch
them all, and then, in company with their god
Belial, they will enjoy the name, title, and privilege of *fools*. There is a national church liturgy
in England, and if ever there should be one adopted
here, the following I think ought to form a part of
it.

> Money, money, is all our cry,
>   Money, the total sum!
> Give us money or else we die;
>   O let thy money come!

But I am rambling from the Capitol. Your son
has drawn it very well, but I wish he had drawn
it on a larger scale, that the order of columns and
windows might have been more distinct. However,
it is the wrong side of the building; it is the east
front and north end that I must paint, looking
down towards George-town, and the place I sketched the view from was just above your house; therefore I must paint the east front and north end.
This, like a fool, I forgot to inform you of; but if
both fronts are to be alike, then what you have
sent will do; if not, then I will thank both you
and him to send me another drawing, at least so
far as the centre of the east front differs from that
of the west.

Since I wrote the above, Mr. King, the painter,
has been in this place, and informs us that both

fronts of the capitol will be the same; therefore, if that be so, what you have sent will answer; and when I come to your place in the fall, I will reward your son for his drawing, or if he choose to make a charge, I will send the money by the post, whatever it may be.

Give my dutiful respects to Dr. Thornton, and tell him that I wish he could see the picture of Washington city when it is finished—I think it will be a grand sight. I am now painting a large view of Chichester, in England, for Governor Clinton; in which his likeness, with those of Judge Miller and Doctor Mitchel, are to be painted on the fore-ground. I wish the doctor could see this paradise scenery also. You talk of coming to York; I wonder if ever I shall have the pleasure of seeing you here. In your last, you ask if I have any communications to send. Perhaps I may have some to send concerning myself, for be assured that if we do not now condescend to go out of our old beaten track, we must fall through thick and thin. When that should be, it would be no sin to do one of the worst things in the world, that is, turn one's own trumpeter.

God prosper you in all your good ways, keep you from all bad ones, and may you live contented, and die happy!

FRANCIS GUY.

Thus you see I have written a letter, and on one

account or another delayed sending it until there is need to write another, to make an apology for the neglect. Indeed, my good wife has been very unwell, and my concern for her made me forget every thing else. This I know you will say is a good and weighty excuse.   **F. G.**

June 10*th.*—News of firing the City of New Orleans, in order to effect a rescue of the pirates, reached this city this day. We hear, also, of the Choctaw Indians fighting, 150 opposed to 150, to avenge the death of an old woman, killed for a witch. They fought until both sides, with the exception of ten or twelve, were all killed.

A man was taken and nearly killed, last week, disguised as the devil, in the act of extorting 150 dollars from a farmer. He was dressed, and spit fire and brimstone, like a proper devil. He is now in prison. A Yankee traveller, lodging for the night, struck this felonious devil to the ground with a club, at the second visit to receive dollars, instead of paper, as at first offered by the farmer for the ransom of his body and soul.

12*th.*—I met again **Mr. Perry** from Carlisle, Pennsylvania. He states that the land and farms there are the best in America; the average of wheat being about eighteen bushels an acre. The best land is to be bought occasionally at fifty dollars an acre, with improvements which have cost all the money; so that the land is given.

Here, he says, an English farmer may, as a farmer, find much animal comfort, but no good society; the mass of the farmers and people being
vile, dishonest, and without any good principles
whatever. All try to rob and wrong you, and
each other, and will do it if you associate, or deal
in any way with them; and they will do it without any shame, being shameless. An honest man,
though rich, must be soon ruined, if he puts confidence in them. " All are tarred with the same
brush." The farmers all work. One, worth ten
or twelve thousand dollars, brought in to Mr.
Perry a waggon load of hay, which he warranted
was a ton, though it was only sixteen cwt. Out
of a farm of good land, consisting of 500 acres, a
farmer does not find above 300 dollars a-year for
the purchase of such necessaries as the family
need from the store. No money is, therefore, to
be made by farming, and the poor live in want all
winter, at which time their labour is to be had for
victuals only, and now for 25 cents a-day. From
sober calculation, he finds that four per cent. is the
most that can be obtained from capital employed
in agriculture, though six per cent. is the legal
interest. He would, a thousand times, rather give
five or six guineas an acre rent, for land at Feversham in Kent, than have it here rent-free; for, after
paying this heavy rent and taxes and labour, he
should have a good living profit in England,
where the climate is good, but here, one year

wears you out more that seven in England.
Grasshoppers too, here, are a plague, destroying
every thing, in the pestilential months of August
and September. There is no money; all is done
by barter.

He would recommend me and others to stick
by England while we can live in it, for he is sure,
that if people in England would attend to their
duties, and condescend to the meannesses and
drudgeries every where practised here, they must
live, and live better at home than ever they can
here. And besides, though things are bad, there
is a hope of better times. Here, there is no hope;
things will be worse; for, with such an unprincipled, vile race of people, how is it possible that
liberty and happiness can be secure? They know
nothing of the nature of liberty, nor want to know.
Law, justice, equity, liberty, are things unknown
amongst them. In England, there is a good
sound core, and seed that must always vegetate;
here, all is rottenness. Mr. Perry believes, that
grazing cattle in Pennsylvania, would pay much
better than cultivating.

18*th.*—I re-visited Dr. Dawes's farm, which
being in a state of complete exhaustion, is unable
to produce again even the seed of any thing sown;
the rye not affording what is commonly scattered
for gleaners in England, while the peas, tares, and
lentils rise not a foot high. This land can only
be restored to fruitfulness by rest, clover, plaster,

and manure, and plenty of cattle and sheep to depasture and manure it.

19th.—This being a beautiful morning, the Doctor ordered out his curricle, and we drove to the seat and plantation of the Right Honourable T. Law, accompanied by Mr. Joel Simpson. I having been introduced to Mr. Law, was appointed spokesman, and stood rapping at the hall of entrance ten minutes before I was heard. At last came a naked, dirty-legged, bare-footed little girl, to say that Mr. Law was not at home, nor likely to be before night. Soon after, came her father, the overseer, who " regretted that Mr. Law was absent at an agricultural dinner, as he was happy to see all callers." He, at my request, shewed us the garden, the farm, and the stock. The farm, about 250 acres, is beautifully situated on high hills, two miles from the Potowmac, but so stony and unfruitful, that its cultivation is a serious expense, rather than a benefit, it being unable to maintain itself. The garden and orchard, a few acres, seem equally poor ; small quantities of its produce are, however, sent from it occasionally to market. At the bottom of it is a spa, or mineral spring, in which the proprietor bathes. The horses are all poor and fleshless, but the cattle and cows, about twelve in number, fat. A cow and a bull of the Yorkshire breed, from England, dislike (says the man) this climate.

The cow gives but little milk, and pines for the sweet, green pastures of her dear native land.

The English labourers, sent over to this farm, are all gone, being drunken and worthless, and withal, so uncivil and conceited, that Mr. Law, who likes men to talk freely with him, could scarcely get a civil answer from any of them. We were at last conducted into the house, and introduced to a pint of whiskey. We saw no house-servants, but heard one, a female slave recently bought, the only slave Mr. Law owns. He lives in great simplicity. The house is better than the best American farm-houses; still, it is not a mansion, but rather something between both. In the centre and front, is a large oblong room, the largest in the house, and resembling a hall of entrance, at each end of which is a smaller room for the winter, and on the other side, being a double house, are three small summer rooms, and chambers over the whole. The road through the farm up to the house is serpentine, and planted with dying shrubs. It is rough, stony, and difficult of ascent, and the entrance-gate (where might stand a porter's lodge) is meaner than a hog-pen-gate. In this retreat dined the President and 200 gentlemen last week. The society admitted here is select, and the principal attraction to it is Mr. Law, who is kind, agreeable, and benevolent to all. In his personal appearance, he is small, lean, withered, and rustic. His nose, however, is noble, like **Lord Ellenborough's,** but his mind is perhaps nobler than that of any of the family, although he lives in greater simplicity than a country squire of England.

21st.—An old Scotsman, a perfect stranger, this morning conscientiously brought back cloth to Mr. ———'s store, to be re-measured, the same containing, he found, several yards more than he had paid for, or expected to find. A mistake had occurred in measuring. An American lady of respectability, also of this city, was standing by, and, in the greatest astonishment, exclaimed: "What! bring it back because there is too much measure? Well, who ever heard the like? I would not have done so, I'll warrant ye." " O, my dear madam," said he, " I could not, would not, have it without paying for it; it is not mine." The proprietor of the store observed, very significantly, looking her ladyship in the face; " Madam, I know of only one rule, and that is, to do unto others as you would that they should do unto you." She blushed, and said no more. This shameless, unprincipled, selfishness is very universal. It is customary, with this people, never to point out defects in goods, or errors in accounts, when such defects and errors exist in their favour. The qualities, honesty and dishonesty, as exemplified in these two characters, seemed as if they were natural.

23rd.—The mayor of this city, Samuel N. Smallwood, Esq. now mayor for the second time, came here, twenty years ago, a pennyless mechanic, but being industrious, grew with the growth, and strengthened with the strength, of this infant metropolis. His mother was a yellow woman, and his origin is still distinguishable in his curled hair, which he keeps close shorn. This, further south, would have been a sin never to be forgiven. He is a man of talent, and lives much respected.

This day I passed a pleasant farm on the eastern branch of the Potowmac, half of it bottom land, and running a mile and a half along the shore, with a good house and offices, orchards, and large gardens. The hills are poor, and covered with woods, amongst which cattle and pigs graze, and breed, and fatten. It contains 667 acres, to be bought at sixty dollars an acre, works twenty, and might work thirty negroes, worth 9,000 dollars. It requires an additional capital of 6,000 or 7,000 dollars, for cultivating. Although much of this pleasant plantation is in wood, yet it is said to produce annually,

		Dollars.
Of Tobacco, ...		3,000
Corn and grain, ...		3,000
Garden-stuff, ...		3,000
Cattle and pigs, bred and fed, . .		2,000
Rent of fishery, ...		500
Butter, ...		1,000
		12,500
If the fishery were fished by the owner, it would make additional		1,000
		13,500

Thus is a capital of 55,000 dollars employed, netting twelve per cent., but the authority relied upon, in thus stating the case, is not the best.

The Patriot pilot-boat, last war, sailed from New York to Charleston city, for the Governor of South Carolina's Lady, Mrs. Allstone, Mr. Burr's daughter, then at Charleston, who, with Mr. Green, her brother-in-law, and servant, plate and specie, sailed from Charleston. They were heard of no more, until last month, when one of the pirates, under sentence of death at New Orleans, confessed that he and others, of the crew of the Patriot, rose upon the captain and the passengers, confined them below, scuttled the vessel, and abandoned her, taking to the boat, in which, with all the money and plate they could find, they landed on the coast of North Carolina, while the vessel, and all it contained, sunk to rise no more.

30th.—I re-visited the seat of Mr. Law, in company with Mr. Elliott, and the Rev. J. Wright. Mr. Law was dining out, three miles from home. I saw him not, but kept possession of the house three hours.

Mr. Law told a friend of mine that he brought 100,000 guineas in gold, but could not now raise, by any means, at a short notice, 1,000*l*. City lots and land allured him almost to ruin. Land seems a substance, but is yet only a shadow in many neighbourhoods.

A common hot day at Washington.—The wind southerly, like the breath of an oven; the thermometer vacillating between 90 and 100; the sky blue and cloudless; the sun shedding a blazing light; the face of the land, and every thing upon it, save trees, withered, dusty, baked, and continually heated, insomuch that water would almost hiss on it; the atmosphere swarming with noxious insects, flies, bugs, mosquitoes, and grasshoppers, and withal so drying, that all animal and vegetable life is exposed to a continual process of exhaustion. The breezes, if any, are perfumed by nuisances of all sorts, emptied into the streets, rotting carcases, and the exhalations of dismal swamps, made vocal and alive with toads, lizards, and bellowing bull-frogs. Few people are stirring, except negroes; all faces, save those of blacks, pale, languid, and lengthened with lassitude, expressive of any thing but ease and happiness. Now and then an emigrant or two fall dead at the cold spring, or fountain; others are lying on the floor, flat on their backs; all, whether idle or employed, are comfortless, being in an everlasting steam-bath, and feeling offensive to themselves and others. At table, pleased with nothing, because both vegetable and animal food is generally withered, toughened, and tainted; the beverage, tea or coffee, contains dead flies; the beds and bed-rooms, at night, present a smothering unaltering warmth, the walls being thoroughly heated, and being withinside like the outside of an oven in continual use. Hard is the lot of him who bears the heat and burthen of this day, and pitiable the fate of the poor emigrant sighing in vain for comforts, cool breezes, wholesome diet, and the old friends of his native land. At midnight, the lightning-bugs and bull-frogs become luminous and melodious. The flies seem an Egyptian plague, and get mortised into the oily butter, which holds them like bird-lime.

Having requested some communication on the subject of farming, and other matters, in Pennsylvania, from a friend, possessing great experience, I was favoured with the following heads, which contain much information in a condensed form.

1*st*. *Pennsylvania.*—The land is of the first quality, and the best farming in the United States is found here. The climate is of a medium temperature, but the extremes meet as in the other states.

2*nd*. *Crops.*—The average produce is sixteen bushels, per acre, of wheat; other grain in proportion; but the crops are very subject to the Hessian fly and mildew.

3*rd*. *Fruit.*—As in the other states, it is inferior to that of Europe, and no dependence is to be placed on crops.

4*th*. *Garden.*—One acre of land in England, produces more vegetables than five acres in the United States, taking the year throughout. N.B. This matter has been most grossly misrepresented.

5*th*. *Grazing Land.*—During five months in the year, there is no pasture for cattle.

6*th*. *Price of Land.*—Varies from 50 to 100 dollars with improvements, that is, with a good house and barn.

7*th*. *Timber.*—Sufficient exists at present; but should the population increase rapidly, it will become a scarce article.

8*th*. *Game.*—Scarce; which is generally the case through the States. No country in the world is worse supplied with game, and in a few years the game will be entirely annihilated, owing to the extreme inclemency of the winters, and there being no cover for them in the woods.

9th. Fish.—Taking the States through, the supply of this article is trifling.

10th. Farmers.—The generality of this class are Germans of the lowest grade ; industrious, but nothing further, and forming no society for an English yeoman. The rest of the population is composed of descendants of the old settlers and of low people of Irish origin.

11th. Residence.—An emigrant requires at the least twelve months. N.B. The United States teem with jobbing lawyers, land speculators, and swindlers.

12th. Grazing and stall-feeding cattle for market.—This line might be followed to advantage with a capital of 4,000 dollars, and with what is of more consequence, the knowledge of dealing or trafficking, for without such knowledge the noble would soon be reduced to nine-pence. A twelve months' residence is, therefore, indispensably necessary, for without being fully initiated in the diabolical arts of *lying out, swearing out, swindling out,* and *thieving out,* ruin is inevitable.

13th. Society.—There is none for an Englishman of the old school, who would scorn to tell a lie, or see his fellow man in want.

14th. Happiness.—Must be found in your own family ; the fruits of your farm will supply every want, and whilst the government of the United States continues as at present, you will be secured in that happiness.

15th.—One matter I had almost forgot, which I must not omit to mention, as you most likely will be asked questions on the subject by many of that most useful and invaluable class, English husbandmen.

1st. Wages.—The highest wages given at this time for *harvest* are, 2s. 3d. per day, English money, and found in provision and bad whiskey.

2nd. Working hours.—From sunrise to sunset, full sixteen hours.

3d. How long does the harvest last?—About three weeks.

4th. Is it warm in harvest time?—Excessively so. The thermometer ranges from 86 to 120. It is impossible to have a just idea of it without actual experience. And, what is of more consequence, an English husbandman would be more *debilitated* in *three years* in the United States, than in *sixteen years* in England.

5th. How long in the year can labour be procured?—About six months.

6th. Are wages paid regularly?—Very rarely. Mostly defrauded.

7th. Then who are the persons that can do?— A man with a family of hard-working children, possessing 300*l.* sterling, and who should reside twelve months in the States before he purchases land. And it is greatly to be feared that both the emigrant and his family must lay in all the low cunning, and earn to defraud and cheat, as prac-

tised here, and entirely forget old English principles
and society, or else ruin and misery will be his
portion.

8th. Mechanics.—Any part of the world before
the United States, for, whatever they may earn,
they will be sure to be defrauded out of half.

9th. Wages.—Not so much as in England, taking the year through.

July 6th.—Visited the house of the President, a
good, substantial, pleasant abode, but neither so
elegant, superb, nor costly as the seats of our nobility.   I saw nothing about it remarkable ; no pictures, save Washington's ; no curiosities, no painted
ceilings. The walls are covered with French paper,
and the rooms are furnished with French furniture.
Its front looks over the Potowmac and Alexandria,
down to Mount Vernon, through a vast extent of
Southern Virginian scenery.   A favourite English butler shewed us all, and regaled us with
good biscuit, brandy, and sherry.

7th.—This morning the Hon. Thomas Law, accompanied by Mr. Elliott, made me a call in return for mine. He very politely regretted his absence when I called, and invited me to come and
spend a day or two with him at his farm, for the
purpose of concluding the conversation now commenced in the following words.

Mr. Law.—" You, Mr. F., saw my farm and
garden. They are poor, but I will improve the
gravelly hills by carting earth on to them from the

valleys. The English labourers sent to me by Mr.
Curwen, I have dismissed. They could do nothing
but plough; they were stupid, conceited, uncivil,
and latterly drunken; whiskey, and the company
they met, seduced them. When I began farming
I knew not wheat from rye, or rye from barley;
but I well know what are the benefits of farming."
" You, Sir, pursue it only for your pleasure?"
" No, Sir, I want profit." " In the present distressed state of agriculture little profit is to be
had." " Truly so; but a paper circulation is
wanted. Mr. Crawford fully agreed with me on
this point, but disingenuously seceded from it in
his report, on which account I have addressed several pointed letters to him, which I will send you
as well as my address to the agricultural society
of Prince George's county."

" On my return home shall I advise and recommend my countrymen to emigrate here?" " Why,
Sir, I cannot answer that question. I have never
recommended emigration, nor caused any to quit
their country; every thing is strange and unsuita-
ble to English farmers and labourers; he can cultivate with success only by slaves." " Have you,
Mr. Law, no regrets at having spent so much of
your time in this country?" " No, Sir, none whatever." " What, Sir, none at the loss of that society which you must have had in common with
your family in England?" Here Mr. Law hesitated a little as if at a loss for an answer. " Why,

Sir, I once with Lord Cornwallis governed India. I returned and saw my acquaintance sliding into commerce, brewers, manufacturers, and merchants, to be cheated; such a course had no attractions for me, and I was opposed to the French war and other government measures. I therefore determined on visiting and ultimately on living in this country, where I have spent my time much to my satisfaction, never being at a loss for amusement. I write and read, and talk and visit, on the most familiar and friendly terms with my neighbours, with whom I frequently stay all night; and whenever I please, I can without ceremony go and talk frequently and freely with the President, Mr. Crawford, Calhoun, and all the heads of the government, and therefore I have the best society the land affords." " But, Sir, there are the honours and emoluments of England which *must* have been yours." " My wants were then, and have always been, very few. I believe I have always been happier than any of my brothers. As I never knew how to say ' My lord' to any man, I did not seek or want honours or emoluments. I saw my family and friends dependant on the funds which are likely some day to beggar them and many others; a situation from which I fled." " What, Mr. Law, is likely to remedy the diseases of England?" " Sir! England is over-peopled. It is not wholly the fault of the government. A famine will be the remedy." " Could not the surplus popula-

tion be transported to the colonies?"   " No, Sir.
A famine is the only remedy."   " But, Sir, is not
a famine calculated to plunge the country into a
dreadful political convulsion and revolution?"   " It
is, Sir, but the government is not blameable."

" Morally considered, or with respect to morals,
do you not think the population of this country
inferior to that of England?"   " The people in the
mass are here more intelligent.   You now see them
at the worst time.   You see them *generally* acting
unworthily and meanly, but their poverty and not
their will consents.   As to slaves, they steal."
" And they have a right to steal," said a third
person.   I answered, " They, to be sure, have
been robbed on a broad scale."   " Why, Sir, the
friends of slavery insist on it that slavery is essential to the existence of liberty.   To what conclusions will they not come?"

" Is there, Mr. Law, no aristocratical feeling in
this country?"   " Yes, Sir, amongst the black population."   " You mean, Sir, amongst the masters
of blacks?"   " Yes, Sir.   You, Sir, have visited
Mr. Birkbeck?"   " I have."   " Is he not a very
pleasant, intelligent man?"   " He is highly so."
" What is he doing?"   " Fast spending dollars."
" Had he raised any produce?"   " None."   " Why?"
" He had been, he said, occupied in settling his
neighbours, who together with himself have been
supplied with provisions from Harmony at 100 per
cent. above their value; but cheaper, they have

said, than they could have then and there raised
them." " I, Sir, do not approve of going into the
wilderness away from market and society, while
land is to be had with both.   What is Harmony?"
" It is a most flourishing settlement, and indeed
the only flourishing one I saw in the wilderness.
What think you, Mr. Law, of the climate?"
" Why, Sir, as Lloyd says,

> " With things at once so hot and cold,
> I can no friendship hold."

Mr. Law talks in an oratorical manner, and with
an energy of action which makes him appear much
in earnest.   He is full to overflowing, and quite
inexhaustible.   " His worth," says Mr. Elliott,
" is not one-tenth of it known, but is thrown away
upon this country."

"It is said, Sir, that the population of this country
is systematically unprincipled, and almost without
virtue." "That, Sir, is not true. In the cities, since
the commercial distress, the people seem dishonest.
The commercial demand from England, and the
withdrawing a paper capital by this government,
have driven the people to desperation. They are
unjustly done by. They were once esteemed good
customers. A circulating medium only is wanted
to heal the breach. In the country the people are
anxious to meet their engagements." " Do you,
Sir, think that no remedy but famine remains for
England?" " No, Sir! no other." " Then the
sooner it comes the better." " But, Sir, (said he)

such confusion, and horror, and calamity, will cha-
racterize the catastrophe as the world has not
seen." " Do you think it will exceed the French
revolution? Will the people of England be more
bloody and heartless in such a struggle than the
French?" " The desperation of their situation will
make them so. Consider, Sir, the rage, anguish,
and collision of so many starving millions, screwed
up into a space not larger than our state of Virginia. Here, Sir, we have plenty, and whether
sleeping or waking are safe in our houses, and
liberty and prosperity are secure. You, I find,
are deputed to collect information. Dine with me
on Monday, and I will get my sons out to meet
you."

Mr. Law finding that I wished a protection or
special passport from the British minister, Mr. An-
trobus, went and applied for it, but did not succeed,
it should seem, because I was acquainted with
———— on the black books of the government.
" Mr. C.," said Mr. Law, " is a very intelligent
man, but I find he carried things with a high, offensive hand in England. He, I believe, Sir, wrote the
Watchman and alarmed the church and the Bishop
of Ely."

Mr. Law seems not to like the radicals. " When,"
says he, " I came to this country from India, it
seemed at first like going down to the grave. I
seemed buried. Tell my family that I drink daily
rye-coffee and whiskey.

Recipe for making rye-coffee, equal to the West Indian, after Mr. Law's fashion.   Swell the rye in warm water before you roast it.

8th.—I received the following letter from Mr. Law.

Saturday, *8th July,* 1820.

Sir,

I wish you, if you see Mr. Elliott of the Patent-office, to desire him to come and dine on Monday. If you can visit me early, I will shew you the neighbourhood, and in conversation you may obtain whatever opinions I have formed from experience respecting this country.   It is most desirable that correct information should be given to those who are necessitated to seek an asylum here.

An European ought not to travel far into the interior, as he must sacrifice every comfort during life.   Want of society, want of hands, want of a market, want of medical aid; in short, almost every want is experienced for many years; discontent soon destroys the harmony of associates, and former attachments to those left behind have double power to excite regrets.

The Americans are a migrating race, and quit their farms to seek rich back lands; but more of this when I have the pleasure to see you.

Yours most obediently,

T. LAW.

Sunday, 9th.—By appointment, I breakfasted with Major Young, 45 years from Ireland, and

2 G

from the first an enthusiast in the cause of America, throughout the revolution up to this time, having been the companion in arms of General Washington, and appointed to the honour of delivering Lord Cornwallis his discharge from his parole of honour. His lordship graciously received it from the Major at his house in London, much pleased that he was not compelled to return to America to discharge his parole, having been exchanged for Mr. Laurens in the Tower. " Major," said his lordship, " I feel obliged to you and others, and will hold myself under obligation to serve you at any time." The Major gave him an opportunity, and was served. Mr. Laurens, while in the tower, was consulted by a friend of Lord Hillsborough, the minister, on this question : " What, Mr. Laurens, would you, as a friend to America, advise England to do at the present juncture." " Why, Sir, the experience of ages proves that an ounce of honey is worth a ton of vinegar." His lordship on hearing this, in great rage rejoined, " America has had too much honey ; she shall have more vinegar."

Mr. John Law, during the attack on Washington, served in the United States' army as a serjeant ; but after the British got possession, he laid aside his uniform, and telling the British officers that he was the nephew of Lord Ellenborough, invited them to his house, where they spent a joyful evening together.

10*th.*—By Mr. Elliott, I was introduced to Major
Roberts, at the public department of engineers.   I
was accompanied by Mr. John and Mr. Edmund
Law, two natives of Asia, to the seat of their father
to dinner, where we met Mr. Carter, Mr. Elliott,
Colonel Heb, and his friend, a Cantab.   Our dinner consisted of lamb, ham and chicken, and black-
berry pie, with claret, brandy, and whiskey, the
latter 15 years old.   Here was all ease and no ceremony.   Every guest seemed as free as if at home,
and eat, drank, and talked as he pleased.   As this
dinner was on my account, Mr. Law placed me
on his right hand as his guest.   The two Asiatic
sons of Mr. Law seem generous, kind-hearted, and
most intelligent young gentlemen, free from all
aristocratic pride.

Mr. John Law, during our ride to dinner, observed that his father's objection to slavery was
rooted in mere prejudice, because, though he
might buy slaves, he could emancipate them when
he pleased.   I told Mr. Law, their father, what
they said of this prejudice.   " Aye," said he,
" call it what they please, I am acting from a good
and proper motive.   Wherever there are blacks,
the white population is seen to decrease.   The
blacks will free themselves in the south; their re-
sistance and insurrection will be horrid and irre_
sistible; the free states will never stir an inch to
oppose the blacks or to assist the planters, who
have no feelings in common with the farmers and

people of free states. The former oppose domestic manufactures, because they think England can give them more for produce than their countrymen, and therefore they are willing that their countrymen should be drained of money for the support of British manufactures."

Free blacks, in all the above states, are an especial nuisance, because they are deemed the cause of insurrection amongst slaves, and act as brokers to them, or receivers of whatever the slaves steal.

Birkbeck and Flower became the theme of the evening. Mr. Law, and all present, regretted that they did not settle in this, or some populous neighbourhood, where they might have lived as the most distinguished citizens, and at a much less cost than now. They might have visited and been visited by the President, and all the heads of departments; had a town and country house, plenty of land, increasing in value, and good markets; plenty of comforts of all kinds; farms, houses, orchards, gardens, and every convenience formed to their hands, at less than the cost of improvements, so that the land is a gift into the bargain. What madness to go into the wilderness! Their land is not advanced in value by their mere residence on it. They might have invested money, on land, in the best western neighbourhoods, and, without sacrificing themselves, their posterity would have reaped the benefit, which must be slow, but which is sure to come with population and population only.

They thought that land must increase in value in
the west, forgetting that there was an infinite supply at the same price; and, besides, how could they
be sure that settlers would follow and give an advance. It was madness so to spend this short life.
They ought to have known that working Yankee
families, who do all the labour themselves, are the
only proper pioneers. Gentlemen-farmers should
not remove into the west, until they can live and
do better there than here. At any rate it is time
enough to go when they can be the third or fourth
buyers of farms; when they can have the improvements at less than the cost, and the land nearly
into the bargain. Society and visiting, so indispensable to such intelligent Englishmen, they
might here have cheaply. " I entertained (continued Mr. Law) the President and heads of departments, and 100 friends besides, to dinner, at
this house, on such a dinner as we have had to-
day, and a little light wine, and the cost of all
was only 40 dollars. My good neighbours, it is
true, sent me hams and rounds of beef, ready
cooked, because they thought I should find it
difficult to cook for so many. If I were in England, I must have my Lord ——, and others of the
same rank; all must be splendid, costly, and pompous; but all this is not the hospitality which I
like and find here. Here we go and come, as, and
when we please; no previous notice is necessary;

we give and take freely of such things as we have, and no one is inconvenienced. In England a house is alarmed by the arrival of an unexpected visitor. As neighbours and visitors we are all equal, and share good things in common."

We walked through the large garden, where Mr. Law boasted that he should have 2,000 celery plants for market at 12½ cents each. All farmers send their garden produce three times a week to market. " What I send (says Mr. Law) pays the expense of the gardener, and puts 100 dollars into my pocket, exclusive of my butter, which furnishes me with butcher's meat, &c. My farm, at present, does not, but it will, more than support my establishment."

He has two women, one white, one black, two or three negro children, and five or six labourers hired at from eight dollars to twelve dollars per month, most of whom are to leave in winter.

At eight o'clock the company departed, except myself. Mr. Law pressed me to stay and spend a day or two longer, so that we might visit Colonel Heb next day, and see the neighbourhood.

We were seated together alone, on the lawn, in the cool of the evening, until ten o'clock, when Mr. Law, with a light in his hand, kindly conducted me to my bed-room. During these two hours we talked freely; first, on the state of England, which, he says, must fall in a few years. " With

such a debt, and so many drones, and having all
the world rivalling and excluding British manufactures, and with such a superabundant population, it is impossible that she can long exist in her
present condition. A famine must certainly sweep
away superfluous millions. It will be brought
about, first, by a scarce year, and secondly, by the
want of specie to pay for foreign grain; for specie
only will do, when manufactures shall not be wanted in exchange for grain. Then the British people,
instead of lying down and dying willingly like the
Hindoos, a scene which I witnessed, will rise with
an irresistible fury, sweeping all authorities before
them." " After such a storm, will they dispense
with monarchy, &c.?" " No, Sir, I think not.
King, lords, and commons, seem acceptable to
the people. The church and the debt only will
be annihilated. My friends and others in the funds
see that this catastrophe is coming. They are therefore unhappy. I see they are eaten up by anxiety;
I am happier than any of them. Many of the rich,
and several of my friends and family, live on the
European continent, to spend their money in ease
and peace. They are all unhappy in their prospects. It is true that I have been unsuccessful in
my speculations here, but my wants are few. I
was advised by General Washington to invest my
money in and about this city, which every one
then deemed a good speculation, and it would
have been so but for the stupidity and blundering

ignorance of this government, which by diminishing the currency, has reduced our estates 50 or 60 per cent. and rendered all unsaleable. There is no money for use. It is impossible that a people can flourish without a circulating medium; a floating capital, which creates a fixed capital. This government, however, will see the need of it and resort to it; for, if the capital once in circulation had remained so, the public lands would have doubled their present value, and the industrious have flourished instead of sinking into ruin. The poor and industrious are the only proper objects of the care and protection of government." " You knew Paley. What think you of his philosophy, &c. ?" " I knew him well; he was a good man, but his philosophy is false. Utility is made its basis; but impulse and feeling furnish the best moral guide. Every feeling in man points him to good. ness." "But, Sir," said I, " is not his philosophy in accordance with Christianity?" " Perhaps it is." I rejoined that I could not help revering it, and that after reading it I thought myself both wiser and better. "That may be." " You knew and esteemed Sir Wm. Jones in India. Was he not a Christian?" " Why sir, Lord Teignmouth has endeavoured to make him appear so; but he was a free-thinker, and unusually vain. Instead of studying his duties and introducing good laws, he was ambitious of learning all languages, and of being a finished antiquarian and poet. He fell a victim to his intense application. He would never travel, except by night; the sun must not see him. He once travelled through my district by night, and I accompanied him. At sunset he would inquire: ' Is my enemy down?' If answered, ' Yes,' he would then start.''

" Did you see M. Volney, during his tour in this country?" " I did; he came, introduced to me by General Washington, and spent some days with me; he spoke our language well, and was a very wise man."

11th.—Mr. Law and myself rose about sunrise. I walked, while he was engaged in writing some materials or arguments for my journal. He writes with great velocity.

After breakfast we rode to the pleasant farm of Colonel Heb to dine, where, with his lady and family, we met a young Cantab, and his lady, who sweetly sung and played for Mr. Law on the piano, with which he seemed enraptured.

We then viewed the Colonel's estate, consisting of 600 acres, of hill and dale, 90 of which are meadow irrigated, and which produces 2,000 dollars in hay annually, while the tobacco * crop is

* From the seed of the best species of Maryland tobacco received from this gentleman, my neighbour, Major Smith, of Somersham, in England, has, unaided by art, planted and manufactured tobacco, of a superior fragrance and flavour, and which he introduces to his friends on special occasions, when it is used as prime Canaster from Havannah.

commonly worth from 100 to 150 dollars an acre.
Here is a marl bank, by which the Colonel has
improved the estate, which, including its first cost,
employs 20,000 dollars, and nets, from 12 to 15
per cent. It is cultivated by from 12 to 20 negroes, who seem happy and well treated, singing
and working merrily. The Colonel thinks slaves
are better off than free-men. All slave-holders
think so, especially those idle men who keep them
merely for hiring out, that they may live entirely
by the labour and breeding of blacks. Free blacks,
in a slave state, are most of them unhappy.

Mr. Law thinks that Colonel Heb saves little
or nothing from this estate, after deducting the
expenses of hospitality, education, and other out-
goings. Part of our dessert, at dinner, was straw-
berries, which, during the summer, bear fruit continually, each month yielding a fresh supply. We
quitted this hospitable abode at seven, p. m., and,
on reaching home, resumed our conversation till
bed-time.

Mr. Law said, that when last in England, he
visited his brother, the now Bishop of Chester,
then living on a small benefice, at Kelshall, near
Royston, where all the neighbourhood seemed
dissenters. "My brother did all he could to please
them, but they would not come to church. My
brother did not like it, and feared that his congregation would be reduced to the clerk and
his own family. Indeed it seldom was more.

What a nest," said Mr. Law, " is the church for hypocrites. All churches are evils, especially when they condemn a difference of opinion, and compel the dissenters therefrom to support the church. Religion is matter of opinion; all have a right to think freely thereon. I wonder how my brother got preferment, when I know he was refractory, and could not submit to the pride and domination of Lord Ellenborough."

" The convulsion in England," says Mr. Law, " will not last long, but it will be horrid; it will sweep away the drones. I saw my friends spending their days ingloriously, and descending to the grave, sick of themselves, and without doing any good to the world.

" My good brother, the Irish Bishop, the most learned of our family, came from Ireland, purposely to see me. He is now dead. There is no independence about bishops. They only seek preferment."

Mr. Law repeated to me some satirical lines which he wrote against the * * *   * * *
" These lines his lordship feared should be shown. He made peace with me and gave up to me. His lordship said, ' I must give up to Tom, or he will expose me to my brother lawyers, and I shall become their butt.' " These lines represented the * * *   * * * as the perfection of pride, and seeking to be Chancellor, being already one in insolence.

" You have not, I suppose, at any time, directly or indirectly, formed a part of this government?" " No, Sir, I would see them at the d—l first." " Is Mr. President Monroe a man of business?" " Yes, Sir. The Presidents are all slaves to their duties, scarcely able to breathe abroad or take air." On passing by the Capitol, I said, " Does this sumptuous Capitol accord with the plainness of republicanism?" " No, Sir, but laying stones one upon another rarely injures any nation; and besides, republics are vain, and public buildings gratify their vanity, and attach them to the country. Inasmuch (said Mr. Law) as this government has left unprotected the manufacturers of the country, and withdrawn the circulating medium from the people generally, it has done all which an enemy to this or any country could do, or wish to see done." I asked Mr. Law if it was worth while to visit Mount Vernon. He said, " Mount Vernon is inviting, but Judge W. knows nothing."

12*th*.—In our ride to the city this morning, with a negro behind us, two gentlemen, Mr. Law's neighbours, overtook us, but being anxious to get on before us, apologized for leaving us. " Oh! gentlemen!" said Mr. L., " we do not want you to wait for us. Go, I pray you, to the devil if you will!"

At parting with Mr. Law this morning, he promised to send me letters of introduction to his

Right Rev. Brother, the Bishop of Chester, and
his distinguished cousin, J. C. Curwen, Esq. M. P.
which letters, together with the following curious
observations, purposely written by him for the use
of this journal, were soon after transmitted to me.

Observations by Mr. Law.—" I have lately
perused an address to the public from the dele-
gation of the United Agricultural Society of Virginia. If, after repeated perusals, I had been
convinced that the exclusion of such foreign manufactures as we can make ourselves, by legislative measures, such as high duties or prohibitions,
would be injurious to agriculturists, I should immediately acknowledge my acquiescence in their
reasoning. To oppose the opinions and arguments of such able men, and of such united members, exposes any one to the imputation of vanity,
and to inevitable ridicule, should his reasoning
prove inconclusive. I have always been an advocate for permitting men to pursue their interests
unobstructed by governmental interference, according to the suggestions of their reason, and to seek
future salvation according to the dictates of their
conscience; and I have always been convinced
that men will employ their capitals and industry
in that business which produces most profit. This
is, indeed, an incontrovertible axiom in political
economy; and the only question to determine, is
whether the exclusion of foreign manufactures be

not a salutary exception to the rule. The dele-
gation above mentioned, accuses the petitioning
manufacturers of soliciting a monopoly. A monopoly, according to my definition of the term, means
an exclusive privilege in favour of an individual,
or a certain class of men, in preference to all
others, who are injured thereby. Now to me it
appears that the duties or prohibitions solicited,
are solely for the encouragement of domestic manufactures, and for the discouragement of foreign
ones; nay, in my opinion, it seems a request in
the name of all Americans, to be shielded from
foreign monopoly. This observation will at first
surprise you, but after my explanation it will, I
trust, have more verisimilitude in it than you
can now imagine. Suppose a sovereign to say
that in a certain county, or department, he would
make a donation of capital for building machinery,
&c. to those who would establish a certain manu-
facture. Should any other of his subjects attempt
rivalship, with his, or their own funds, could not
those, who had their capitals gratis, undersell the
competitor or competitors? Say that the buildings
and machinery cost 100,000 dollars, and that
50,000 dollars, current capital, were required to pay
workmen, and buy materials. The former aided
by the sovereign, if they made ten per cent. on
their current capital, would receive 5,000 dollars
per annum, but the latter, if he obtained only a

profit of 5,000 dollars on his 150,000 dollars laid out, would only receive three and a third per cent. Now the foreign manufacturer has a capital from his father, which is useless to him, if not employed. Say his buildings, machinery, and 50,000 dollars current capital, produce him 15,000 dollars. If he finds foreigners, who heretofore purchased from him, attempting to set up for themselves, will it not be good policy in him to reduce his profits two thirds, to ruin his incipient rivals? Mr. Brougham, in the House of Commons, used the following language, when speaking of the loss to merchants by an excessive exportation of manufactures:—*it was worth while to incur a loss, in order, by the glut, to stifle in the cradle those rising manufactures in the United States, which the war had forced into existence, contrary to the natural course of things.*

" Would it not have been humane and judicious in Congress, to have prevented this ruinous glut, which contributed, with the order to resume specie payments, to crush our manufacturers, merchants, and storekeepers, and to injure farmers, &c.? How have foreigners obtained above 30,000,000 of our stocks, but by manufactures? The importation of manufactures is now much diminished, and manufactures are rising, and the price of labour falling. Will, however, any prudent man commence manufacturing till shielded from a glut? Our manufactures, till then, cannot prosper, and we must remain dependent on foreigners. If all men relied upon handicraft, as formerly, then the general rule, before alluded to, would apply, and we might be supplied by home-spun. Were all patriots, the nation would prefer home-spun, if even a little dearer than foreign articles of a similar kind; but, as many will prefer their own to the general interest, the general government must, in respect to foreign commerce, interfere. The farmer in England obtains from 8s. to 10s. a bushel for his wheat; our farmers obtain 4s. 6d.; the manufactures in England amount to about 100,000,000l. sterling; ours, to less than that amount in dollars.

" The distress occasioned by the sudden reduction of our circulating medium from 100,000,000 dollars, to 45,000,000 dollars, has reduced all property far below its intrinsic value; the banks are prosecuting to recover sums loaned, mortgages are foreclosed, and landholders in debt are compelled to sell. When an European purchases land in the western countries, he has to clear and fence, and to build house and barn and stable, at a great expense. In the old states, as they are termed, the land is sold at so much per acre, and the house, barn, &c. are thrown into the bargain. Land, from four to eight miles from this city, may be averaged at twenty dollars an acre, ready to be occupied. Navigation is near; the market is near; the newspapers, as essential almost to an Englishman as his breakfast, may be received three times a-week by market-carts. Society is good ; the expense of a long journey, and a thousand inconveniences experienced by new settlers, are avoided. Horses and oxen, I believe, can be bought cheaper in this neighbourhood. If a man wants to remove his family and to sell, he can find purchasers more readily than in the western wilds. Sickness almost always occurs on the first exposure of new land to the sun. State taxes and county levies fall heavily on settlers in a new country, requiring public buildings, roads, bridges, &c. ; labour is dear, and not always attainable. A New England man succeeds in a new country, because he is a jack-of-all-trades; he can make his own log-house, mend his cart, &c. There is an old adage, that " fools build, and wise men purchase." Suppose 150 acres, purchased in this neighbourhood, at twenty dollars an acre, making 3,000 dollars, the fencing, and building, and clearing, would cost at least that sum. When three or four Englishmen wish to purchase together, they ought to keep it a secret, and to employ some American, not in high life, who can be confided in, to sound persons wanting to sell; for if a stranger offers to buy, it is immediately reported over all the neighbourhood, and prices are raised, and it exaggerates the value. Americans are remarkably shrewd.

Englishmen, in general, are credulous and sanguine. All bargains ought to be legally formal, under signature and seal.

" Question. Is Great Britain capable of sustaining its national debt for any length of time?

" There are operating against the possibility of this,

1st.—The rivalship of manufactures of other nations, knowledge and skill not being an exclusive advantage.

2nd.—The encrease of poor-rates, by a superabundant population, and reduction of wages.

3rd.—The augmentation of payments abroad to British residents, who avoid taxation by removing to foreign countries.

4th.—The transfer of sums by the timid and enterprizing, who, foreseeing embarrassments at home, make purchases abroad of stock and lands. The British funds yield less than five per cent.; the French and American yield six.

" These four causes, combining against British prosperity, almost preclude the hope of supporting the immense load of taxes. The army cannot, with safety, be much diminished, for as discontent increases with the addition of burthens, the power of the government must be increased. It is surprising that the " tight little island" prospers as it does; there cannot be a stronger proof of a good internal management.

" The industrious classes cannot support, in

any community, more than a certain proportion
of drones. The important question is whether the
army, navy, state creditors, hierarchy, servants,
residents abroad, tax-gatherers, &c. can be supported by the industrious. The rapid increase of
poor rates, evinces that a nation has arrived at its
acme.

" The arrival of monied men in this country, to
purchase lands and to avoid an apprehended convulsion, is ominous of the approaching crisis. It is
painful to forebode misfortune, and an unwelcome
task to predict evil. Could I anticipate improvements similar to those of Arkwright, &c. to be
long exclusively enjoyed, and were there lands
still to be cultivated, to support augmenting po
pulation, I could indulge the hope of liquidating
the debt. At present I behold an inverted pyramid,
propped by machinery, which is giving way. Your
own journey, your own inquiries, must make a
forcible impression, that present profits are pre-
carious, and that happiness is alloyed with appre-
hensions for the future."

13th.—During a conversation this day with Dr.
Thornton, of the post-office, he observed that this
city, like that of ancient Rome, was first peopled
with thieves and assassins, and that, during his
residence in it, he had found more villains than
he had seen in any other part of the world. When
he was a magistrate, such instances of unblushing
villainy and want of principle amongst the people

had come to his view, as he could not suppose existed any where. " There are, however," said the docter, "many good men now in it." There is a disposition generally amongst the citizens to live above their income. Persons who live as independent gentlemen, often run into debt with their butchers, &c., to the amount of several hundred dollars, and delay a year and a half before they attempt to pay, suffering themselves to be dunned continually, always promising payment, but never being punctual in performance, and ultimately paying by instalments of five, ten, or fifteen dollars ; a mode of payment from which the meanest man in England would shrink.

15*th*. — I received a farewell visit from Mr. Thompson, late of Boston, who states that he finds the inducements to emigrate much fewer and smaller than he expected. Society, as it at present exists, shews great want of organization, great want of religion, honour, and virtue, and the country generally seems destitute of English comforts and advantages. Yet he is now about to make a commercial attempt, by way of experiment, which, if not successful, he will return into his former sphere, well content to remain in it, without again wandering five miles from it. He believes that none of the tables in America afford the comforts of an English table. He thinks that the government in its neglect of seminaries entails imperfection on the people. A bitter sectarian spirit prevails, and is more vicious than in England, and there is a miserable, petty feeling of aristocracy. It seems to him that republicanism is suited only for an infant people.

This evening 1 took my farewell of the claret club, the focus of liberal principles and of friendly feelings.

Sunday, 16th.—Accompanied by Mr. Elliot and the Rev. J. Wright, I drove to Mount Eagle, the hired seat of Ferdinand Fairfax, Esq., on our way to Mount Vernon. This gentleman, an English lord, gave us an introductory letter, penned on the top of a post, to the supreme Judge, Washington, who received us coldly and reluctantly before he read the letter, and said, " 1 do not like to see people on this day, but you may walk round." He then turned away while Mr. Elliot muttered, " We consider it no act of impiety to visit the tomb of General Washington, and thus to come on pilgrimage to the shrine of your illustrious ancestor." On reading the letter his severity relaxed, and he sent two of his servants to conduct us to the tomb, through the house and gardens, and to point out whatever was curious. The road, through the estate, leading to the mansion, is rough and worn into gullies. Every thing bespeaks the neglect and apathy of the present owner. The land is poor; the estate is separated on all sides by a rail fence, that is, rails split and mortised into posts; and the gardens are sur-

rounded with evergreen cedar fences, all of which
are the work of the late General, for whom every
thing here seems to mourn. The house contains
nothing curious save the huge old iron key of the
French Bastile, kept in a glass case, and the recollection of its being once the abode of General
Washington. Instead of carpets, you see Indian
matting on the floors. The furniture is mean and
common, and was brought here by Judge Washington.

The exterior of the house is of wood, sanded
over, in imitation of stone. It suffers for want of
paint, while bricks seem falling from the chimneys
without being replaced. Here are no pictures of
any value. The only likeness of the late General
is cut from a Chinese pitcher! The grass upon
the lawn and garden, in front and rear of the
house, is rotting and seeding down; it is never
mown.

The tomb containing the General, and his lady,
and brother, and others of this renowned family,
might be mistaken for a dog-kennel, or a mound,
much resembling a potatoe grave in England. It
is situated at the extremity of the garden, and on
the brow of a hill. No monument marks it. Ever-
green cedars of Lebanon grow thick upon it, a
branch of which is often stolen as a sacred relique.
I bore away one for the king of England. In like
manner did the Russian minister carry one to his
Imperial master, Alexander. No pilgrim is for-

bidden thus to pilfer. The tomb is formed by excavating the earth, and then arching it over with bricks; three feet of earth is then cast on to the arch, which completely hides every thing but the entrance at one end, through a door, formed of half inch fir board, now rotting away. Such a door would disgrace an English pig-stye. Were pigs to range here, they would soon enter the tomb, which was built by the brother of the late General, the latter of whom is to sleep here until a national grave is made by lottery. Graves and cathedrals are raised, in this country, by means of lotteries!

While seated on this monumental hill, I exclaimed with Gray. "The paths of glory lead but to the grave." Mr. Elliot replied. "Why, Sir, I look on my grave, *already made*, with pleasure, and in the same manner as a weary traveller does to a down bed at the end of a long journey. I anticipate, with joy, the rest which there awaits me." "Such a feeling," said I, "is desirable, but how few the number of those who so feel!"

We were next taken to the green-houses, which in winter, are filled with all species of choice exotics, from all quarters of the earth, gifts to the late General. They now stand out in front of the green-house, with myrtles, oranges, and lemons, ripe, and in great abundance. There are aloes too of enormous size; plantains, mace, and coffee trees.

I gathered ripe coffee, which is contained in a kind of rich fruit or berry, of delicious flavor. The pine-apple also bears in the green-house, but it seemed in a withering state.

The approach to the house is marked by negro huts, and negroes of all ages, male and female. In the General's time, all was well managed, particularly the farm and gardens. He, the Cincinnatus of his time, was up early, and always vigilant. Now all is ruin, and ruin personified mourns for him.

The Judge is cold and reserved in his manners, and more than commonly plain in his dress. He seems to be between 50 and 60 years of age, of small stature, and lean habit of body. His features possess but little expression, and he is, indeed, as unlike the late General, as any man in the United States.

After having seen all we wished, we re-entered the house to thank the Judge, but he appeared no more, simply sending a message that we were " welcome, and he hoped pleased." He is, we were informed, an amiable, good man, but of limited knowledge. We appeared, in his esteem, as sabbath-breakers. On this account he excused his inhospitality to us; and, besides, the saying of the late General, " I would not trust any man an inch beyond my nose, who would set an open example of sabbath-breaking," might rise in his recollection much to our prejudice. I felt the

Judge's answer to us as a reproof, because I hold it essential to the good of society that Christian sabbaths should be respected.

The scenery in the neighbourhood of the house and estate is very interesting. The umbrageous mount, on which the house stands, is a mile high from the shores of the great Potowmac, which is here two or three miles broad.

The British, and all the foreign diplomatic personages, visited this spot by water, and with the marine band saluted it with solemn dirges. Our guide told us that none but *great gentlemen* were permitted to see the house and gardens on Sunday. I asked if the Judge preached or kept a parson? He himself reads prayers, morning and evening, and therefore keeps no parson.

From an attentive perusal of the American history, and a close examination of the character of Washington, says Mr. ——, it appears to me that the principal faculty of his mind was judgment, which always led him to avoid the dangers of precipitancy, and the errors which sometimes result from a more vivid and brilliant imagination. The dictates of that judgment constituted the line of his conduct, which was of course marked with the most consummate prudence. This virtue seems never to have deserted him, either as a statesman or a warrior, in a public or private capacity. His prudence and caution were particularly observable in his military career, and, like Pericles, he never

willingly came to an engagement, when the danger
was considerable, and the success very uncertain;
nor did he envy the glory of those Generals, who
are admired and applauded, because their rash
enterprizes have been attended with success. He
had many difficulties to encounter, but these difficulties were readily surmounted. Patriotism animated him, and prudence conducted him to tri-
umph. With a limited education and little patron-
age, he paved his way to greatness, and by his
virtues, cast a blaze of glory around his character,
which time can only increase, and which posterity
must contemplate with enthusiasm and rapture.
There is no parallel for such a man in the annals
of the world; so singular a combination of virtues
with so few vices. Such disinterested patriotism
and such unimpeachable integrity, with so many
temptations to swerve and so many inducements
to betray, were never before united. Immoveable
in the hour of danger, no difficulties could shake,
no terrors appal him. He was always the same,
in the glare of prosperity, and in the gloom of adversity. Like Fabricius, he could not be moved
from the paths of virtue and honor, and like Epa-
minondas, he made every thing bend to the interests of his country. His country was his idol,
and patriotism the predominant feeling of his mind.
Personal aggrandizement and individual resent-
ment and interest, were alike sacrificed to this
overwhelming passion, which no difficulty could

weaken and no neglect destroy. Washington was
reserved, without being haughty; religious, without being bigotted; great in all stations, and sublime in all his actions, whether he moved in the
sphere of domestic obscurity, or employed his
energies in wielding the destinies of his country.
Antiquity would have made him a god. Posterity
will make him more. Every nation can boast of
its heroes, its statesmen, and its bards, but there
are few that have produced their Washingtons.
He stands alone in the history of the world, and
will be venerated while virtue and patriotism have
an influence on human action.

" You will, (says the same eulogist,) no doubt,
be astonished to understand, that the remains of
this great and excellent man still repose in a
humble sepulchre on the estate at which he re-
sided, and from which, like Cincinnatus, he was
several times called by his country. The Americans are certainly not ungrateful, but they seem
to have an aversion to perpetuate a man's name
by " monumental brass," or to express their gratitude by splendid tombs, or ponderous and magnificent mausolea. Your long acquaintance with
Westminster Abbey, where the high and the low,
the great and the obscure, the good man and the
villain, are alike honoured by their country or
their friends, may, perhaps, draw from you a burst
of indignation, at the imaginary apathy and indifference of this great republic, to the memory

and past services of its illustrious dead, but I
question whether it be not correct policy. To
begin would be to have no end, and the erection
of a monument to Washington might terminate,
as in Russia, with a monument to a dog. Since
the invention of writing, and the present extent of
knowledge, the " storied urn and animated bust,"
have become almost useless. History will record
with fidelity the illustrious actions of him who
has deserved well of his country, and his name
will be as perpetual as if Pelion had been piled
on Ossa, to preserve his memory. It was doubt-
less owing to the want of this art, that the humble
tumuli of the Celts, and the massy pyramids of
the Egyptians, were formed; they had no other
mode of expressing their gratitude, or of perpetu-
ating the memory of their dead. After all, perhaps, the best monument is "to read their history
in a nation's eyes."

" It is but justice, however, to state, that though
the American government have refused to erect a
monument to the memory of their illustrious hero,
his countrymen have not been quite so fastidious;
and the citizens of Baltimore, with that enthusiasm
and public spirit which have done them so much
credit, are now engaged in building a monument
that will, at once, evince their gratitude, their patriotism, and their taste. It may be safely asserted,
that the Americans pay less attention to the depo-
sitories of their dead, than almost any other nation.

They seem to be no sooner laid in the earth, than they are forgotten; and the tear of sorrow, and the hand of affection, neither bedews nor decorates the sward, under which the friend, the parent, or the relative reposes. Among the ancients, you will recollect, this was a part of their religion, and we owe to the tenderness and affection of a Corinthian nurse for her deceased charge, the rich and splendid capital which beautifies the Corinthian shaft. It is in vain to look into the burial grounds of this country, for the pensive cypress, or the melancholy willow, the virgin weeping over the urn of her departed lover, or the mother hanging over the grave of her darling child. No flower blooms, bedewed with the tear of affection. All is waste and dreary, and dead as the sunken grave over which you pass; and a few stones, on which are engraved the name and age of the deceased, are all that remain to manifest the affection of the living, to those who have passed away and are no more.

"Bushrod Washington, the present proprietor of Mount Vernon, is the nephew of the General. He seems to be about 60 years of age, is below the middle size, and apparently nervous and feeble; his complexion is pale and cadaverous, but his countenance has the lineaments of benevolence and good nature. He has long been one of the judges of the supreme court of the United States, and has, during that period, discovered no defi-

ciency in his acquaintance with the law. His decisions are, I believe, generally correct, though not
very remarkable. I know not whether he ever
was distinguished for his eloquence at the bar;
but little seems to be known of his powers as an
advocate or a lawyer, and that little does not tend
to place him much beyond the grade of mediocrity.
Satisfied with the reputation which the fame of his
uncle, the situation he holds, and the wealth he
possesses, cast around him, he feels no motive to
exertion, and no desire to render himself illustrious
by his own efforts. He appears to be one of those
men to whom the pleasures of the domestic circle
are more seducing than the fitful, though captivating splendour which surrounds the temples of
the statesman or the warrior, and he prefers what
the world would term the inglorious repose of
domestic felicity, to the feverish agitation and
sickly turmoil of public life.

" Mount Vernon has become, like Jerusalem and
Mecca, the resort of travellers of all nations, who
come within its vicinity. Veneration and respect
for the memory of the great and illustrious chief,
whose body it contains, lead all who have heard
his name, to make a pilgrimage to the shrine of
patriotism and public worth, and to stroll over
the ground which has been consecrated by the
repose, and hallowed by the ashes, of heroism and
virtue. A twig, a flower, or even a stone, becomes interesting, when taken from the spot

where Washington lived and died, and no man quits it without bearing with him some memento to exhibit to his family and friends."

17th.—I was revisited yesterday and to-day by Mr. Law, who, in speaking of my new acquaintance Mr. Fairfax, says, " he is an amiable, good, and learned man, but like Charles II. ' he never said a foolish thing, nor ever did a wise one.' He is ever unprepared to protect himself from cheats. This gentleman is the great great grandson of the famous Sir Thomas Fairfax, Cromwell's favourite general; he was once the richest man in America, but exchanged 100,000 acres of Virginia land for the same quantity in the west country, which he was told abounded in iron, silver, and other mines; he thus parted with a substance for a shadow." " He still," says Mr. Elliott, " possesses 100,000 acres, and one of the warmest and truest hearts in the world. He was brought up at Mount Vernon, a favourite of General Washington's, who predicted great things of him." But, says Mr. Law, he has long been living in prison bounds. His lady lamented to us on Sunday her want of a carriage, and the hot walks she had to make to town. This gentleman's brother, Thomas Fairfax, Esq., commonly known as Lord Fairfax, who, in his own right is a British peer, possesses large unproductive estates, and lives frequently in disgrace, but both, though lords in England, would feel themselves highly insulted were they so to be addressed here. Both are staunch republicans.

I yesterday added to my acquaintance a lord-chancellor, a lord, and two princes of the Ossage nation of Indians, who with two other chiefs, last week, went in state (naked) to the Secretary of war, and stamped, and said, in great anger, they came not here to be cheated out of their lands. They are fine dignified fellows, speaking only their own wild language.

Mr. Law, during conversation this day, observed that if this government would, and he believed they would, adopt his financial system, the people here would soon flourish again, and every wild spot become a garden. " Mr. Crawford, the Chancellor of the Exchequer, although he has recommended a contrary measure, is exactly of my opinion. We are both as much alike on this subject as pea to pea."

I said, " Mr. Law, would not a visit to England be agreeable? Would it not tend to lengthen your life?" " O, Sir, it would, but I could not now live in England; I must be active, and doing that which I deem for the good of mankind. My opinions would run counter to the powers which be." " But, Sir," rejoined I, " is it not our duty to be prudent and to seek the peace of the land we live in? Because in its peace we shall have peace." " Certainly! such is the duty of every good man.

Why should he sacrifice himself and family? Mr.
A——, your envoy here, seems suspicious of you
on account of your acquaintance with Mr. ——
I am sorry Mr. —— should have given such toasts
at the dinner on th e4 th of July, in favour of the
radicals. What have the radicals to do with
America? These toasts will be sent home by
A——. Envoys have nothing to do but to watch
the conduct of British subjects and give reports.
I am sorry that Mr. ——, who is a good, kind-
hearted, polite man, should thus expose himself,
and you, and other friends, to suspicion and misrepresentation."

19*th.*—I received the following letter from Mr.
Law, addressed to me at Mr. ——'s.

Washington, 18th July, 1820.

Dear Sir,

I enclose you a list of garden seeds; if you will
make a statement of the probable amount, I will
pay now, or answer your draft after the purchase.
A pound or two of Swedish turnips and of Norfolk turnips may be added. I shall be happy to
pay every attention to any of my countrymen
coming here, and to give them any information in
my power. I regret that I formed your acquaintance so late. My hay turns out better than I expected, and I hope to have four or five acres of
turnips, as I am sowing between my rows of corn.
Any farming information I shall be very thankful

2 I

for. I remain, with wishes for a safe and speedy
voyage,

Your most obedient servant,

T. LAW.

Pray write to me by what vessel you send the
seeds.

The following letter from Edward Meacher,
gardener to Mr. Law, is a specimen of the easy
freedom and familiarity of Yankee labourers. It
is addressed

To Thomas Law, Esq.

July, 1820.

Sir,

Considering my ill behaviour towards you the
other day, I consider myself culpable; therefore to
prevent such like trouble in future to you, I shall
declare upon oath against spirituous liquors, such
as brandy, rum, gin, and whiskey, *except three
drams in the course of each day,* as long as I live
with you. Three drams a day will not injure my
health or temper. Upon these conditions I expect
not to displease you in future, which will be a
cause, I hope, for you to encourage me in your
employment.

Sir,

From your faithful servant,

EDWARD MEACHER.

20th.—This day I bade farewell to Washington city and America, and to all the bright and vivid spirits I found in it.

21st.—In company with Mr. E. Dumbleton, and my wicked, beautiful, silver grey squirrel, a native of Maryland, whose brushy tail is his nightcap, and who eats razors, buttons, bibles, &c., and is therefore sentenced to transportation for life, I embarked on board the good ship *Minerva* of Boston, to Amsterdam bound, and from Alexandria sailed gently down the great river Potowmac.

After a passage of about 30 days, we arrived at the Isle of Wight. Here I had the honour to present my most gracious Sovereign with a precious relic—a cedar-cane cut from the grave of General Washington; together with six gallons of " elegant, mighty fine claret," purposely sent on a Yankee voyage of 10,000 miles, to ripen for the use of British royalty.

CONCLUSION.

Having reached home, partially recovered what seemed irrecoverably gone, my long lost health, and told my story, there seems little or nothing to add, except a few retrospective observations, summarily bearing on the preceding descriptions, opinions, and decisions, which throughout are frankly and fearlessly rendered, chiefly aiming to enlighten the ignorant, and to abash the wicked. " But," says the reader, " to emigrate or not to emigrate? That is the question!" It is easier to propound than to answer this inquiry. To seek a refuge from danger, and to fly from the coming storm, is on the one hand in accordance with one of the first laws of nature ; and on the other hand, it may be said, that to abandon our hearths, homes, and altars, because our country mourns and is in trouble, is cowardly. That numbers have gone, are now going, and will continue to go, is certain ; for when there is a surplus population, and the hive swarms, what shall set bounds to the free-born? To those, then, who are inevitably destined to roam, friendless, homeless, really lone strangers in a strange land, and to see their old, much-loved homes, and the tombs of their fathers no more, I would say: Study the preceding well-meant pages. I know your wants and feelings. Study, then, I

would say, by every attainable qualification, principle, and sentiment, to fortify your minds, and
make yourselves all which you ought to be. Plague
not yourselves nor the land of your adoption, by
importing and giving perpetuity to home-bred prejudices. A nest you will find; but every where, like
that of the nightingale, a thorn within it. Learn,
therefore, yourselves to forget, and as far as in you
lies, teach your posterity also to forget, and to remember only what they ought to remember. A
British origin will be ever honourable in their he-
raldry. This is well worth remembrance, and may
they never stain, never dishonour it; but into
whatsoever lands they wander, may they seek the
good and peace of that land, for in its good and
peace they shall have peace themselves!

To those whose disgusts and moral and physical
disabilities point them homewards, as prodigals to
the house of their fathers, the broad Atlantic, in the
words of the Hon. J. Q. Adams, offers a highway
for their return; having undergone a process by
which they shall, perhaps, learn the vast sum and
value of English homes and comforts.

The old family quarrel has evidently made the
natives of both countries somewhat incommiscible;
else how is it that the French, Dutch, Germans,
Irish, and strangers of any other land, are more
acceptable to America than the children of the
common parent, Great Britain. For to the latter
the most distinguished Americans have heretofore

proudly traced their pedigree, unless some rank
and cancerous blemish was in the root and core of
it. Hence all grades blush not to own and call her
mother, though she is denounced by many, and it
must be owned with some justice, as an unnatural
parent. But those events have long since become
matter of historical record, and it is not good policy to visit the sins of the fathers upon the children, from generation to generation. Let both
countries wisely learn to think correctly of their
several governments, and kindly of each other.
Peace and goodwill, in all their fruitful ramifica-
tions, will ever bring more silver dollars to the one,
and more golden guineas to the other, than fire-
ships, torpedos, battles, blazing cities, and heroes
covered with glory!

" Well! I guess, after all," exclaimed a Yankee
friend, " it is a good land with small faults; necessary evils; seeming evils; good in disguise."
" Yes, it is a good land," rejoined another, in love
with it at first sight, " mine eyes have seen it for
myself, and not another. I am fascinated with it.
My return from it would be impossible, but for
the adamantine chain which binds me to my country. My heart tempts me, but my duty forbids me
to break it." Hasty conclusions like hasty matches,
are rarely happy, and so it was with our enthusiast; for in less than two years of patient trial
and perpetual travel, he very gladly returned to
his native country, joyfully repeating,

——————— " Whoe'er thou art,
Cling to thy home. If there the meanest shed
Yield thee a hearth and shelter for thy head,
And some poor plot with vegetables stor'd,
Be all that heav'n allots thee for thy board,
Unsavoury bread, and herbs that scatter'd grow
Wild on the river bank, or mountain brow,
Yet ev'n this cheerless mansion shall provide
More heart's repose than all the world beside."

Finally; were, however, America, of which I now perhaps take my leave for ever, every thing that the purest patriotism could make it, yet the climate is an evil, a perpetual evil, a mighty drawback, an almost insurmountable obstacle to the health, wealth, and well-being of all, except the native red and black man, the genuine aboriginal, and the unstained African, for whom alone this land of promise, this vast section of the earth, this new and better world, seems by nature to have been intended. Otherwise, it is argued, would noisome pestilence annually desolate its cities and districts, and every where unsparingly and prematurely people the grave? In spite, however, of climes, tropical or changeful, torrid or frigid, and of constitutional predisposition to sickness, health, physical and moral, is much more at the command of mankind than she is generally supposed to be. Temperance, abstinence, and exertion, approximating to labour, in free air, are the essential handmaids to health, and enable a man to laugh at doctors, and to withstand the effects of climate. Hence, then, in whatsoever climes, stations, or circumstances, my reader may be found, let him learn to think health worth a sacrifice.   To persons, whose fortune it may be to encounter the risks of this dangerous and debilitating climate, I would especially say: Let ablutions and affusions of pure, cold spring water, become habitual with you, and as a beverage, let water be substituted for wine, whiskey, and alcohol in all its forms.   Let milk supply the place of tea, coffee, and other stimulants; and let tobacco, snuff, and all the family of narcotics, be abandoned.   Surely health is ever, what a late venerable friend of his species was often wont to call her, *the Sugar of Life.*   He who thinks and acts otherwise rarely finds health, and never deserves her.

FINIS.